A DURKHEIMIAN QUEST

A DURKHEIMIAN QUEST

Solidarity and the Sacred

W. Watts Miller

berghahn
NEW YORK · OXFORD
www.berghahnbooks.com

Published by

Berghahn Books

www.berghahnbooks.com

©2012, 2014 W. Watts Miller
First paperback edition published in 2014

Library of Congress Cataloging-in-Publication Data

Watts Miller, William, 1944-
  A Durkheimian quest : solidarity and the sacred / W. Watts Miller.
    p. cm.
  Includes bibliographical references and index.
      ISBN 978-0-85745-549-9 (hardback) — ISBN 978-1-78238-528-8 (paperback) —
      ISBN 978-0-85745-567-3 (ebook)
  1. Durkheim, Émile, 1858-1917. 2. Sociologists–France. 3.
Sociology–History. 4. Ethics–History. I. Title.
  HM479.D87W37 2012

                                                            301.092–dc23

British Library Cataloguing in Publication Data

A catalogue record for this book is available from the British Library.

Printed on acid-free paper.

ISBN 978-0-85745-549-9 hardback
ISBN 978-1-78238-528-8 paperback
ISBN 978-0-85745-567-3 ebook

Contents

Contents

List of Tables and Figures

Tables

Figures

Acknowledgements

Thanks are due, for direct and indispensable support in the evolution of this book, to Marion Berghahn, Bill Pickering and Rob Stones. Thanks are also due, for their own particular contributions to the whole business of a project's floating around, shaping, discussion, critique and encouragement, to Stéphane Baciocchi, Massimo Borlandi, Cecilia Busby, Irène Eulriet, Kieran Flanagan, Mike Gane, Sue Stedman Jones, Philippe Steiner and Ed Tiryakian. At the same time, the work would have been impossible without anchorage in the understanding of my partner and wife, Elizabeth Watts Miller.

Along with all the importance of what is owed to individuals, however, there is a collective dimension. A specific debt is to two overlapping groups, one made up of fellow members of the British Centre for Durkheimian Studies, Oxford, the other the network of colleagues, at universities and at the publishers, who help to produce the journal, *Durkheimian Studies*. Participation in these groups has been an essential stimulus in keeping up to date with new research and as a source and testing-ground of ideas.

A more intangible influence is to do with the career of Durkheim himself, not just during but after his lifetime, in a vast, diverse, long-running and continuing history of interest in his work. How individuals are drawn into these collective currents of interest and select a way through them is to some extent a matter of the biography of individuals themselves. In my own case, at any rate, what is hoped to contribute to a collective effort is also a personal affair.

August 2011

Introduction

An Encyclopaedia Entry

An encyclopaedia entry on Durkheim would not be doing its job, if it just gave his name and dates of birth and death:

Durkheim, Emile (1858–1917).

It should at least give a reason for having heard of him:

Durkheim, Emile (1858–1917) One of the founders of sociology.

A detailed entry can then pick and choose its way through various kinds of more or less 'factual' biographical information. For example:

Durkheim, David Emile (1858–1917) One of the founders of sociology, he was born in eastern France, the son and grandson of rabbis yet nonetheless from a relatively modest social background. Although given the biblical, at the time identifiably Jewish, forename of 'David', he was known in his family, as also in his public career, simply as 'Emile Durkheim'. He was a firm supporter of the Third Republic, established in the 1870s, was sympathetic with certain forms of socialism, and was often the subject of right-wing antisemitic attacks.

   In 1876, aged eighteen, he left his home town of Epinal to become a student at Paris. In 1882, he graduated from the prestigious Ecole Normale Supérieure, and went on to teach in various provincial high schools, where he gave courses on philosophy. In 1885, aged twenty-seven, he published his first academic article, and by this time had already converted to sociology, as well as started his doctoral dissertation on the division of labour. In 1887, he got his first academic appointment as a lecturer at the university of Bordeaux. In 1902, aged forty-four, he returned to Paris with an appointment at the Sorbonne, where he eventually became a full professor and was increasingly active and influential in the university's affairs. He died while still only in his fifties and at the height of his intellectual powers.

Durkheim founded a new sociological journal, the *Année sociologique*. He also gathered around him a group of young talented scholars – including his own nephew, Marcel Mauss – and encouraged them to develop his vision of sociology through detailed specialized studies. His four main works are *The Division of Labour* (1893), *The Rules of Sociological Method* (1895), *Suicide* (1897), and *The Elemental Forms of Religious Life* (1912).[1]

But at this point an encyclopaedia entry runs into problems. As well as listing Durkheim's main works, should it not also highlight his most influential ideas? Yet how does the encyclopaedist decide what these are?

It can come down to a report of the views of selected 'authorities'. So in a way, it can come down to the question: whose Durkheim?

But taking another approach, the more basic question is: which Durkheim? This involves a sociology of his representation through the quite different concerns and conventions of an encyclopaedia entry, a student textbook, an examination essay, a chat at a conference break, a fashionable piece on how to develop and apply his insights nowadays, an article in a learned journal on the history of ideas. Accordingly, it is possible to suggest three ideal-types of the character in question – a mythological Durkheim, a living Durkheim, and an actual historical Durkheim.

The Mythological Durkheim

'Elemental Forms of Sociological Life'

If sociologists continue to talk about Marx, Weber and Durkheim, it isn't thanks to an interest in history. It is because they are totems of the tribe. On the surface, they are 'founding fathers' of sociology. At bottom, they are mythic ancestors whose real present-day function is to symbolize a collective identity, constructed and reconstructed in a variety of ways.

These include rites of initiation – not least, the examination. New recruits are subject to ordeal by essay, tested for their acquaintance with the tribe's special arcane language, and obliged to show they have heard of figures such as 'Durkheim' and can impress their elders with opinions on them.

In general, though, the life of the tribe fluctuates between times of dispersal and times of assembly. In times of dispersal, its scattered members get on with the ordinary everyday business of teaching, research, administration, making a living, and plotting a career. True, throughout these self-interested individualistic times, they may still be linked in the solidarity of a division of labour and of networks of ordinary everyday activities and relations. But what must not be forgotten is the role of collective memory.

Consider, for example, the shelves of sacred texts in a professor's office. It is simple-minded to think they are there to be read. A key job is to constitute the professor's own particular identity, say with Weber in a place of honour, Durkheim down near the waste-paper basket. But it is above all to act as a constant reminder – to students, to colleagues and to the professor – of the individual's participation in a collective tribal life, and of authority through relics of the sacred dead among the latest productions of the living.

Even so, collective memory doesn't just run on its own. What must also not be forgotten is the importance of times of assembly – above all, the conference. Members of the tribe's various clans, sections and departments gather together in a making and remaking of a collective identity through formal as well as informal rites. Whether in a sort of effervescence during star performances in the conference hall, or in conversations over drinks at the bar, there is a solidarity in the middle of disagreements and a communication with one another through a whole set of collective representations, concrete symbols and common canonical references.

Thus a key role of symbols like 'Durkheim' is to act as shorthand for rival positions fought over in sociology. But this is also how they help to create a shared identity, in helping to create a shared discourse of conflict and division. So the mythological Durkheim still does his bit, even as a negative reference. For a while he served as the ancestor the tribe most loved to hate, the founding father as whipping boy and symbol of errors of all sorts – empiricism, positivism, determinism, functionalism, conservatism, an ideology of the status quo. Things might change, yet stay the same. Whatever happens, it is futile to argue against the tribe's mythic Durkheim as an unrecognizable transfiguration of the actual historical Durkheim. This is not just because it is hard to dislodge 'mythological truths', embedded in a group's rites, practices, institutions and sense of identity. It is above all because the tribe isn't interested in the historical Durkheim, but in a representation of the past driven by the concerns of the present.

Comment

This story of the ritual-symbolic life of a modern 'tribe' deflates sociology's own self-image as enlightened rational enquiry. But in the process it involves two quite special ironies. It constructs a mythological Durkheim through ideas that in fact come from Durkheim himself. At the same time it undermines one of his most basic commitments. With its picture of how even sociology runs on clouds of myth, it undermines his belief in reason and his hope not only in social science but in movement towards a society with transparent self-understanding.

Indeed, it involves an inherent ambivalence in *The Elemental Forms* itself. This still comes with *The Division of Labour*'s commitment to an enlightenment of secular rational transparence. Yet it also comes with a sense that society always and inevitably runs on myth, thanks to energies of the sacred that in the very process of creating a social world act to transfigure it. In other words, it can be seen as fundamentally ambivalent between a sociology of transparence and a sociology of transfiguration.

There is a need to recognize this ambivalence, inasmuch as it is just there in Durkheim's actual work. But there is also a need to decide what to do about it, in attempts to take up and apply his work nowadays. That is, it is an example of issues that arise in the relation between the 'historical' and a 'living' Durkheim.

The Interrelation between the Living and the Historical Durkheim

It can sound quite exciting to want to rescue Durkheim from the museum, and to develop his work in ways that are relevant to present-day concerns. In fact, however, the historical Durkheim doesn't exist fixed immutably in the past. As much as anything, he is a forever changing creation of continuing scholarly research into his life, work and times. The two 'Durkheims' involve an ongoing interaction with one another, whether in an individual's own research or in a collective division of labour.

In the process, it is important to avoid sweeping indiscriminate talk of 'presentism' and 'historicism'. A route to mythology might be reasonably and specifically identified with a presentism that interprets a work just through the context within which it is nowadays read, and in ignorance of the context within which it was originally written. A route to incoherence is to brush aside such concerns as historicist and in an insistence that the past is inaccessible, since inevitably a construction of the present. It has no way to distinguish interest in a living Durkheim from mythology. This interest depends on research investigating the historical Durkheim himself, as a basis of claims to offer a neo-Durkheimian reworking of his ideas.

There are still some major problems. A way to kill off a living Durkheim is to demand adherence to his ideas in their entirety, however questionable or dated some of these might now seem. The nature of the project entails a choice of what is emphasized and taken up from his work, and what is downplayed or discarded. Yet is there any point in trying to write a *Rules of Selective Method*? In principle, any number of factors can come into the development of different versions of a neo-Durkheimian sociology and their evaluation as theoretically fertile, interesting and important. In principle, in other words, there is an irreducible element of judgment in looking for both historically based and theoretically fertile lines of 'neo-Durkheimian' enquiry.

There is also a different type of issue to consider. To the extent that there is a market for studies either of the living or the historical Durkheim, it is not least thanks to his myth-enshrouded canonization as a 'founding father of sociology' and accordingly as a magnet for continuing references in present-day sociological arguments and debates. There may be many reasons for a time lag of many years between these references and up to date specialist research on his work. In any case, it was for a number of reasons that I eventually decided to focus most of this book on an effort at fresh new investigations of his work itself – his main claim to fame, rather than his social background, personal life or psychology – while it is also to focus on his own individual contribution to what, through the group he gathered round him, developed as a collective achievement. These investigations are then followed up with a set of essays that draw on Durkheim but also a range of other authors, to explore how his work might generate various apparently quite different yet interlinking lines of enquiry on modern times.

Investigations of a Project

Durkheim's project for a social science is a key to his work as a whole, yet is also where it is especially enveloped in clouds of mythology. So I decided to begin with a fresh look at what a 'founding father' of sociology thought the new science was about. However, an essential way to investigate an overall work is through particular works. Accordingly, I decided to focus on his search for solidarity in *The Division of Labour* and quest for the sacred in *The Elemental Forms*. At the same time a question is how he got from one to the other. The answer has to do with an intellectual crisis, undermining his old core view and forcing him to begin to create the new sociological world that eventually emerged in *The Elemental Forms*.

The Idea of a Social Science

A number of things might be emphasized in pointing ahead to a fuller exploration of Durkheim's idea of a social science. It is not just a matter of going over his abstract programmatic statements on how to do social science in theory. It requires investigation of works in which he sets out to show how to do social science in practice. But at the levels both of theory and practice, it also means coming to grips with what he repeatedly described as a new scientific 'rationalism'.

This involves his insistence on actual empirical studies of social phenomena. But it is together with his insistence on digging underneath the surface of external 'social facts', to try to bring to light a hidden

internal social logic and dynamic going on in them. At the same time it
is in belief in an evaluatively committed, critical social science. It has a
key public role in identifying deep-rooted modern ideals, in diagnosing
a far-reaching crisis and malaise, and in pointing to the action required
to bring about social change and reform.

All the elements of this vision of social science were in place early
on in his career, in his project for a group of works centred round *The
Division of Labour.*

The Creation of a Work, Questions of Context, and an Intellectual Crisis

Durkheim had to submit two pieces of work for his doctorate – a subsidiary thesis in Latin, and a main thesis in French – and it is clear that he
wrote them to complement each other. One lays out the basic principles
of a new social science. The other shows how to get on and do it in practice. Thus his subsidiary thesis involves his first full-length programmatic
statement on social science, and in the process legitimates it as a form of
enquiry with roots in the Enlightenment. His main thesis was *The Division of Labour* itself, with its story of the emergence of the modern world,
but which ends with scenes of social and moral crisis and with insistence
on the need for reform. His plan was accordingly for a follow-up companion work, looking to reform through the intermediate occupational
groups of a new guild socialism. He never completed this, but left a
whole trail of material that gives a picture of its ideas.

In sum, Durkheim launched his sociological career with a project for
a set of three interrelated works. Like a triptych, the main central panel
is *The Division of Labour,* on the creation of the modern world. One of
its side panels is on enlightenment and a new social science. The other,
sketched-in side panel is on achievement of the good society through a
new guild socialism. This wider project is part of the story of *The Division
of Labour* itself. A route to misunderstanding is to view it in isolation. It
needs to be seen, like the main panel of a triptych, along with its two side
panels, and as the centrepiece of a vast overall composition.

In general, a way to understand a work is to find out about its creation. At the same time this is bound up with questions of context. In Durkheim's case, these involve questions about the particular intellectual milieu he inhabited, but also about a wider social and political background
– the continuing legacy of the French Revolution, the establishment of
the Third Republic, the rise of socialism, the conflict of church and state,
the crisis of the Dreyfus Affair… It would be a recipe for intellectual in-
digestion to try to introduce everything all at once. It is instead hoped to
build up a gradual familiarity with some of the more important references
along the way, in the course of discussing his work itself.

It is nonetheless worth emphasizing, at this stage, a basic difference between the contexts that are relevant in asking about the creation of the sociological landscape of *The Division of Labour* and the sociological landscape of *The Elemental Forms*. One is especially rooted in Durkheim's efforts to champion social science in France. The other is especially rooted in his encounter with anthropology in the English-speaking world. This is an altogether key context of the creation of *The Elemental Forms*, without which, indeed, it is entirely inconceivable. The reason is to do with an intellectual crisis, sparked off by the arrival, via England, of shock news from Australia. It came in the form of Baldwin Spencer and Francis Gillen's *The Native Tribes of Central Australia*, published in London, to rave reviews, in 1899, and appearing to consign Durkheim's whole core view of evolution to the scrap-heap of old, out-of-date theory. Throughout the early 1900s, he tried out various ways to come up with a response and in various ways began to change his ideas. His solution eventually emerges in a course he started to give in 1906. This can be established, using a battery of textual methods, as the earliest known version of *The Elemental Forms*. It then took him several years to prepare the manuscript of a final version, completed in 1911 and published in 1912.

In sum, the story of the creation of the work is again a way of getting to understand the work itself. But it is also a story of how the transition from *The Division of Labour* to *The Elemental Forms* was a long, drawn out, complex affair. In Durkheim's actual sociological writings between 1893 and 1906 there is little evidence of a dramatic change, or experience of a sudden miraculous 'revelation'.

Arguments, Discourses and Problematics

It is of course important to address a work's explicit arguments. But it is also important to investigate the discourse in which these are embedded, complete with its key terms, examples, metaphors and themes. What is perhaps most important of all is to get to grips with a work's underlying problematic, or set of problematics.

So, for instance, the investigations of Durkheim's thesis examine how and why he took up the already established yet highly controversial term, 'collective consciousness'; the way he interlinked this with a 'segmental structure'; his use of the Jews of ancient Israel as his model example of a tradition-bound socioreligious world, and of contemporary France as his main example of modern social life; the meanings he built into his metaphor of 'mechanical' versus 'organic' solidarity; and his theme of a growing emancipation from the 'forces of tradition', revised in a later edition to emancipation from the 'collective yoke'.

But a major concern is with the discourse of solidarity itself. By the time of his thesis, there were three core meanings that had become packaged together in the single French term, *solidarité*. It can be established by systematic textual analysis of the work that it draws on all three of these core meanings, while in the process reshaping them in ways that set up its whole underlying problematic of a modern solidarity. After all, his thesis sets out in search of a modern solidarity thanks to the division of labour, yet fails to find it in modern everyday scenes of alienation, anomie, class war and a far-reaching crisis. The problematic, then, is to do with how the division of labour constitutes his dynamic of the modern world, how it is therefore necessarily implicated in a modern crisis, and how it is nonetheless a route to reform through a new guild socialism's web of intermediate occupational groups and associations.

The investigations of *The Elemental Forms* examine, among other things, Durkheim's changing view of 'effervescence'. But in his enthusiasm for it in the eventual work itself, effervescence is bound up with the sacred and a discourse of energy, force, power. Although already evident in *The Division of Labour*, this discourse becomes central in *The Elemental Forms*. It is the extraordinary energy of special effervescent times that constructs the sacred, yet that in the process helps not only to create but to transfigure society. So does the work itself construct a story of the inevitable transfiguration of any and every social world? Or, as the author insists, is it nowadays possible to move towards the transparence of a more enlightened, self-understood society? This ambivalence is at the heart of *The Elemental Forms*, and its problematic modern quest for the sacred.

Texts

It was necessary, in undertaking fresh investigations of *The Division of Labour* and *The Elemental Forms*, to go to the texts as originally published, rather than to rely either on modern editions or on translations. However, there were four editions of *The Division of Labour* that appeared during Durkheim's lifetime. Although I have consulted all of these, I decided to use as well as cite the original thesis dated 1893 together with the revised edition dated 1902.

It is nonetheless unfortunate that so far there is no critical edition of Durkheim's work as a whole, systematically showing variations between texts, dealing with misprints and other errors or inadequacies, and providing notes as and when appropriate. The good news is that this is now being planned, under the direction of Massimo Borlandi and with the collaboration of a whole team of scholars. It will run into many volumes and take many years, or even never come to an end. Discoveries of lost, forgotten or unknown texts still keep turning up, as well as discoveries about existing texts. At least a start has been made in establishing a scholarly textual basis of interpretations of Durkheim's work, but also of more accurate and informed translations.

Meanwhile, another issue is that this is a study of Durkheim in English, and I have decided to keep it in English throughout, but using my own translations of passages from Durkheim as well as from others. In the end, this is because it is necessary to take responsibility for ways in which an effort to translate is inevitably an effort to decode a text and interpret a work. An example is whether to decode *Les Formes élémentaires* as *The Elementary Forms* or as *The Elemental Forms*.

There are at least two core meanings contained in the single French term, *élémentaire*, and an English decoder needs to decide between emphasizing the basic, early and elementary or the basic, continuing and elemental. But a French decoder faces a similar choice. Nor is it simply a matter of looking up a dictionary. It above all depends on an effort to understand Durkheim's project as a whole, through analysis of the final published version of the text but also of any earlier versions or fragments of versions, and through investigation of his project's origins as well as the work's creation. In brief, he was all along committed to the importance of digging around in the basic, early and elementary, yet not just as of interest in itself, but to get to the bottom of the basic, continuing and elemental. So is it better to emphasize his method – digging around in the elementary? Or is it better to emphasize his aim – discovering the elemental?

Another factor is that his project is not just about basic forms of social life, but basic forces and energies at work in creating and shaping it. In a way this is a difference between what is to be described and how it is to be explained. Again, it seems to me better to emphasize his interest in discovering not only elemental forms of social life but elemental forces always at work in creating and shaping it. However, I leave readers to make a decision for themselves, while trying to make clear my own.

Essays on Modern Times

Durkheim's work has been criticized and even denounced in any number of ways, while it has also been defended, taken up and developed in any number of ways. It would be a formidable task to investigate and try to do justice to all of them. Besides, whatever the importance of investigations, there is still a role for the essay. This is less about answering questions, more about opening up questions themselves and playing around with ideas and approaches in exploring them. At any rate, the essays on modern times are not intended as investigations of modern times, let alone as a manifesto of a sweeping new 'neo-Durkheimian' theory. They are explorations of some issues to do with modern times, and draw on a variety of sources, including some that are not Durkheimian – or even sociological – at all. But they are anchored in concerns arising from his work, especially in a tension between *The Division of Labour* and *The Elemental Forms*.

One of these concerns is to do with his continuing worry over a modern 'crisis', but continuing insistence it was only a 'crisis of transition', and would go away. A hundred years on, however, isn't the 'crisis' permanent and here to stay?

It is possible to speculate that, despite his public air of confidence, a sense of despair was an underlying factor in transforming his search for solidarity into a quest for the sacred. In any case, the essays explore how it is still possible in modern power struggles to hang on to hope, take refuge in art, and keep looking for signs of the sacred. All the same, it can seem a losing battle against forces of the mundane and what he once described as a 'sordid commercialism'. The last article he published, in 1917, was entitled 'The Politics of the Future'. The conclusion to my book as a whole is in a way an update, but in a mood near to despair. Yet this is a reason for hanging on to his belief in a critical social science, with a key public role. It is also why, however stimulating it might be to go to *The Elemental Forms*, the problematic that underlies and haunts *The Division of Labour* doesn't belong to the museum, if only because capitalism doesn't belong to the museum. The overall relevance, interest and vitality of a neo-Durkheimian sociology depends on keeping going a tension between approaches inspired by and rooted in these works.

PART I
INVESTIGATIONS OF A PROJECT

CHAPTER 1

The Idea of a Social Science

The Division of Labour begins:

> This book is above all an effort to treat the facts of moral life according to the
> method of the positive sciences. (1893a: i / 1902b: xxxvii)

So in investigating Durkheim's work, a way to begin is with an effort to understand his very idea of a social science.

It is meant to be objective. Yet it isn't neutral. It is committed. This is made clear from the start. He emphasizes how a science of moral life, far from having a merely academic interest, can help to identify the ideal. His ambition is to explore a route from 'is' to 'ought'. He attacks 'mystics' who just assert this is impossible, and who accordingly 'put human reason to sleep' (vi / xli).

Social Science as Social Vision

In Durkheim's work, solidarity is a basis of any social world and so a basis of any ideal of the good society. Thus books 1 and 2 of his thesis are about the division of labour as the place to look for a solidarity of modern times. But book 3 is about a failure to generate this, in modern everyday scenes of alienation, anomie and class war. On the one hand, then, he insists it is a 'crisis of transition' and looks to a solidarity of the future. On the other, he also insists that the only way to achieve this solidarity is if the modern world meets its own deep-rooted aspirations to freedom and equality. So in effect he comes up with a vision of a society of free autonomous persons, justice, and solidarity.

This echoes the Revolution's *Liberty, Equality, Fraternity*. Or rather, it re-echoes it. The famous trio of ideals had re-emerged in the Third Republic, to become adopted as its motto in 1880 and to form part of the wider political context of Durkheim's thesis. For the republic's conservative opponents, the motto was a ragbag of dangerous, impossible and contradictory notions. And throughout the 1880s, there was a sustained collective effort to answer such attacks. Durkheim's thesis was a contribution to this effort. It mobilized his new science of moral life, to offer a sociological defence of the ideals expressed in the Revolution. True, this involved reworking them, to form a coherent whole and accordingly to form a practical vision to strive to realize. But it above all involved seeing them as an expression of the aspirations of modern times, built into our world's underlying structure and dynamic.

So this also involves the wider intellectual context of his thesis, since it is clearly a version of nineteenth-century stories of progress. In turn, these have roots in the eighteenth-century Enlightenment. Thus it is instructive to pick out the writings on enlightenment and a 'philosophical history' of progress by Immanuel Kant, given his general importance in the French philosophical milieu in which Durkheim was educated. Indeed, an interest in Kantian philosophical history is especially evident in a work by one of Durkheim's examiners, Henri Marion's *Moral Solidarity* (1880). Moreover, there are basic similarities between the philosophical history and Durkheim's own line on a modern age.[1]

Kant's philosophical history is 'teleological', in that it is about humankind's progress towards an end. And Durkheim went out of his way to reject teleological stories, in that he emphasized a 'mechanistic' dynamic of obscure hidden forces. Yet so did Kant, in emphasizing a dynamic in which most of the time humanity stumbles blindly along in unawareness of an end. It is only eventually that there arises a modern 'age of enlightenment', increasingly conscious of the human ideal, and preparing the way for a future 'enlightened age', increasingly realizing it in practice. But in a seeming contradiction for a story of evolution that is so mechanical, a basic force in things is the growth of the human kernel of freedom. And this takes us to Kant's whole concept of 'autonomy', which he explicitly tied in with a vision of a union of free autonomous persons – a 'kingdom of ends' – an ideal he first formulated in 1785, on the eve of the Revolution.

It also takes us back to Durkheim himself. It is this vision of a kingdom that became reformulated in the French milieu he inhabited, and in which he took up, interpreted and engaged with Kantian ideas. Emile Boutroux – another of his examiners – converted the kingdom into a 'republic of persons'. Charles Renouvier – Durkheim's left-wing philosophical hero – recast it as a 'society of persons'. Either term will do for his own vision of an enlightened world of free autonomous persons, justice and solidarity. But it is also possible to draw on the English and American radical tradition to evoke this as a commonwealth of persons.

Although the term was never used by Durkheim himself, it might be used here. It helps to encapsulate what he saw at stake in his vision of a modern future, but also in his critique of the state we are in now.

Social Science as Social Critique

'Every society is a moral society', according to the conclusion to book 1 of his thesis (1893a: 249 / 1902b: 207). This is because every society runs on solidarity, in turn the source of morality. Nor does he contradict himself in book 3's scenes of malaise. He still sees a world of society. It is just that it can have only an 'imperfect, troubled solidarity' (421 / 369).

This is an understatement for what comes across as a crippled solidarity. In any case, where does he locate the sources of a deficient present-day solidarity? The answer is to do with his worry over a lack of 'intermediate groups', and is how to understand his worries over alienation, egoism and anomie.

Alienation, Egoism, Anomie and a Lack of Intermediate Groups

In Durkheim's overall work, an essential point about a web of intermediate groups is to link the individual with a wider society, through involvement in a web of particular definite interlinking milieux. Otherwise, there is only a mass of atomized individuals plus an authoritarian centralized state – a situation the new preface to his thesis describes as a 'sociological monstrosity' (1902b: xxxii).

Part of the background is his story of how the guilds of the old regime were swept away, without replacement, in the Revolution. Nor was there any role for such groups in the ideal of a republic in Rousseau's *Social Contract* (1762), which became a Bible of the Revolution. In a key essay, he sees Rousseau and the Revolution as paradigmatic modern cases of how 'individualism combines with an authoritarian conception of society' (1898c: 260). In lectures on *The Social Contract*, probably given around 1897,[2] he comments that its republic attaches individuals to society but not to each other: 'they are linked with each other only because they are all linked to the community, that is, alienated within it' (1918: 143).

This is one of the few occasions in which Durkheim mobilizes talk of alienation. But since it can include his more familiar yet changing uses of the term 'egoism', it helps to express what he sees as the most basic modern pathology of all. This is a real enough modern tendency to lone, atomized individuals, cut off from everyone else and wrapped up in their own thoughts, desires or interests. Alienation is the opposite of solidarity. At its most extreme, it is the absence of everything he looks for in modern solidarity – attachment to one another, attachment to intermediate groups, and attachment to a wider society.

This set of attachments is fundamental to his vision of a modern solidarity, but also to his critique of modern pathologies, including anomie. At its most general, anomie is about a lack of social and moral regulation, in a breakdown of a detailed code that governs relations with one another but also the individual's own life and character. On the one hand, then, anomie is bound up with lack of attachment in webs of relations and so with alienation's radical separateness. The two, together, are at the same time sources of his account of different pathological forms of individualism – cut off in a private world of thought and the imagination, or ruled by emotion, impulse and desire, or driven by a calculation of interest. On the other hand, however, it is all very well to develop a negative critique of these and their various modern philosophical expressions, such as theories of the self as a radically separate atom. But he needs to construct, more positively, an alternative account of the modern self.

What he comes up with is the *individual personality* – forming a distinctive individual consciousness and developing as a distinctive individual character, but precisely in the social attachments, webs of relations and different roles and outlooks of a division of labour. It could be seen as a 'liberal-communitarian' self. In that it is communitarian, it is about an internal sense of attachment that is deep-rooted in the personality, since deep-rooted in webs of relations. In that it is liberal, it involves both each individual's difference, through a distinct personality, and everyone's sameness, through the shared status of a person. Thus running through Durkheim's work as a whole there is concern both with how a modern division of labour can make for attachment as individual personalities and with how a modern collective consciousness can make for attachment through a common belief in everyone's status as a person. His various particular writings come with differences of emphasis on these two elements. But a basic constant is that he simultaneously defends a modern individualism to do with the personality / the person, while attacking other modern individualistic forces that he sees as pathological and associates with a world in crisis.

These especially include what he calls a 'sordid commercialism' – code, perhaps, for capitalism – but in any case how he describes an economistic, interest-driven individualism (1898c: 262). It is a form of individualism that he attacked throughout his career, starting with his first sociological publication. This describes a conflict of 'unfettered egoisms' – here, quite clearly code for capitalism – generating class war, but in the process also generating pressures for control by the state and a 'despotic socialism'. The only escape from these alternative nightmare scenarios is a new network of intermediate occupational groups (1885a: 371). It was this early critique of 'unfettered egoisms' at the heart of modern economic life that then became a general critique of anomie as a lack of regulation in whatever sphere of life. But it remains basic to the account of anomie in book 3 of his thesis. It reappears in the conclusion to *Sui-*

cide, on the need for new occupational groups (1897a: 434–51). It then becomes the whole focus of his new preface to *The Division of Labour*. In once again making the case for new occupational groups, this describes scenes of anomie and class war at the heart of modern economic and industrial life, and so at the heart of modern society itself (1902b: ii–v). The crisis cannot be solved by the state, or by reliance on vague general abstract ideals of justice. It requires, through new intermediate groups, a social organization with the power and legitimacy to translate, articulate and develop these ideals into an effective moral code.

Durkheim continued with this campaign in lectures that were given throughout the 1900s. But it was also during the 1900s that he became increasingly absorbed in issues, to do with the sacred, that eventually led on to *The Elemental Forms*. Even so, it was in no way to see the solution to a far-reaching crisis in a bit of ritual and symbolism. It was in looking to a whole new effervescent explosion of energies for escape from a present-day time of 'transition and moral mediocrity' (1912a: 610). When, in a sense, an explosion of energies came, in the Great War, the need to reconstruct society by tackling the economic and industrial crisis described in *The Division of Labour* is again the theme of his last article, 'The Politics of the Future' (1917c).

In sum, Durkheim all along hoped in life after capitalism – or at any rate, life after a 'sordid commercialism' – in a continuing critique of the way things are now and in a continuing campaign for social and moral reform.

Yet isn't his 'crisis of transition' here to stay? Or why treat contemporary capitalism as pathological when it is so widespread and, in a sense, so 'normal'? And how can the same type of society – modern industrial society – generate such different possible scenarios as a commonwealth of persons, capitalism, totalitarian socialism or whatever else might seem described in his work?

A way to explore these questions is through what could be called his social science's 'internalist' programme. In turn, this helps with understanding what is at stake in what he himself called his social science's 'rationalist empiricism'.

An Internalist Programme

Durkheim's idea of social science commits him to empirical indicators. But their rationale is to track down something else, so that it is always necessary to ask what this is. What he above all wants to track down, in his search for modern solidarity, is an underlying and unfolding logic of the division of labour as a dynamic of the modern world.

In his subsidiary thesis, he sets out a programme of how to do social science. This attacks theorists who try to explain malaise just in terms of circumstances that are exceptional, and so in some way accidental, contingent, external. On the contrary, 'disease, as much as health, is part of the nature of a living being' (1892a: 55). In other words, let us say, a basic rule of sociological method is always to look for an internalist explanation of things – to dig around within a social world's own nature and dynamic for ways this can explain both its ideals and its pathologies.

So does the author of *The Division of Labour* break a basic rule of his own sociology's 'internalist' research programme? He invokes a modern dynamic to explain our ideals, yet asserts that in itself it has nothing to do with our pathologies:

> The division of labour does not produce these consequences as a result of a necessity of its nature, but only in exceptional and abnormal circumstances. (1893a: 417 / 1902b: 364)

And for good measure, he repeats the claim in his new preface (1902b: v).

It is important to notice this explicit argument of the author, even if a deviation from one of his own work's rules of method. But it is more important to notice ways in which his work's actual underlying arguments are in line with the rule, in providing an internalist explanation of how the division of labour is itself a source both of modern ideals and modern pathologies. Two examples have already been encountered. Thus a general theme of his work is how the dynamic of the division of labour frees things up, so that it helps to generate modern individualism in all its forms – not just those he endorsed, but complete with others he viewed as pathological. Or again, it is the division of labour's freeing up of things that he saw as underlying the attack on the guilds of the old regime and their abolition in the Revolution – leading to his nightmare scenario of the atomized individual plus the authoritarian state, with no effective intermediate groups.

Accordingly, here is a sketch of an internalist retheorization of the division of labour as his dynamic of the modern world. Its underlying and unfolding logic necessarily involves the possibility of going in different directions and crystallizing in different scenarios. But the logic isn't equally realized in these. On the contrary, it continues to generate pressures for a commonwealth of persons.

So it still makes sense to talk of a 'crisis of transition'. Even if it has settled in for some time, energies for change do not go away and visions of an alternative do not disappear. This can be put another way. Contemporary capitalism isn't an accident, with nothing to do with the division of labour and its internal logic. But it isn't the only possibility built into the logic, and still comes out as pathological. With its economistic individualism, flourishing injustice and crippled solidarity, it is a deformation of our world's dynamic, in comparison with its realization in development towards a commonwealth.

In the end, it is this comparison that counts in *The Division of Labour*, in its concern with energies for reform and aspirations to an ideal with roots in modernity's dynamic itself:

> There are no needs so well founded as these tendencies, since they are a necessary consequence of changes that have taken place in the structure of societies. (1893a: 434 / 1902b: 382)

In sum, Durkheim's social science comes together with social vision and social critique. This normative element isn't just a personal value-added extra. It is integrally bound up with a search for an underlying social logic of things, in an idea of social science as rationalist empiricism.

Social Science as Rationalist Empiricism

Durkheim aimed to develop an empirical social science, yet in opposition to empiricism as usually understood. This is why he variously described his approach as 'rationalist empiricism', 'scientific rationalism' and a 'new rationalism'. It modernizes classic rationalism.

His Latin thesis was concerned with Montesquieu's *The Spirit of the Laws* (1748), a leading work of the Enlightenment. But it was also to set out his own first major programmatic statement of social science, quickly turned into French to become *The Rules of Sociological Method*. This appeared as a set of articles in 1894. It then came out as a book, together with a preface answering his critics and insisting on his approach as 'scientific rationalism' (1895a: viii).

But although it now had a name, it is basically the argument of the Latin thesis that is repeated in *The Rules*. Both of them work their way through the study of social facts as things, the classification of societies into types of social world, the distinction between the normal and the pathological, the nature of social explanation, and how it is above all causal explanation – understood as a search for necessary intelligible connections in an underlying logic of things.

Of course, it wasn't his Latin thesis but *The Rules* that became famous. Indeed, it is often treated as if a unique infallible Bible of his social science. This is a mistake. Durkheim didn't necessarily follow his own programmatic statements of method. But also, he came up with several of these during his career and a detailed investigation of them all would fill a large volume. In any case *The Rules* is not the place to go to grasp his idea of social science in its essentials. Instead, it is the short essay that identifies his approach as 'rationalist empiricism' (1897f: 79–80).

Rationalist Empiricism as a Programmatic Statement

Durkheim's basic objection to empiricism is that it is a determination to stay at the surface of things. It assembles facts, works out statistical correlations, forms theoretical concepts and puts together operational heuristic models. But it doesn't go beyond this, in search of explanation. It refuses to dig around in the evidence to try to uncover intelligible connections in an underlying logic and reality. Indeed, it denies any underlying logic in the world at all. It insists its theoretical terms and operational models are useful but artificial constructions, which 'do not correspond with anything in reality' (1897f: 75). Thus even when its supporters go on from the physical world to apply its methods to the intelligible human realm of the mind, it is still to stick with mere behaviourist sense-data:

> If it extends to everything, it enlightens nothing. Under the guise of positivism, they spread mystery everywhere. (78)

So it is also to spread mystery and mythology to label Durkheim an empiricist. He declared war on empiricism, precisely because he believed in an empirical social science as a search for explanation.

This is why it is also wrong just to emphasize his rationalism. True, his opposition to empiricism stems from belief that 'the real is intelligible', and from concern with internal connections in a 'logic of things' (75–76). But it was in attacking the sort of rationalism that claims to uncover all this without bothering to dig around in mere facts, and without the sweat and toil of actual empirical detective work. Instead, it goes for the quick philosophical fix of an analysis of concepts. It assumes that the logic of ideas is the same as the logic of things – that is, ways of thinking, feeling and acting it is impossible for us to change just at will, thanks to their deep far-reaching roots in our psychic and social life. Thus it has no real sense of a world of the mind with 'obscure, profound depths', and fails to grasp how this is 'not so clear, so transparent, so easy to penetrate' (78–80).

Durkheim was still hitting out at this simplistic philosophical rationalism in his last manuscript, on *Ethics*, written in 1917. But his campaign against it was already well under way in his Latin thesis. This insists on an ineliminable role for reason, to help science with 'ideas that guide research through the obscurity of things' (1892a: 59). It is above all to guide the empirical detective work required to dig around for clues to an underlying logic, and in an effort to bring to light its secret connections:

It is not our claim that social things are in themselves irrational. But if a certain logic lies hidden within them, it is different from the one we use in deductive reasoning; it does not have the same simplicity; perhaps it even follows other laws. Thus we need to find out about it from things themselves. (64)

Yet how does rationalist empiricism, as a programme, work out in practice?

Rationalist Empiricism in Practice
In exploring Durkheim's use of empirical indicators, a paradigmatic case to take is his thesis on the division of labour and its indicators of solidarity itself. In line with ordinary usage of the time, he understood *solidarité* as a moral term, involving both an internal sense of attachment and a web of social relations. But he stresses the problem of accessing solidarity as an internal phenomenon, and comes up with the solution that 'its visible symbol is law' (1893a: 66 / 1902b: 28).

So two basic points need to be made. One is about the function of his indicators of solidarity, the other about their nature. In book 1 chapter 1, their general job is to track down an internal sense of attachment, rather than a more readily observable web of relations. In book 1 chapter 2, their specific job is to track down the internal beliefs and sentiments of a collective consciousness, to do with a traditional 'mechanical' solidarity through likeness. By book 1 chapter 5, however, it becomes clear that their function is to track down an entire set of moral phenomena – beliefs, sentiments and webs of relations – in both a traditional solidarity through likeness and a modern solidarity through the division of labour. What his thesis above all attempts, as an exercise in a developing, increasingly complex, empirical investigation, is to track down, measure and compare the relative influence of different types of solidarity in different types of social world as these evolve through history and in a long-term dynamic of things.

In order to undertake such a vast comparative investigation, it is necessary to find empirical indicators that are both convenient and appropriate. Durkheim's solution certainly involves the convenience – for an armchair anthropologist, sitting in a study reading through archives – of books and statutes of law as the 'visible symbol' of morals. Yet the indicators must also be appropriate, and let us focus on this aspect of their nature.

Durkheim himself discusses them as 'signs' or 'symbols', and this seems thanks to his rationalist empiricism. He doesn't consider anything that might somehow act as an accidental yet nonetheless regular indicator of another phenomenon. Instead, he wants something he can construct an intelligible theoretical story about, to see it as intrinsically connected with what he aims to access. In other words, it is a sign or symbol of this – not a mere 'empiricist' indicator – since it is intrinsically and inherently bound up with it in his story of things.

This approach gets going in the original introduction to his thesis. His problem is just to get started with a science of moral life, by finding an empirical way to identify and access its very subject matter. His solution is the sanction, as an outward 'symbol' of an internal moral sense of obligation (1893a: 25).

In brief, his introductory theoretical story is that moral life is an affair of rules of conduct that come with an internal sense of duty and obligation. Accordingly, the breach of a moral rule necessarily generates disapproval or outrage or an even more severe and punitive response. In any case it necessarily generates a sanction, as a visible symbol of the rule, and so of morality itself.

Thus although it is only to get started, it is already quite a complex story, manoeuvring through numerous difficulties and open to many objections. But as Durkheim gets on in earnest with his project, he needs the empirical indicators of an even more elaborate detective work, to track down the things his developing arguments point to as crucial. And this involves him in even more elaborate interpretative stories, to link visible signs and underlying meanings. The result – in *The Division of Labour* itself, but also in *Suicide* and *The Elemental Forms* – is that his social science becomes an increasingly interpretative study of social life.

So, in line with his programmatic statements, it is still a search for a logic of things – whether these are beliefs and sentiments, webs of relations, social structures, or long-term historical processes of change. But in contrast with his programmatic statements, it isn't as 'fact-driven' as they imply. In the effort to uncover a social logic, it involves a whole interaction, indeed a fusion, of empirical detective work and theoretical interpretative reason.

But it remains an *effort*. It isn't about sticking with initial stories; it is about using these to kick-start a developing process of investigation. So it is also a route to the creativity of rethinking things, asking new questions, forming new concepts, and opening up new lines of research.

This creativity is more readily observed in action if a work's drafts and redrafts are available for analysis along with the eventually published text. It is nonetheless evident enough from any close examination of Durkheim's writings. True, his own programmatic statements on how to do social science stress the sweat and toil of patient investigation according to strict rules. But perhaps this was to discipline his own enthusiasm for ideas and love affair with reason.

At any rate, here is what he says about his science as rationalist empiricism:

Without condemning reason to give up, without even setting limits to its future ambitions, it puts it on guard against itself. It gives it the sense of a surrounding darkness, while recognizing its power, little by little, to spread light. It gives satisfaction in this way to two contrary sentiments, which can be seen as the great driving forces of intellectual development – a sense of the obscure, and faith in the power of the human mind. (1897f: 79)

Rhetorical, no doubt. Yet effective. Besides, isn't it merely innocent to imagine science as bare, naked, transparent discourse, stripped of all metaphor? An elemental metaphor of science is transparence itself.

Social Science and the Ideal of Transparence

A work of science is like a work of art. Meaning is bound up with the form of discourse itself. An entire worldview is embedded in the grammar, style and vocabulary of a work on economics and accounting. Indeed, a way to kill off all sense of solidarity and the sacred is to write about them in the manner of a work on economics and accounting. An effort will be made later to go into Durkheim's own discourses of solidarity and the sacred. Meanwhile, there is a need to ask about a basic metaphor and theme of his social science – bringing the hidden to light, in an ideal of transparence.

Enlightenment and Modernity
In Kant's philosophical history, humankind stumbles blindly along until the emergence of an age of enlightenment, increasingly conscious of the human ideal, then hopefully followed by an enlightened age, increasingly realizing it in practice. But what is Durkheim's message? Is his new social science merely a secret esoteric knowledge, limited to sociologists? Or does is it involve a spread of understanding throughout society, and if so, how?

As he writes early on in his thesis, science is nowadays a highly specialized knowledge within a vast division of labour, and by its nature unavailable to the lay multitude. So this can be called 'esoteric enlightenment'. Yet as he writes on the very same page:

It is essential that intelligence, guided by science, takes a greater role in the processes of collective life. (1893a: 53 / 1902b: 15)

This entails a spread of social understanding, but guided by the sociologist, and so can be called 'expert-led enlightenment'. Yet as he also writes on the very same page:

So that societies can live in the conditions of existence that now apply to them, it is necessary that the field of consciousness, whether individual or social, becomes greater and clearer. (53 / 14)

This sees a whole wider movement in which society itself generates its own more or less transparent self-understanding, and so can be called 'civic enlightenment'. What, then, is the form of enlightenment that wins out in Durkheim's work as a whole? A key case is how, throughout his career, 'god' is a transfigurative metaphorical representation of society.

Enlightenment and God

A famous saying from the Enlightenment is attributed to Voltaire: 'If God did not exist, it would be necessary to invent him'. It must have been known to Durkheim. Certainly, it is echoed in his thesis. He describes events that generate extraordinarily intense collective energies, which get represented as a transcendent sacred power or 'god'. The representation is illusory, yet the illusion is necessary. It has a basis that is real and a function that is essential. Although ideas of 'god' are metaphorical, they drive home a sense of a power over and beyond the individual, and what they represent is society (1893a: 107–8 / 1902b: 68–69).

Yet what sort of enlightenment is this? It comes in book 1 chapter 2, which starts his story of a traditional collective consciousness and traditional consensual dogmatic beliefs. So is it an esoteric enlightenment, confined to sociologists? Try as they might, it is impossible to spread the news that 'god' is a social construction. Nobody will believe them, precisely thanks to the social entrenchment of belief in God's reality. Or is it an expert-led, but self-defeating enlightenment? News indeed seeps through to the lay multitude that 'god' is a social invention, undermining the very idea that belief in God is a social necessity. In fact, reading on in his thesis, it is concerned with civic enlightenment.

It soon transpires – in book 1 chapter 5 – that 'god' is an illusion we can do without. Religion at first governs everything, but loses its influence as the processes of the division of labour take hold. Science itself is part of a whole wider modern dynamic that generates a world of secular life, individualism and free thought (183–86 / 143–46). Or, reading even further on, to the work's conclusion, it doesn't end with a call for a return to religion. It ends with a call 'to build ourselves a morality' (460 / 406). And if it is really necessary to spell this out, it is a call to build ourselves a *secular* morality.

However, taking Durkheim's career as a whole, what is the relation between a modern secular morality and a modern secular religion? In a debate around the time he began drafting *The Elemental Forms*, he remarks:

> I see in the divinity only society transfigured and thought of symbolically.
> (1906b: 75)

Yet a secular religion, while dropping 'god', keeps the sacred. So is it just another way to transfigure the social world in clouds of mystification? But if the sacred can come with transparence, is there any real difference between a secular ethic and a 'secular religion'?

In *The Elemental Forms*, religion constructs the sacred through symbolism, ritual and effervescent energies and emotions. So it can seem guaranteed to generate a fog of mystification. This reading is repeatedly encouraged by remarks of the author himself. Yet, at crucial points, it is also explicitly denied by him. In the middle of the work's whole centrepiece on symbolism, ritual, effervescence and the sacred, he insists on the possibility of a secular religion that comes with all these things, but 'without transfiguration of any kind' (1912a: 306). His example is the French Revolution, and so is an example of civic enlightenment. The only trouble is how he associates it with an idea of secular religion that seems a contradiction in terms – a transparent faith, complete with altars, symbols and rites, yet without mystification of any kind.

The picture is different in the account of secular religion and a modern cult of the person in his essay on the Dreyfus Affair.[3] This describes the whole business of symbols and rites as 'superficial', indeed a mere 'external apparatus'. The core of religion lies elsewhere:

> Essentially, it is nothing other than a set of collective beliefs and practices
> with a special authority. (1898c: 270)

So here is a slimmed-down view of religion, with a far-reaching significance. Its idea of an enlightened secular religion is indistinguishable from an enlightened secular ethic. The key is again what actually constructs the sacred. It isn't, of course, the illusion that is 'god'. But it also isn't the mere paraphernalia of symbols and rites. Nor, therefore, can it be the mere rhetoric of talk of the sacred itself. What, then, constructs the 'special authority' of beliefs and practices centred round everyone's sacredness as a person?

> This cult of man has, as its first dogma, the autonomy of reason, and, as its
> first rite, free enquiry and examination. (268)

So this is indistinguishable from enlightened secular ethics, since the source of its authority is autonomy. The message is the same in his lectures on moral education, probably given in 1898–99,[4] then throughout the 1900s.

Moreover, the significance of the lectures is not just their content. It is also their audience. Year in year out, Durkheim gave the course to students intending to become teachers – spreading throughout France, to provide future citizens of the republic with an enlightened education. And his opening lecture makes clear what this entails. It is necessary to develop a secular ethics that cuts through the fog of religious symbolism, so as to understand the nature of morality in 'rational language' – indeed, to reveal it in its 'rational nakedness' (1925: 10, 13).

He then embarks on an account of elemental forms of moral life, which he identifies as discipline, attachment, and the modern aspiration to autonomy. But at the same time he worries about a modern movement of essentially negative deconstruction and critique. It strips away religious symbolism, yet in the process leaves a moral void. What is necessary, instead, is to look for a rational equivalent of the mysterious power that once was 'god'. Predictably, this involves him in appeal to the scientifically accessible moral power that is society (119, 138). However, it also involves him in an issue that was central to the essay on the Dreyfus Affair: where, in the modern world, to find the source of the authority of the sacred. But now, revealed in its 'rational nakedness', his basic problematic is Kantian: where, in the modern world, to find the source of the authority of the ethical. And his key to things is again Kantian. The only possible modern source of this authority is autonomy, as the necessary condition of 'free, enlightened acceptance' (137).

It is true that Durkheim can be irritating in the way he so often just invokes 'Society'. But it is an error to assume he therefore locates ethical authority in any actual social world whatever. On the contrary, and as in the lectures, the modern social world can achieve this only to the extent that it is on the way to meeting an essential modern aspiration – a self-understood, transparent commonwealth. In a version of Kant's ideal of a 'kingdom of ends', Durkheim's source of ethical authority is neither Reason nor Society but a union of autonomous persons.

Enlightenment and Autonomy

This aspiration is why Durkheim insists on what he calls a 'progressive autonomy', evolving and developing in history (1925: 130). It is also why he criticizes what he sees as Kant's radical dualism. It locates autonomy in a mysterious 'noumenal' realm, while leaving us imprisoned in the chains of determinism of the actually experienced 'phenomenal' world.

So perhaps, in the lectures, he wanted to concentrate on getting across to students an issue that is undoubtedly central to engaging with Kant's thought. But in the process he leaves out Kant's philosophical history, where the kernel of a freedom inside everyone evolves and develops through a dynamic of the sociohistorical world itself. In fact, there are many ways of seeing an interlinkage between Kantian and Durkheimian stories of a progressive autonomy on the road to a commonwealth of persons.[5] But a basic point is how, like Kant, Durkheim wants to a find a way to reconcile human freedom with scientific explanation in terms of necessary causes. It is another piece of mythology just to label him a determinist. Instead, his 'progressive' autonomy is about the socially conditioned development of a power of human agency. In turn, this is about a socially conditioned development of a power of critical thought and enquiry, and the emergence of science itself. Thus 'it is science that is the source of our autonomy' (132). But also and more generally, 'it is thought that is liberator of the will' (136).

Even so, and again focusing on his thesis on the division of labour, how do these programmatic statements work out in practice?

His own explicit testimony is that his thesis originated in the issue of the relation between solidarity and autonomy (1893a: ix / 1902b: xliii). But it is important to dig around for other evidence.

It must have been quite soon in working on his thesis that he had the idea of distinguishing two basic types of solidarity, and calling them 'mechanical' and 'organic'. The proof is a lecture in which he recaps the previous year's course on social solidarity, begun in 1887. He reminds his students that 'mechanical' solidarity through likeness is about the primitive and a group's total control of the individual, while 'organic' solidarity through the division of labour is about the modern and an independence of the individual within the unity of a complex whole (1888c: 10). However, it is also in going to this early text that it is possible to notice a significant change in the final, written-up version of his thesis. Mechanical solidarity is still about a primitive, total collective control of the individual – but now he emphasizes it as amounting to control and possession of a thing. Organic solidarity is still about a modern, free independent sphere of action of the individual – but now, in contrasting it with control of a thing, he mobilizes talk of autonomy (1893a: 139–41 / 1902b: 100–1).

So an implicit reference is to a Kantian contrast between heteronomy as if things and autonomy as persons. This is an underlying meaning of Durkheim's whole 'mechanical'/'organic' metaphor. It encapsulates a message of his whole story of an evolution from one type of solidarity to the other. Leaving behind a world of mechanical solidarity is about emancipation from a mechanistic determinism – that is, from heteronomy as if things and from imprisonment in chains of causation that cannot be controlled since they are not understood.

Durkheim's official plan of his thesis is that book 1 tackles the division of labour's 'function', book 2 its 'causes and conditions', book 3 its 'abnormal forms'. Of course, it isn't quite so neat as this, in the actual way it builds up and increasingly weaves together all his many concerns, themes and arguments. In the case of book 2, his concern with 'causes and conditions' involves working through a series of factors to build up a picture of their interaction in an overall process in which, as it gathers momentum, the division of labour takes over as a dynamic of the modern world. But his first main business is to try to pick out which of these factors set the whole process in motion. In turn, this involves two main aims. One is to pick out the factors that trigger a long-term transformation of structure, underlying a transformation of consciousness. The other is to insist on momentous changes that take place without understanding of the forces that drive them. There is no notion of their far-reaching consequences. So it is absurd to invoke a 'teleological' explanation in terms of a consciously pursued end or ideal. On the contrary: 'Everything happens mechanically' (299 / 253).

However, this is in book 2 chapter 2, before all of his story has been told. In the conclusion to book 2, in chapter 5, he writes:

> A mechanistic conception of society doesn't rule out the ideal, and it is an error to accuse it of reducing man to a mere inactive witness of his own history. (380 / 331).

So he still wants to talk of 'mechanistic' as against 'teleological' explanation. But it is in a choice between two terms that are equally inadequate to describe what is actually going on in his argument. Whatever might set in motion the division of labour's evolution as a modern dynamic, things are different once the dynamic takes hold, complete with the development of new social ideals, individualism, a cult of the person, free thought and science itself. The job of book 2's final chapter is to bring a complex of interacting factors together, but also to prepare the way for what is to come in book 3 and the work's conclusion – a critique of a world in crisis, and a call for action for reform.

Social science can help with guiding this, since, as in the preface, it can clarify aspirations and ideals. However, it isn't its job to concoct detailed blueprints of the good society. Reform can only take place gradually and spontaneously, through pressures from within society itself that make it necessary. But this is why there is a need for a new web of intermediate groups, to develop adequate and effective processes of collective argument that are necessary to articulate these pressures, to work out reforms and to translate ideals into a moral code. In practice, it is the main route to a form of civic enlightenment in which, as insisted early on in the thesis, the field of consciousness becomes 'greater and clearer'. The need for new occupational groups surfaces at various points in his thesis, helping to prepare the way for a follow-up companion work on them. In any case, it is his long-held view of these groups – as the key to a developing spontaneous process of reform, made necessary by forces arising within society itself – that is the context of the call for action that brings his thesis to an end:

> In a word, our first duty at the present time is to build ourselves a morality. Such a work cannot be concocted in the silence of the study; it can arise only on its own, little by little, under the pressure of internal causes that make it necessary. But the service that thought can and must render is to set out the goal it is essential to attain. This is what we have tried to do. (460 / 406)

In Sum

In order to understand Durkheim's project for a social science, it is necessary to explore and interrelate the elements of vision, critique, rationalist empiricism and, not least, the theme and metaphor of transparence. It is in his very emphasis on obscure forces that his aim is to bring the hidden to light, which at the same time helps to free us from blind mechanisms and bring these under control. In the end, however, it is not so much science that is liberator of the will. It is intelligence guided by science, but together with empowerment by adequate and effective processes of collective argument. This still involves what might nowadays seem an idealistic view of science's social role. Yet it is the historical Durkheim's idealistic sense of a mission that was behind his youthful conversion from philosophy – leading eventually on to his canonization as 'a founding father of sociology'.

CHAPTER 2

The Creation of *The Division of Labour*

A way to get to know a work is to get to know about its creation, and a way to investigate the creation of *The Division of Labour* is through three basic questions. When was it written? How was it part of a larger project? What was its context?

The Career of a Doctoral Dissertation: 1882 to 1892

Durkheim arrived as an eighteen-year-old student in Paris in 1876, in the middle of a period of crisis that finally saw the establishment of a new Third Republic. He was later to recall his feelings of youthful enthusiasm during these events of 'twenty years ago' (1898c: 276). It was in this atmosphere of hope and sense of a world on the move that he turned his mind to what, after graduation in 1882, to do for a doctorate. According to his nephew, he originally thought about the relation between individualism and socialism, but soon fixed on the relation between the individual and society. He then drew up a first plan of his thesis in 1884, completed a first draft in 1886, and began work on a final version in 1888 (Mauss 1928: v).

What other evidence is there to back this up? It is now possible to go to recently discovered student notes of a college philosophy course given by Durkheim in 1883–84. These come with a revealing discussion of individualism versus socialism. Individualism treats society as an artificial construction and fails to see it is a complex living reality. Yet socialism so exalts society and the state that it denies individual rights and crushes the individual personality. However, 'the solution to this problem is the division of labour' (2004: 258–60).

This fits in with Durkheim's own testimony that his thesis originated in the problem of how the individual can be more autonomous yet also more attached to society, and how the solution is 'the ever increasing development of the division of labour' (1893a: ix / 1902b: xliii–xliv]). But the most important piece of evidence is the lecture where he recaps the course on social solidarity that he began in 1887, when he got his job at Bordeaux. It is clear that he had set out to teach his students the ideas of his thesis:

The analysis of these two types of society then led us to discover two very different forms of social solidarity, one that is due to the similarity of consciousnesses, to the community of ideas and sentiments, the other that is on the contrary a product of the differentiation of functions and of the division of labour ... It is in the great modern societies that we can best observe this higher solidarity, child of the division of labour, that allows its individual parts their independence while reinforcing the unity of the whole. (1888c: 258)

His summary runs to three pages and reports the basic ideas of books 1 and 2, on the division of labour's function, its causes and conditions, and its evolution as the modern world's dynamic. He says nothing about book 3's modern pathologies. But he must have already been worrying about these. This is on the evidence of his early articles, including his first article of 1885, with its call for new occupational groups to tackle a modern crisis.

Indeed, a problem for him must have been how to handle all his material within a single work. Thus according to his own testimony, it was while writing his thesis that he decided on a companion follow-up volume on occupational groups. But are there any other clues to how his project was taking shape?

Durkheim's publications start to trail off in 1888 and come to a halt in 1890. They don't get going again until after he handed in the work for his doctorate in 1892. So this suggests a period in which he concentrated on completing a detailed, polished version of *The Division of Labour* – while having to get on with his Latin thesis, and to continue to do his teaching. In turn, it also suggests it was when he finally decided on a companion volume on occupational groups.

The detailed polished arguments taking him to the end of book 2 took up so much space that they converted into four hundred printed pages – roughly 85 per cent of the eventual text. So on the one hand, he was running out of room for book 3, and in fact it remains a sketch of a world in crisis. On the other, he wasn't running out of ideas and material on this. It is evident from what he was doing in his teaching that he was developing his account, in earlier articles, of the nature of a deep-rooted crisis and of the need for reform through new occupational groups. In sum, there are various ways of trying to back up his own personal testimony of deciding on a companion volume – a decision crucial to the entire structure and content of *The Division of Labour,* shaping not only what went into it but what was left out.

However, to return to the story of his thesis itself, the copy in the library of the Sorbonne records that it was handed in – or more precisely, was 'seen and read' and given an *imprimatur* by the university authorities – on 24 March 1892.

The Career of a Sociological Text: 1893 to 1911

The thesis was printed with the date '1893'. Yet this was over nine months after the manuscript was handed in. There is also a page reference to it in his Latin thesis, printed in 1892 (18, n.1). But let us just take its date as correct. What counts is that it was circulated in time for study by his examining jury, which met on 3 March 1893. A commercial edition, by the newly successful Dr Durkheim, was then brought out and put on sale to the public. So, contrary to the usual impression, there were two printed versions of *The Division of Labour* that appeared in 1893.

It is nonetheless convenient just to refer to the 'university edition' (of the thesis), while continuing to talk about the 'first edition' (of the commercial book). What matters is if there are significant differences between the two texts. And there is one that is obvious. The thesis is simply called, *De la Division du travail social.* It is only the book that comes with the subtitle, *étude sur l'organisation des sociétés supérieures* ('study of the organization of higher societies'). But so far there has been no systematic check for other differences.

In a way we enter more familiar territory with the second edition. It is well known that Durkheim made two main changes – extensive cuts in the introduction, and a new preface on occupational groups. It is not so well known that in cutting the first edition's subtitle, he went back to the original unadorned title of his thesis. In any case, these were not the only changes. Some were noticed in the first English translation, by George Simpson (1933: viii). But he overlooked others. And again there has been no systematic check for all the differences between the texts, just as there has been no systematic check for misprints and other mistakes.

In a letter of March 1901, Durkheim confesses he has just started work on the new edition, yet the deadline for getting it to the publishers was only around a month away (1998: 279). Two weeks after the deadline had passed, he asks his nephew – 'if you have a moment to spare' – to go through the entire original edition to correct it for errors (283). There is no indication that Mauss even attempted such a task. And Durkheim somewhat coolly informs him, just over a week later, that he has sent everything off to the publishers (286). Evidently, he did the preparation of the new edition in haste.

It is doubtful if he did anything at all for what is announced on the frontispiece as 'the third edition'. The last in his lifetime, it was published in 1911 while he was completing *The Elemental Forms* and looks like a reprint of 1902. The same applies to subsequent posthumous editions, except that they come with mysteriously introduced misprints and other changes of their own.

It is impossible to rely on them for scholarly historical purposes. A modern critical edition is still awaited, as part of the project directed by Massimo Borlandi. Meanwhile, this study's investigations have been anchored in the original university edition of the thesis (1893a), together with the second edition of the book (1902b). At the same time references and quotations have involved a check on all four editions appearing in his lifetime, in a lookout for significant differences. It is only a sample digging around in the texts that constitute the material substratum of the work. But it is better than no digging around at all.

The Latin Thesis

It has already been suggested that the creation of *The Division of Labour* was like the creation of the central panel of a triptych, so that it has to be understood, not just on its own, but together with its two 'side panels'. And let us start with his Latin thesis. Submitted in November 1892, it focuses on a seminal work of the French Enlightenment, Montesquieu's *The Spirit of the Laws.*

In reading through other works of the time on Montesquieu, it becomes striking how the thesis is so different and original in comparison. Indeed, its line on Montesquieu is very much driven by Durkheim's own ideas, and links with his thesis on the division of labour in two main ways. It has already been discussed how it uses Montesquieu to set out Durkheim's own programme of social science. So let us now concentrate on its other job, which is to construct Montesquieu as a totemic founder of social science. A way to legitimate Durkheim's own project was to find respectable ancestors. The aristocratic baron de Montesquieu – a voice from the old regime, yet also of a new era – was an ideal candidate.

Montesquieu as a Totemic Founder of Social Science

Durkheim was appointed to a new post in social science at the university of Bordeaux in 1887. His opening lecture introduced his students to the course on solidarity in which he taught them the ideas of the thesis he was working on. But it was also a high-profile public occasion, and in effect the ritual of an inaugural lecture – perhaps why it was printed and has survived. Appropriately, then, for an inaugural lecture, he outlines the history of his discipline and goes on to explain the role and mission he sees for it.

His story of sociology gets going in earnest with the French Enlightenment, to take a swipe at Rousseau, followed by honorific mention of Montesquieu and Condorcet. But he especially picks out Montesquieu, in a mix of praise and criticism, as a founder of a 'science of societies' (1888a: 80). He then gets on to Comte, who had given sociology a name. But when he brings the story up to date, there is a long discussion of the Englishman Herbert Spencer, as well as a long discussion of various Germans. Yet except for a brief mention of Alfred Espinas – a leading member of the university, who had helped to get Durkheim his post and who was presumably sitting in the audience – he says nothing at all about any live, rather than dead, French social theorist. The clear message is that the new science is forging ahead outside France, while lagging behind in France itself, the very place, in the story, where it began. The future author of *The Division of Labour* then concludes with a stirring vision of a renascence of sociology in the country that gave it birth. And it would not have been too difficult for his audience to work out that he saw himself as going to lead this renascence.

The Latin thesis begins with the same basic message of how the new science nowadays flourishes in Britain and Germany, while in France it is regarded with suspicion and it is forgotten that 'it started up in our own country' (1892a: 7). This is then the cue to introduce Montesquieu. But it also takes us to a problem. The title of the thesis announces that it is on Montesquieu's contribution to *political* science. So is it really about this, rather than, as in the inaugural lecture, his contribution to *social* science?

It is mistaken to see Durkheim struggling to express himself in an ossified language. He had been given a long, thorough classical education, and his thesis is written in clear and indeed elegant Latin. So to understand what is going on in it, let us start with his use of a set of key terms – *res politicae, res civiles, civilia facta, socialia vincula, societas* and *sociologia. Res politicae* straightforwardly translate as 'political things'. *Res civiles*, while literally 'civil things', take us towards 'social things'. And *civilia facta*, while literally 'civil facts', take us towards 'social facts'. But there is no ambiguity at all about *socialia vincula*, which are the 'social links' central to his whole account of solidarity. Nor is it hard to translate *societas* and *sociologia*. The issue, instead, is their role in his argument. He was playing some sort of subversive game with the very idea of 'political science', to deconstruct this and shift the ground towards social science.

Thus once we get past his dissertation's title and frontispiece, we read in the main text's very first page that it is about a science eventually given 'its own – if somewhat barbarous – name of sociology' (1892a: 7).

But what counts is his argument's whole development. This takes us through issues of subject matter, classification, explanation and method. And he starts with how the new science's subject isn't merely government, but everything 'bound up with the nature of societies' (17). He then goes on to praise Montesquieu's classification of three real enough 'types of society' (40). But he criticizes Montesquieu's actual discussion of these as a republic, monarchy and despotism. This misleadingly tries 'to distinguish forms of society through forms of government' (41). The story is the same when we get to issues of explanation and method. Montesquieu is seen and assessed for his contribution to a science that goes beyond politics, to become a science of society:

> He opened the way to his successors who, in inaugurating *sociology*, did not do much more than bestow, on the kind of study undertaken by him, a name. (66)

But it is even more evident that the thesis is about Montesquieu's construction as a founder of social science, if it is read in the context of other approaches at the time and Montesquieu's construction in the Third Republic as a symbol of a modern liberal democratic politics.

Montesquieu as a Symbol of Liberalism and a Modern Age of Democracy

It is significant that the battle for the republic saw the first effort to publish an edition of Montesquieu's *Complete Works*, brought out in seven volumes between 1875 and 1879. It is a key part of an old regime aristocrat's reconstruction as a symbol of liberalism, and of the aspirations but also anxieties of a modern age of democracy. What is perhaps even more significant is the identity of the editor, Edouard Laboulaye. It was Laboulaye who organized something even more monumental, the gift from France to America of the Statue of Liberty. As a symbol, this is opposed to images of Liberty as a bare-breasted woman-warrior, leading the people at the barricades and trampling triumphantly over the bodies of dead reactionaries. It recasts her in unmistakably liberal form, as a stately figure with a torch of knowledge and enlightenment in one hand and a book of laws – evoking Montesquieu's *Spirit of the Laws?* – in the other. It was this new colossus that gradually rose up to dominate the skyline of Paris while Durkheim was a student there in the early 1880s, to be re-erected with much ceremony in New York Harbour in 1886. Moreover, a work by a jury examiner that Durkheim took care to consult for his thesis clearly identifies Montesquieu's editor, Laboulaye, as a champion of modern liberty and democracy *à l'américaine* (Janet 1887: vol. 2, 738).

But the handiest contemporary guide to this whole terrain is Albert Sorel's *Montesquieu*. Entirely ignored in Durkheim's thesis, it was by one of France's star historians. Highly acclaimed and quickly translated into English, it was the work to go to for an accessible, informed, up to date account of Montesquieu and his importance – even, or especially, in recognizing his limitations:

> Montesquieu did not foresee the rapid advent and wonderful development of modern democracy, still less did he believe in the establishment of democratic republics in extensive countries. (Sorel 1887b: 98)

Or again:

> Democracy was only for Montesquieu a kind of historical phenomenon: it
> reigns now in some of the greatest nations of the world, and aims at invading
> all the others; the monarchy he describes was in his day the prevailing form of
> government in Europe; it has now almost entirely disappeared. (101–2)

But the picture changes when Sorel moves on from Montesquieu in his
place and time, to a history of his different constructions during and
after the Revolution. In going over uses of Montesquieu to defend some
or other form of monarchy, he attacks their determination to ignore the
nature of modern society and the democratic forces at work in it. Yet
this is also why he attacks attempts, in the Revolution, to invoke Montesquieu's ideal of a republic of virtue as if ancient Sparta could re-arise
in modern France in abstraction from actual sociohistorical conditions.
Instead, he goes on to see a genuine modern successor to Montesquieu
in Tocqueville, author of *Democracy in America* (1835–40). It is because
Tocqueville, despite his own royalist and aristocratic attachments, was
inspired by the spirit of Montesquieu's approach to try to understand
the nature of the modern world and the advent of modern democracy.
In turn, this has inspired a whole flourishing of contemporary political
and historical studies. So, as he concludes, it is above all through Tocqueville that Montesquieu is 'connected with and influences the France
of the present day' (Sorel 1887b: 172).

The main heavyweight academic study of Montesquieu at the time
is to be found in Paul Janet's *History of Political Science*. Running to two
volumes, and in a new, revised and expanded third edition, it was by
one of Durkheim's examiners and is frequently cited in his thesis. Yet
the thesis, in contrast with both Sorel and Janet, takes no real interest in the implications of Montesquieu's approach for understanding a
new democratic era. Indeed, Durkheim's Montesquieu is someone who
would have seen modern France as a monarchy and 'would not have
counted it a republic' (1892a: 32). This is because Durkheim's Montesquieu is a sociologist, using 'monarchy' as a term to describe modern
society itself and a world where 'the division of labour tends towards its
fullest development' (37).

But there is an even more revealing example of how the thesis is
above all about sociology, rather than politics. It is to do with the issue
of how to read Montesquieu on 'despotism'.

Durkheim treats this as about a real enough type of social world,
the vast societies and empires of the East. He ignores Janet's argument
for a different interpretation, that Montesquieu's talk of despotic rulers

of China or wherever is about the king of France in disguise. Indeed, Janet makes this a key to decoding Montesquieu's text, to ask why its aristocratic author had so much to say on despotism in far off lands, yet was conspicuously silent about Louis XIV. 'These Chinese names, aren't they there in place of other names that one doesn't care to mention?' (Janet 1887: vol. 2, 365). He goes on to emphasize despotism as 'a spectre' that haunts Montesquieu. It is in no way just a story of the East. It is a nightmare scenario built into the very nature of monarchy and of the modern Western world itself.

This is a general line of interpretation that perhaps started to get going as soon as *The Spirit of the Laws* was published in 1748. In any case, it took hold with the experience of a series of authoritarian regimes during and after the Revolution, and became especially influential through Tocqueville. The 'spectre' of despotism is thus very much part of how – after the collapse of another empire in 1870, and in the effort to establish a new republic – Montesquieu was transformed into a symbol of the aspirations but also the anxieties of a modern age of democracy.

Yet there is little or no trace of any of this in Durkheim's thesis. Why? Part of the mystery is how he also has next to nothing to say on Montesquieu's defence of intermediate groups. Or is it part of the answer? The issues of modern democracy, the spectre of authoritarianism and the need for powerful intermediate groups are all bound up with one another. Investigation of this whole problematic calls for a full-scale work of its own. And it is something he intended to undertake, though not in a subsidiary thesis in Latin, nor in his main thesis on fundamental long-term social change through the division of labour, but in a companion volume.

In sum, a note in the *History of Political Science* says that Montesquieu is 'one of the ancestors of our modern sociologists' (Janet 1887: vol. 2, 405, n.3). Durkheim's Latin thesis doesn't just expand on this idea. It hammers it home with a sort of single-minded brilliance. In concentrating on Montesquieu as an ancestor of sociology, it deliberately left out well-known issues involving Montesquieu's construction in a modern politics. These were to be done justice elsewhere, in a work conceived as part of a triptych centred round *The Division of Labour*.

The Projected Companion Volume on Occupational Groups

Durkheim wrote *The Division of Labour*'s new preface in the spring of 1901. He explains it is about occupational groups, and continues:

> If, originally, we touched on the problem only by way of allusions, it is because we intended to take it up later and make a special study of it. Since other things have

arisen to divert us from this project and we do not see when it will be possible for us to carry through with it, we would like, with this second edition, to take the opportunity to show how this question links with the subject dealt with in the course of the work. (1902b: i–ii)

This more or less announces the abandonment of his project. A preface does not have the same impact as a full-scale work. Nor has anybody brought together all his material on occupational groups in a single collection. It remains scattered in different places, again with an inevitable loss of impact. What can be attempted here is to identify this material, from his first academic publication in 1885 to his last manuscript in 1917.

A New Guild Socialism

Durkheim began his sociological career with a long enthusiastic review essay of a work by the German social theorist, Albert Schaeffle. The essay picks up on a crisis with origins involving the suppression of the old guilds and corporations. This helped to unleash two extreme tendencies – a conflict of 'unfettered egoisms', arising from individualism but generating class warfare, and a 'despotic socialism', centralizing power in the state. There is only one solution to the crisis:

> It is to re-establish the corporations. Correctly understood, there can be no question of reviving them just as they existed in the middle ages. But it is not impossible to find them a new organization, less narrow and fixed, and better adapted to today's mobile life and far-reaching division of labour. (1885a: 371)

So this reads like an abstract of *The Division of Labour*'s new preface. But it is significant in other ways.

It comes in the context of a law of 1884 that, after a long struggle for the right of workers to form organized trade unions, at last lifted the ban on these and won them legal recognition. At the same time it marks a change in Durkheim's own attitude to socialism, away from the attack on it as entailing a monolithic state in his college lectures of 1883–84, and towards support for a guild socialism on the lines advocated by Schaeffle. Indeed, in a series of articles, he went on to criticize leaders of French liberal opinion not only for their lightweight ideas on reform and failure to understand the depth of the crisis, but for their woeful ignorance of socialism and attack on it as entailing a monolithic state. Instead, he went out of his way to defend Schaeffle and his version of socialism (1885b: 179–81; 1886a: 208–10; 1888b: 377–83). Thus Durkheim's first essay wasn't a one-off affair. It combines with these other early texts to make clear that he looked to reform through occupational groups from the outset of his sociological career, and in the process very publicly identified himself with a particular form of socialism.

But the most radical evidence from this period involves his course on the family, given from 1888 to 1892. In the concluding lecture, he sees the occupational group as a way to develop a collective yet decentralized ownership and control of wealth. It is necessary to tackle private individual inheritance through the modern nuclear family and the ways in which it creates massive social inequalities that are unmerited and unjust:

> This injustice, that appears more and more intolerable to us, is becoming more and more irreconcilable with the conditions of existence of our societies. (1921: 45)

Nor is it a coincidence that his critique of these inequalities is the same as in *The Division of Labour*. He handed in his thesis in March 1892, and gave the lecture in April 1892. But where the thesis states the problem, it is his lecture that offers a solution, in the occupational groups of a new guild socialism. It also suggests he was getting ready to get on with a follow-up work on these as the key to reform.

After The Division of Labour

Durkheim's first publication after *The Division of Labour* was an essay on socialism. It attracted attention as a sympathetic yet non-sectarian attempt to understand the socialist movement in all its many forms. Yet this is why it draws a veil over which of these he himself supported, with only a brief allusion to a guild socialism of new occupational groups (1893c: 232–33). It is similarly discreet about the kinds of socialism he opposed, though he was public enough about them elsewhere, and even more forcible in private letters (1998: 225–26). On the other hand, it is precisely as a general overall survey of modern socialism that the essay can be seen as preparing the ground for future, more detailed investigations.

In fact, a revised version is put to work to introduce the course on socialism begun in 1895 and continuing into 1896 with lectures on the early nineteenth-century socialist movement led by Saint-Simon. These are of considerable interest, but not least because Durkheim explicitly rejects Saint-Simon's idea of a return to religion. Instead, he again insists that the solution to the crisis of modern industrial society lies elsewhere, in new occupational groups (1928: 296–97, 351–52).

It was also in 1896 that he was busy writing up the manuscript of *Suicide*, completed early the following year, as we now know from his letters

(1998: 43-45, 51). It was again to reject the idea of a return to religion as a solution to modern pathologies, again in a call, instead, for new intermediate occupational groups. But at the same time it suggests his continuing commitment to a full-scale work on them. The conclusion to *Suicide* is significant as the first major sustained account of his ideas on these groups (1897a: 425–51).

In turn, it fed into what now survives as his fullest treatment of the whole issue. This is his course on occupational and civic ethics. It was published long after his death as *Lectures on Sociology* (1950). But according to his nephew, it is the text of a manuscript written up in 1898–1900.

So in a way it is ironic that, just after putting in all this effort, and in rushing to get out *The Division of Labour*'s new edition, he seems to have abandoned his project for a companion work. However, and again according to his nephew, the manuscript of the lectures is the definitive version of a course given throughout the 1900s. He especially mentions how it was given in 1912–14 – just at the time, it might be noted, of the appearance of *The Elemental Forms* – but the last occasion was in 1915–16 (Mauss 1937: 500–1).

This takes us on to Durkheim's last article published in his lifetime, 'The Politics of the Future' (1917c), and his last manuscript, outlining the project of a new great work, 'Introduction to *Ethics*' (1920). The article continues to analyse the problems of the modern industrial world in terms of the sociological landscape of *The Division of Labour*, and in the process discusses occupational groups. The manuscript makes clear Durkheim's intention to draw on his material on these, but as part of a larger project. Indeed, it is possible to see the follow-up companion volume to *The Division of Labour* as a new great work on *Ethics*.

The Revolution and the Republic

In a way, the creation of *The Division of Labour* was a continuing process, going on long after it was first drafted, written up and published. However, let us return to its origins in the 1880s, and to the world in which it took shape and made an appearance. This was the world of a new Third Republic, complete with its motto re-adopted from the Revolution, *Liberty, Equality, Fraternity*. The legacy of the Revolution is a basic context of Durkheim's search for a modern solidarity.

'1789'

As every French schoolchild was expected to know, the Revolution began in 1789. It then generated a succession of regimes – three republics, as many monarchies, and two empires.[1] Durkheim himself was born and

brought up during the Second Empire, run by the moustachioed Napo-
leon III in alliance with the Church and with the great crusader against
liberalism and revolution, Pope Pius IX. The regime collapsed in defeat
in 1870, involving two events that became engrained in French collective memory. One was the loss of Alsace-Lorraine to the Germans. The
other was the uprising of the Paris Commune, suppressed in 1871. A National Assembly, elected the same year, took upon itself the task of deciding a new form of government. Right-wing parties had a majority. Along
with their opposition to a republic, they shared a general longing for the
'Moral Order' of a hierarchical, conservative, Catholic France. Yet as well
as hating a republic, they hated each other. This was in a division against
themselves that wasn't merely poisonous, but insurmountable, thanks to
the claims of two rival kings and one would-be emperor. As the stalemate
dragged on, their position weakened. After an attempted *coup d'état* – a
last stand of reaction, with the blessing of the Church – the parties of the
right were swept away in the election of 1877. Then, between 1878 and
1881, a whole series of events confirmed the arrival of a Third Republic,
to the elation of the young Durkheim. All the same, what can a school-
book story of *1789 and All That* tell us about the creation of an elaborate
university thesis?

'1789' and the Battle of Rites and Symbols

Durkheim's first major publication after submitting his thesis was the essay on socialism. His last publication beforehand was an essay on the Revolution. More precisely, it was a review of Thomas Ferneuil's *The Principles
of 1789 and Social Science*, a book that appeared during the celebrations
of the Revolution's centenary in 1889. Yet Durkheim's essay makes no
explicit reference whatever to this great jamboree of ritual, symbolism
and collective memory, coming complete with its new thrusting image
of the republic and icon of progress, the Eiffel Tower. The story is the
same with his thesis on the division of labour itself. He is keen to talk
about things such as law as a 'visible symbol' of morals. But he says nothing about a whole effervescence of ritual and symbolism going on in the
society around him.

This amounted to a battle of rites and symbols, in conscious efforts
to win over hearts and minds.[2] In 1879, for example, the new republic
adopted *The Marseillaise* as the national anthem. But it soon faced growing competition from *The International* as a socialist anthem. In 1880,
after much wrangling between left-wing, moderate and conservative re-
publicans, it was decided to select 14 July and the Fall of the Bastille
as the national holiday. However, one of many challenges to this was
the development of May Day as a socialist holiday. And while the motto

Liberty, Equality, Fraternity was engraved on public buildings throughout France, there were banners at socialist conferences that instead proclaimed *Liberty, Equality, Solidarity*. At the same time and throughout the entire period there was the upsurge of activity of the Church and her faithful, in a wave of new saints, miracles, centres of mass pilgrimage, festivals, basilicas.

Perhaps Durkheim ignored all this, together with all the contemporary comment on it, since he quite deliberately dismissed it as unimportant and superficial for understanding the world around him. Digging around in his early work can come up with the remark: 'what must concern us is not the symbol, but what it translates and covers over' (1886a: 193). But another possible and less conscious reason is that it just wasn't the sort of thing one discussed in the earnest intellectual environment he inhabited. Thus ritual and symbolism also get short shrift from the author of *The Principles of 1789 and Social Science*. In his preface he goes out of his way to dissociate himself from the junketings of the Revolution's centenary and insists it is mere coincidence that his book has come out the same year (Ferneuil 1889: v–viii). In any case, there is a need to understand '1789' as constructed in Durkheim's own particular milieu.

'1789' and Social Science

A place to start is again with the work by one of Durkheim's examiners, Janet's *History of Political Science*. In the course of a long, scholarly, yet impassioned argument, his introduction notes the approach of the Revolution's hundredth anniversary. And it is to call for a defence of its ideals.

This is against the fashionable critique of them as mere abstract formulas, with no basis in reality. On the contrary, the ideals of 1789 were abstract expressions of concrete facts, and of profound, deep-rooted social needs. Far from just being an exercise in abstract chimerical principles, the Revolution was about 'the freeing, the emancipation of a living, real, concrete society that had developed imperceptibly for several centuries and that had then come to maturity'. As Tocqueville had shown, this society was already in existence *before* the Revolution, and so the old regime's official institutions were already 'in contradiction with the actual social situation of the country'. In sum, although the French – like the American – Revolution expressed itself in a way of thinking characteristic of the time and in an abstract philosophical form, this had a real social foundation (Janet 1887: vol. 1, xlv–lv). Indeed, it is the mere dismissal of the Revolution's ideals thanks to their expression in an abstract way of thinking that is itself abstract, unhistorical and unscientific. It is instead the genuinely empirical approach of modern historical and political science that generates a defence of the ideals of 1789 as ideals of the modern era, together with a need to continue to develop them in light of issues they continue to open up. 'The society conceived and proclaimed in the Revolution was so little a chimera that it is the one that exists today' (lxiii–lxiv).

Durkheim's own essay on the Revolution might then be read as an entirely unacknowledged use of arguments stolen from Janet. He criticizes Ferneuil's book as unhistorical and unscientific, in just dismissing the ideals of the Revolution as abstract formulas, and in just complaining about a way of thinking that was characteristic of the time. On the contrary, the ideals of 1789 were abstract expressions of an underlying reality, and social science should study them as a social fact (1890a: 218, 223).

It is nonetheless clear that Durkheim makes his own contribution to all this, based on ideas of a thesis already first drafted in 1886 and being taught in his lectures on solidarity in 1887. Thus in the essay itself, the Revolution's ideals have not gone away but have gathered force and spread far and wide. They must therefore depend on 'some general change that has taken place in the structure of European societies'. But work is needed to show whether these ideals are 'pathological' or 'indeed, on the contrary, if they simply represent a necessary transformation of our social consciousness' (1890a: 224). This work was of course his thesis, which showed they were indeed, on the contrary, a necessary transformation of our social consciousness. Durkheim had already mapped out a sociological defence of the ideals expressed in the Revolution, without having to steal it from Janet. Indeed, a fundamental error is just to ask individualistically about the originality of his arguments. It is essential to investigate how they express a general collective current of thought in his milieu, looking to a new empirical science to defend '1789' and the new era it represents.

Ferneuil himself was part of this milieu, and Durkheim's review of his book is on the whole enthusiastic. But it is also misleading. If we go through the book itself, it is only the first sixty pages that focus on the Revolution. The three hundred pages that follow are all to do with its legacy, and with mobilizing social science to address issues in the present day. Yet Durkheim's review gives the impression that Ferneuil just concentrates on the Revolution. And although saying a lot about his attack on abstract philosophical theorizing, it says little about his campaign for a sociological approach itself. Of course, a review can't cover everything. However, it is revealing to note some of the things Durkheim leaves out. He passes over the book's support for the idea of a collective consciousness (Ferneuil 1889: 86–88). He omits its concern with a web of intermediate groups as a necessary condition of a modern democratic society (145–50). He is silent on its case for new occupational groups as the way to solve the crisis of capitalism and evolve a socialism of the future (218–55). But also, he says nothing whatever about its argument for a modern solidarity due to the division of labour.

Ferneuil makes this a main theme of his conclusion, in a sort of return to discuss the ideals of '1789', but to discuss them as re-adopted in the motto of the new Third Republic itself. And it is to reconstruct and defend them sociologically as ideals of the modern era, but best encapsulated as *Liberty, Equality, Solidarity*.

A key, commonly made point at the time – as in Durkheim's own thesis – is that the ideals of '1789' can't just be separated from one another. They come as a package, and as a whole interlocking set of modern needs and aspirations. Even so, let us focus on Ferneuil's concern with solidarity. His objection to 'fraternity' is that it is religious-like cant and sentimentalism about some sort of vague fellow-feeling. Instead, solidarity is about a sense of attachment embedded in definite social links and definite moral and legal obligations, while at the same time entailing an interdependence of parts in an organic whole. Indeed, this is why he argues that solidarity is weak in 'primitive' societies. Individuals do more or less the same things, and so aren't interlocked in a division of labour:

> In contrast, when the differentiation of functions and the division of labour tend increasingly to become the law of modern societies, each individual, unable to be self-sufficient, is subject to the need to call on the services of the other, and to become attached to members of the social body through links of solidarity. (Ferneuil 1889: 342)

Perhaps Durkheim's review failed to mention these ideas because, compared with his own thesis, he saw them as basic and commonplace. Yet it is precisely a reason for their interest here, to help with understanding *The Division of Labour* as an articulation of general collective currents of thought in the author's milieu. This approach is important for understanding Durkheim's sociological defence of '1789'. It is altogether elemental for understanding his notion of solidarity itself.

Three Core Meanings of Solidarity

There are three core meanings that by Durkheim's time had become packaged together in the single French term, *solidarité*. All three meanings are mobilized in his thesis. But before asking about his own particular use of the term, there is a need to try to grasp it as a collective representation. One way to do this is to trace the development of entries on *solidarité* in French dictionaries from the seventeenth to the nineteenth centuries. At the same time it is essential to draw on the scholarship of modern French reference works on the language's history and etymology.[3] In brief and in simplifying things, here, roughly, is the story.

Solidarité began life in the late seventeenth century as a term of jurisprudence for a form of collective legal obligation. But it doesn't get an entry in a dictionary of 1690, or even in one of 1694, which is around when it started to appear. These instead record *solidité*, which for a while was the established term, hanging on until the Revolution. Thus a dictionary of 1788 concedes that *solidité* is still the official usage, but maintains that *solidarité* is the term normally as well as correctly preferred. By 1835, even the crusty and conservative dictionary of the Académie Française records that *solidité* is obsolete as a legal expression, having long been replaced by *solidarité*.

Moreover, it was in taking over as the established legal term that *solidarité* also took on what became its ordinary meaning – as a moral term for a sense of attachment involving definite links, responsibilities and obligations. Again by 1835, the dictionary of the Académie Française registers that *solidarité* has these two meanings, the legal and the moral. And it registers the moral meaning as the one employed in ordinary language.

However, it says nothing about a third meaning. This is to do with ideas of a reciprocal interaction and of an interdependence of parts in a whole. On the one hand, then, there had been scientific and philosophical talk of *solidarité* along these lines since at least the early nineteenth century. On the other, it didn't have enough impact to make it into the dictionary of the Académie Française. But moving on to when Durkheim was writing his thesis, Littré's dictionary of 1885 records *solidarité* as having all three core meanings. It is nonetheless the moral meaning that remains dominant, in that it is again recorded as the one employed in ordinary language. But it is not just a mere sentimentalism of fellow-feeling. Instead, it is about a solidarity of links and mutual responsibilities.

This is a framework for understanding Durkheim's own use of the term, but also that of other writers. Thus the work of one of his examiners, Marion's *Moral Solidarity*, is above all a development of the philosophical idea of interrelation in a totality. Indeed, it is why Marion begins with 'individual solidarity', to investigate the individual as an organic whole, then proceeds to 'social solidarity', to investigate a social world as an interrelated whole. So it is not surprising that he looks down on ordinary usage. Given solidarity's everyday moral meaning, 'individual solidarity' is a contradiction and 'social solidarity' is a tautology.

Certainly, in the case of Ferneuil's work, this just talks of solidarity. The reason, as can now be brought out, is that he is above all concerned with solidarity in its ordinary moral sense, as attachment in definite links, relations and obligations. But since he sees these as involving both moral and legal obligations, he still taps into its origins as a legal term. At the same time he draws on the relatively newfangled idea of solidarity as interconnectedness in a whole.

This is also a basic pattern in Durkheim's case. True, his thesis refers in its official discourse to 'social solidarity'. But in fact, like Ferneuil, he often just talks of solidarity. And although he mobilizes all three of the term's core meanings – the legal, the moral, and the holistic – in the end what counts, as in his concern with a web of intermediate groups, is attachment in a web of definite links and relations.

CHAPTER 3

In Search of Solidarity: *The Division of Labour*

Durkheim's thesis sets out in search of a solidarity of modern times. Yet what it ends up describing is a world in crisis, in everyday scenes of alienation, anomie, class war and injustice. This is why it is necessary to dig around in search of its whole underlying problematic of a modern solidarity.

The Problematic of Modern Solidarity

All three core conventional meanings of *solidarité* soon turn up in a single page of his thesis. Solidarity is discussed both as an internal moral phenomenon outwardly symbolized by law, and as a holistic integration of society (1893a: 66 / 1902b: 28).

A way to bring out what is at stake is to introduce, along with his talk of the 'internal', the terms 'microsocial' and 'macrosocietal'. His thesis is concerned with solidarity as an internal sense of attachment in webs of microsocial relations. At the same time it is about solidarity as a world's macrosocietal interconnectedness. It is how the internal, the microsocial and the macrosocietal dimensions of things might come together that helps to constitute the problematic of modern solidarity at its most fundamental.

In turn, this involves what could be called the work's 'moral', 'functionalist' and 'republican' discourses of solidarity. The moral discourse is concerned with internal attachment in webs of microsocial relations as a basic continuing elemental form of solidarity – even or especially in evolving from a traditional solidarity through likeness to a modern solidarity through difference and the division of labour. The functionalist discourse pictures the division of labour in terms a harmony of roles in an overall integrated system, and describes the individuals filling these roles as 'the parts of a whole', indeed, as 'the organs of an organism'. It is the republican discourse, however, that in the end is crucial. Modern solidarity depends on what is eventually revealed as the 'spontaneous' division of labour. This is discussed and defined in terms of republican concerns with freedom, equality, justice and the ideal of a society of persons.

Macrosocietal Interconnectedness

Book 1 of the thesis discusses the division of labour's 'function' and sees it as a way of generating a unified 'solidary system' (1893a: 249 / 1902b: 207). Yet what sort of social world is this about? It is all very well to talk of a modern global village and to invoke a vast macrosocietal interconnectedness. A brute theoretical fact is that it doesn't guarantee microsocial attachment, and can come instead with book 3's everyday scenes of anomie and alienation. On the one hand, then, it is still a world of interconnectedness thanks to the division of labour and globalizing forces. On the other, it is not what Durkheim has in mind in a discourse of interconnectedness in which his key terms are 'integration' and 'cohesion' – as in repeated talk of 'the general integration of society', 'the general cohesion of society', etc. That is, it is in no way a discourse of just any world's interconnectedness, but of a society's integration and cohesion as a solidary system.

Moreover, it is also in an idea of an internal core logic that constitutes the very process of the division of labour. Book 3 envisages a world in which 'nothing comes from outside to denature' this, attributes scenes of crisis to 'abnormal and exceptional causes', and denies they have anything to do with the division of labour as such and 'in itself' (417 / 364). Yet whatever the internal core logic might be, isn't the division of labour very much implicated in the problems, crises and conflicts of modern times? And isn't this evident from the thesis itself?

In going over key examples, a start might be made with the politics of identity. A mistake is to assume that Durkheim's general abstract references to modern 'society' are in fact to the nation-state, with France as his paradigmatic case. Even if he usually seems to mean this, he is explicit about other possibilities. As he sums up in his conclusion, where he links the division of labour with the emergence of ideals of human fraternity:

> We have already seen that what is tending to form in a spontaneous movement going beyond European peoples is a European society, which even now has a sentiment of itself and the beginnings of an organization. If the formation of a single human society is forever impossible – which has not been shown – at least the formation of ever larger societies takes us continuously closer to this goal. (455–56 / 401–2)

This brings out two basic elements of his idea of a 'society' – as a social world with *both* an organization *and* a consciousness of its identity. Yet it is precisely to discuss a process going beyond established 'societies'. It is about the division of labour as a dynamic underlying a continuous modern reconstitution of 'societies'. This macro dynamic necessarily has a micro dimension. It is the inevitability of different collective currents of sentiment over *which* 'society'/'societies' can claim an individual's loyalties of attachment. In sum, the work generates an argument in which it is the vast globalizing process of the division of labour itself that helps to create the conflicts of a modern politics of identity.

But there are also other things that get in the way of book 1's functionalist dream – or nightmare? – of society as a unified system, all of whose members are its happy and obliging servants, each casting themselves merely as 'the part of a whole', and 'the organ of an organism' (250 / 207). One of the things getting in the way is how the work links the rise of the division of labour with the rise of collective currents of individualism. These are not and cannot just be a functionalist affair of a system's different interlocking roles. Book 3 sums up why:

> Functional diversity entails a moral diversity that nothing can prevent, and it is inevitable that one grows at the same time as the other. (405 / 352)

That is, the division of labour's functional diversity comes with a moral diversity of personalities, attitudes, lifestyles, beliefs and worldviews. In turn, this feeds into the work's own mixture of responses to individualism. These include all the attacks on forms of individualism driven by ideas of a radical separateness. At the same time they include the functionalist fantasy of mere members of a system and organs of an organism. But they also include the whole republican concern with an individualism that can combine autonomy with solidarity in aspirations towards a commonwealth of persons. Here, however, the basic point is that the work's story of the division of labour links it with the rise, not just of the individual, but of different, conflicting individualisms.

Finally, it is essential to consider book 3's account of a crisis going on in economic and industrial life and so, in Durkheim view, at the heart of the modern social world. Indeed, it is a reason for seeing the problematic that haunts *The Division of Labour* as the problematic of capitalism. In any case, it is about forms of the division of labour that he insists are 'abnormal', when instead they might seem part of its whole historical development. A key argument goes beyond general worries about an interest-driven individualism, to pick out two factors that feed into and fuel one another in a rapidly accelerating process. One is the growth of a mass market. The other is the growth of mass production. Their combined effect is a crisis in solidarity. The rise of a mass globalizing market creates a radical separation of producers and consumers, without meaningful social links between them. At the same time the rise of large-scale mechanized industry creates a radical separation in the sphere of production itself. It generates worlds of labour and capital that aren't mere economic abstractions. In actual concrete social terms they are worlds set apart, and almost different social planets, without meaningful contact between them (411–15 / 359–62).

Yet how can it make sense to claim that the division of labour is not bound up in all this? Isn't the division of labour an essential condition of the rise of mass markets and mass industry? Certainly, the argument brings out why it is crucial to distinguish macrosocietal interconnectedness from microsocial interlinkage and attachment. Its story of globalization is a story of a vast interconnectedness that actively destroys particular social links. Its worry about an absence of these links is a worry about a radical separateness, and so, in effect, about alienation.

True enough, Durkheim doesn't headline it as alienation and instead fits it into his chapter on anomie. This is to emphasize how the crisis in modern economic and industrial life is to do with a lack of regulation. But his explanation of why there is a lack of regulation is largely to do with the breakdown in social contact. That is, his explanation of economic anomie is largely to do with the creation of a vast social gulf and separateness amounting to alienation. In turn, this is a key to his entire elaborate thesis. The solidarity that is basic to everything, and that counts above everything, is the solidarity of microsocial attachment.

This is the solidarity that is essential for any effective moral regulation of life, and for the task, nowadays, of rebuilding morality. It is the lack of this solidarity that characterizes a world in crisis, complete with its 'abnormal' forms of the division of labour. It is the redevelopment of this solidarity that is at stake in the campaign for a web of new occupational groups, helping to translate ideals of justice into a code governing everyday life and practice.

Microsocial Attachment

Book 1 chapter 1 helps to launch the thesis in a number of ways, but not least through a discussion of what Durkheim sees as paradigmatic cases and exemplars of solidarity. These are clearly cases of solidarity as microsocial attachment. They are the close intimate relations of friendship and marriage.

He wants to introduce the idea of two types of solidarity, one based on likeness, the other on difference and a division of labour. But he is especially keen to show how friendship and marriage, as paradigmatic cases of solidarity, can involve solidarity through a division of labour. An essential idea is that individuals 'complete' one another through the particular qualities they each contribute to a relationship. They constitute distinct personalities that are interdependent rather than separate. And though their relation in a division of labour entails an exchange, this is 'only a superficial expression of an internal, more deeply rooted state':

> The image of the other who completes us becomes inseparable in us from our own, not just thanks to frequent association, but above all because it is its natural complement: it becomes an integral and permanent part of our consciousness, to such a point that we are unable to do without it and look for everything that can increase its energy. (1893a: 63-64 / 1902b: 25)

Indeed, this suggests an internal, deep-rooted attachment in an interpenetration of selves.

Durkheim then goes on to make a quite sweeping generalization: 'There can never be solidarity between another and ourselves unless the image of the other unites with our own' (64 / 26). This very much raises the stakes. It is all very well to insist on solidarity as an interpenetration of consciousnesses in the case of intimate relationships. Yet how can there be anything of the sort among all the individuals and strangers, passing one another in the night, in vast modern worlds?

Book 1 chapter 2 again sees solidarity as an 'interpenetration of minds' (111 / 72). But it is in developing an account of solidarity through likeness, associated with traditional small-scale communities. Accordingly, what happens in book 1 chapter 3, where Durkheim gets on with an account of solidarity in large-scale societies and through the division of labour?

This introduces yet another distinction, to do with what he calls 'negative' as against 'positive' solidarity. Put another way, it is to do with respect as against attachment. It involves a set of rights with a negative rather than a positive function. It isn't to encourage cooperation, but to limit conflict:

> It isn't to join the different parts of society with one another, but on the contrary to detach them from one another, to mark out clearly the barriers that separate them. (127 / 88)

Thus it is about the importance of a social space between individuals, entailed in attitudes of respect for persons and rights. But this generates a paradox. How can there be a shared respect for rights, among individuals set apart by them?

Durkheim sees the only possible solution in the dependence of negative respect on positive attachment. It is why he is so hostile to theories that imagine society could run on 'mere respect for rights' (129 / 90). These pluck 'respect' out of philosophical thin air, just taking it for granted and without understanding its social roots in a collective, deeply engrained moral attitude:

> In reality, for men to recognize and mutually guarantee rights, it is first of all necessary that they care about one another, that, for whatever reason, they are attached to one another and to a same society of which they form part. (130 / 90–91)

So this complicates the search for a solidarity of modern times. It is about attachment, but together with separateness and 'barriers' between one another entailed by respect for persons and rights. So it again raises the stakes in the case of vast modern worlds, and how, if at all, these might constitute worlds of society. It rules out the minimalist morals of trying to make do just with respect; it insists there must also be a positive solidarity of attachment.

This prepares the ground for the development, in the chapters that follow, of one of the main themes of Durkheim's thesis as a whole. It is how it is the division of labour's collective dynamic that generates individualism. But put another way, it is how it is the division of labour itself that generates a problem he looks to it to solve. It creates the individuals he looks to it to unite.

Thus it emerges, in book 1 chapter 5, that his search for solidarity through the division of labour is a search for solidarity in what is inevitably a 'growing multitude of individual disputes' (187 / 147). One reason is that the division of labour's functional diversity entails moral diversity, inevitably coming with different personalities, attitudes and beliefs. However, another reason is that the division of labour's increasing development entails a transformation of the collective consciousness. It is increasingly an affair of vague general abstract ideas, open to different interpretations and in effect also opening the way to individual differences and disputes.

This whole argument is central to his thesis, in limiting the role of a collective consciousness nowadays and in insisting on the division of labour as the main place to look for a modern solidarity. A paradox is that it is not least to remain attached and stay together in disputes, yet it itself is the basic underlying source of these disputes.

Accordingly, a way to understand ambivalences, tensions or even contradictions in the work is how Durkheim oscillates, in this situation, between functionalist and republican discourses of solidarity. It is the functionalist discourse that identifies the division of labour with attachment as an organ of an organism, to imagine the integration of a solidary system. It is the republican discourse that identifies the division of labour with attachment as a social yet distinct individual personality, to complicate things through respect for rights, through freedom of thought and autonomy in a multitude of disputes, and a moral diversity's whole far-reaching liberal pluralism.

A flash-point in the tensions between these discourses occurs when he first reveals, in book 1 chapter 5, that at the core of the modern collective consciousness there is a religious-like cult of the individual. His functionalist concern with integrated organs of an organism prompts an initial attack on such liberalism – 'it is not to society that it attaches us; it is to ourselves' (187 / 147). But his thesis ends up sympathizing with a cult of the person (450 / 396). After all, his republican project is to combine solidarity with autonomy, and so with the modern self as something more than a mere atom. The cult attaches us to society and not just to ourselves, precisely thanks to his whole republican account of a socially attached yet distinct individual personality.

A crucial battleground between his functionalist and republican tendencies involves what happens in book 1 chapter 7. This is book 1's final chapter, and brings it to a close with a vision of a promised land of solidarity thanks to the division of labour. But it is through an attack on yet another version of minimalist morals, which yet again tries to do without the solidarity of positive attachment. Instead, it pictures a society that runs on contracts and an interest-driven exchange. Accordingly, it rests on a fundamental misconception of social and moral life.

> If interest draws men closer, it is never for more than a few moments; it can create only an external link between them. In the act of exchange, the different agents remain separate from one another and, their business done, each makes off to resume life as before. Consciousnesses are only superficially in contact; they neither interpenetrate, nor strongly attach themselves to one another. (222 / 180–81)

Just as Durkheim launches book 1 with cases of solidarity in intimate relationships, so, in concluding it with a vision of solidarity in large-scale modern worlds that do indeed constitute societies, he continues to insist on a division of labour that entails an internal deep-rooted attachment and interpenetration of selves.

Yet how does he see this as possible, and why does he see it as necessary?

> Even where society is most completely based on the division of labour, it doesn't dissolve into a mass of juxtaposed atoms, between which it can establish only external and transient contacts. Instead, its members are united by links that extend far beyond the few brief moments when exchange is transacted. Each of the functions that they exercise is in ongoing dependence with others and forms with them a solidary system. (249 / 207)

On the one hand, this expresses his core view of the division of labour as a source of attachment through webs of ongoing contacts and relations. On the other, it is served up in a purely functionalist discourse, imagining a harmonization of the microsocial and macrosocietal thanks just to the exercise of their 'functions' by 'members' of a 'solidary system'.

It nonetheless comes with ominous warnings. These point ahead to book 3's world in crisis and to a follow-up work on the need for new intermediate groups. Indeed, their main discussion in his thesis is in book 1's final chapter, clouding its functionalist sunniness with how actual social and economic life is in a state of malaise. The breakdown in solidarity can only be tackled by new groups to replace the old guilds, swept away in changes 'that required, not so much this organization's radical destruction, as its transformation' (238–39 / 196–97).

In any case, book 3's account of a world in crisis is where the thesis itself runs into a crisis. Book 1's functionalism can't deliver the goods. It turns out that modern solidarity depends on what is now explained as the 'spontaneous' division of labour, defined and discussed in terms of a republican discourse to do with freedom, equality, justice and the ideal of a society of persons. But it is especially in a theoretical crisis centred round issues to do with justice.

It can seem from some of Durkheim's arguments that he looks to a revival of a traditional collective consciousness, as if, out of sociological thin air, the modern world can come with a detailed consensus in the interpretation of its abstract ideals of justice. This risks collapsing his entire thesis about a modern solidarity through the division of labour, even or especially in all the disputes it spontaneously generates over interpretation of a collective consciousness's shared but vague abstract ideals. It is hopeless to try to isolate justice as a special case. It is part of a whole web of modern aspirations to freedom, equality and human rights in an ideal of a commonwealth of persons. The only coherent approach is to look for a negotiation of inevitable modern disputes through an effective, morally legitimate organization, and so through something like the web of new intermediate groups he had envisaged for so long and planned to write about in a follow-up work.

In sum, this approach is again essentially republican, necessitated, not least, by his own repeated insistence that functional diversity entails moral diversity. It is also especially concerned with tackling what book 1's functionalism of 'organs of an organism' is unable to explain, namely, the everyday scenes of alienation, anomie and class war going on in contemporary economic and industrial life, and so at the heart of modern society.

Yet if in the end what counts is the search for a modern solidarity in what is not so much a functionalist as a republican worldview, it is still rooted in a moral discourse in which the basic continuing elemental form of solidarity is attachment in microsocial webs of relations. Indeed, it is again in terms of a republican worldview that the thesis sees a modern emancipation of the individual-in-society from the overwhelming conformism of traditional community.

In the Beginning: *The Division of Labour*'s Elementary Forms of Social Life

The Division of Labour constructs an evolutionary grand narrative in which, in the beginning, the basic unit of social organization is the clan and life runs on a solidarity that is overwhelmingly through likeness. An essential part of the story is to do with the nature, role and career of a 'collective consciousness'. So a way to start is with some background on this notion.

The Very Idea of a Collective Consciousness
Durkheim didn't invent the idea of a collective consciousness. It had been around for some time. Yet although it had its supporters in France, it was mainly regarded with suspicion. Thus although defended in a work he reviewed (Ferneuil 1889: 86–88), it is dismissed as nonsense in a work more representative of established opinion, by one of his thesis examiners (Marion 1880: 153–54). The underlying reason for the hostility is brought out in the long discussion of the issue in one of the time's best-known texts on sociology, Alfred Fouillée's *Contemporary Social Science* (1880: 192–257). The idea of a collective consciousness is German, authoritarian and metaphysical. True, Fouillée tries to do something to rescue it, but in urging a switch to the term 'social consciousness'. In getting away from German authoritarianism, this flags up a liberal expression of the 'social ideal' – a combination of 'the maximum individuality of each' with 'the maximum solidarity of all'. In getting away from German metaphysics, it ditches the unscientific mystical notion of a collective group mind. A social consciousness exists only in individual consciousnesses. It isn't thinking *by* society, but thinking *about* society. Although society is real, it is only the individual who reflects on the social world and forms a consciousness with 'the unity of a subject' (246–48).

There are a few brief, unfavourable references to Fouillée's work in the thesis, but no explicit mention of it at all in Durkheim's own discussion of a collective consciousness. It is nonetheless an implicit reference. It was impossible to ignore its important, influential campaign for a social consciousness, and attack on the very idea of a collective consciousness.

It is against this background that a number of things become noticeable about the way Durkheim introduces and presents the idea. He says he won't come up with a new term, but 'will keep the expression most in use' (1893a: 85 / 1902b: 47). In fact, however, he is keen to break its usual association with the idea of a group mind, an issue he buries in a footnote (85, n.2 / 47, n.1). Instead, his main text emphasizes his concern with a collective consciousness as it exists in individual consciousnesses. It is about whatever beliefs and sentiments are held in common by individuals. Indeed, this is perhaps why he often just talks of it as a 'common' consciousness.

In any case, it is why it is necessary to pick out a collective consciousness, as against a social consciousness. A 'collective consciousness' refers only to beliefs that are shared, while a 'social consciousness' covers all beliefs with a social content or character, complete with individual variations between these. Indeed, this is why it is an error 'to assume the collective consciousness is the whole of social consciousness'. In the modern world, a collective consciousness is a 'limited part' of a social consciousness (84 / 46).

So although Durkheim makes no mention of Fouillée, it is significant that he introduces a collective consciousness in relation to a social consciousness, buries the idea of a group mind, and shares a similar liberal republican vision of a modern combination of the solidarity of all with the individuality of each. In effect, then, he introduces it through a discourse of three interlinked terms – 'collective', 'social', 'individual'. In the beginning, in his narrative, everyone is so alike that almost all beliefs are shared and a collective consciousness covers almost everything. Nowadays, a collective consciousness is only a small part of a social consciousness and individuality flourishes. So it might be expected that he would go on to tell a story of a long-term change from a collective to a social consciousness. Yet this is more or less the last we hear from him about a social consciousness. Instead, he squeezes it out of the picture, and sets up a dualism reducing things to the issue of the collective versus the individual.

Tracking a Collective Consciousness

Durkheim's original introduction to his thesis gets things going with a story of how internal moral sentiments of obligatoriness can be tracked through the visible symbol of the moral sanction (1893a: 26–27). Book 1 chapter 1 begins to rework this into a story of how internal moral phenomena can be tracked through the visible symbol of law (1893a: 66 / 1902b: 28). Book 1 chapter 2 elaborates it with a controversial, even intentionally shocking story of crime and punishment.

Durkheim first attacks a commonsense view:

It shouldn't be said that an act offends the common consciousness because it is criminal, but that it is criminal because it offends the common consciousness. We don't condemn it because it is a crime, but it is a crime because we condemn it. (86 / 48)

As if this story of crime isn't scandalous enough, it is rounded off with a story of punishment in which it 'remains for us what it was for our forefathers', 'an act of revenge' (94–95 / 56). Its basic underlying function isn't to reform the criminal. And it isn't to deter crime. The real role of punishment is to give vent to collective moral outrage, and accordingly 'to maintain social cohesion intact in maintaining the common consciousness in all its vitality' (115–16 / 76).

An immediate objection to his story is that it takes no interest in who or what gets punished, as if the sacrifice of anyone or anything will do to maintain the collective consciousness 'in all its vitality'. In other words, it takes no interest in issues of justice and responsibility. True, he was aware of cases such as the trial and execution of animals. But they get only a passing mention in his thesis, without any serious attempt to understand them. They constitute a particularly striking example of how, again, a major theoretical gap in his story of crime and punishment is that it leaves out beliefs to do with responsibility and the ways different sociohistorical worlds classify men, women, children, animals and things as accountable or non-accountable for their action. But a study along these lines was undertaken by one of Durkheim's close associates, indeed, his successor at the Sorbonne. This is Paul Fauconnet's *Responsibility*, and he says that it was inspired by lectures on responsibility given by Durkheim in 1894, when he was a student of his (Fauconnet 1920: iii). It is unfortunate that these lectures have been lost. Like Fauconnet's work itself, they would have helped to fill a gap in *The Division of Labour*'s opening, simplistic account of crime and punishment.

However, there are other criticisms that can be made. Durkheim's theory, in rough, is that traditional worlds dominated by a collective consciousness involve a pre-eminence of criminal law, punishment and what he calls 'repressive' sanctions. Modern worlds increasingly running on a division of labour involve an increasing role of civil law and what he calls 'restitutive' sanctions. In practice, though, he doesn't undertake a detailed systematic investigation of sanctions themselves – such as torture, execution, imprisonment, fines and so on – despite the fact that these are his official 'signs' and 'symbols' to track the career of a collective consciousness. His investigations centre round crime itself, along with civil law.

Book 1 chapter 5 comes with an important table, spread over three pages (166–68 / 127–28). It attempts to group, in a complex set of types and subtypes, all the many things that in different sociohistorical worlds have been classified as crimes. It therefore represents what must have been a considerable research effort. Yet it is often ignored by commentators, as if empirical detective work is of less interest than arguing over theoretical issues in the abstract. But it is this table, with its extensive background research, which is the focal point of a key theoretical discussion in the same chapter. Although Durkheim draws on its material in a number of ways, a basic concern is with what has been declassified as crime. But this raises two further questions. One is about a hard core of things always categorized as crime. The other is what has been reclassified to become crime.

He emphasizes how his table shows that in traditional worlds the law is permeated by religion, with all sorts of things condemned as criminal and sacrilegious. At the same time it shows a long-term process of secularization, decriminalizing offences against religion. But he is about to reveal a modern cult of the individual constituting a sort of religion and sacralizing everyone as a person. A problem, then, is how to analyse offences against the person.

His explicit solution is that violation of the person belongs to a hard core type of action always and everywhere criminalized thanks to the very nature of social life. But it is implicit that what is in fact involved is a reclassification of crimes through a reclassification of persons. As he goes on to discuss, there is a move away from societies that exclude children, slaves and others from legal protection, to a modern universalizing extension of the status of a person to everyone (180 / 140–41).

In sum, instead of merely criticizing his thesis, it can be seen as a source of issues and questions for further investigation. These include the issue of responsibility, explored in the lost lectures that inspired Fauconnet. They include questions about the history and career of sanctions, not least the case of the birth of the prison, touched on in Durkheim's 'Two Laws of Penal Evolution' (1901a[i]). And they include questions about the history and career of the person, explored in Mauss's 'A Category of the Human Mind: The Notion of the Person' (1938), as well as in Fauconnet's *Responsibility*, but also in *The Elemental Forms* itself.

Indeed, there is a whole set of questions raised by *The Division of Labour* as a sort of starting point of *The Elemental Forms*. These centre round three claims. (1) In the beginning, social life is identical with religious life. (2) It is governed by a collective consciousness's same shared detailed beliefs. (3) The collective consciousness is embedded in a particular social structure, based on the clan.

The World of the Clan

Durkheim briefly speculates about the earliest, simplest type of society as a single homogeneous mass he calls 'the horde' (1893a: 189 / 1902b: 149). He quickly moves on to what he regards as the earliest, simplest societies that are known through historical or ethnographic evidence. He identifies them with a social structure made up of groups that are all essentially alike and that are each internally homogeneous. At an abstract theoretical level, he discusses these groups as 'segments', forming an overall society with a 'segmental' structure. But it is necessary to penetrate this fog of abstract theoretical talk, to understand his actual picture of things. In the beginning, and as he himself emphasizes, there are '*segmental societies based on clans*' (190 / 150).

His thesis sees the clan as the early elementary unit of both social and religious life. This remains his core view of things in *The Elemental Forms*, subtitled *The Totemic System in Australia*. Yet it is clear that, in writing his thesis, he knew next to nothing about anthropological theories of the time in which the world of the clan is a world of *totemic* society and religion, and a paradigmatic case is Australia. He makes no mention of 'totemism', and has only a single brief footnote reference to a study of Australia.

His core view of the socioreligious world of the clan as the beginning of things must therefore have had other origins. What, however, were these? With its vast scope, his thesis draws on a wide-ranging secondary literature. But it also involves digging around for himself in primary sources. Noticing what was overwhelmingly his primary material is suggestive about his own sense of self-identity. In the case of modern society, it is France's Civil Code. In the case of traditional society, it is the Pentateuch – that is, in another guise, the first five books of the Old Testament. Indeed, his paradigmatic case of the world of the clan is the case of ancient Israel.

In turn, this is a clue to a systematic change between editions of *The Division of Labour*. The thesis almost invariably talks of 'the Jews'. The new edition deletes most of these references, to replace them with talk of 'the Hebrews'. So maybe the reason is to make totally clear that what is at stake is the world of the people of ancient Israel – not the present-day individuals seen as their descendants, many of whom, like Durkheim himself, had come to see themselves first and foremost as citizens of a modern republic.[1]

Certainly, this is what is at stake in the account of segmental societies in book 1 chapter 6, and also involving other changes between editions. Durkheim runs through various cases of worlds of the clan – including his brief mention of Australia – to lead up to and conclude with a long discussion of ancient Israel. In both editions, he emphasizes that in ancient Israel the basic social unit is indeed the clan, which he complains is improperly translated in secondary literature as 'the family'. On the contrary, it is a group that can consist of thousands of persons, and that is seen as a group of kin since seen as 'descended, according to tradition, from a same ancestor'. Moreover, it is in a segmental structure in which a group of clans forms a tribe, and in which 'the union of the twelve tribes forms the whole of Jewish society' [revised to the 'Hebrew people'] (194 / 153–54).

The thesis then continues with a passage deleted in the new edition. Once again it brings out that his paradigmatic case of solidarity in worlds of the clan is the case of ancient Israel. At the same time it involves a counterpart of the problematic of modern solidarity. It is a problematic of traditional solidarity, in which ties of community need not help with attachment to a wider society. Clans can be almost entirely cut off from one another, in a lack of webs of interlinkage between them, and any wider cohesion 'varies from an almost absolutely chaotic state to the perfect moral unity shown by the Jewish people' (1893a: 194).

But the problematic makes crystal clear that microsocial interlinkage is his key to solidarity, just as it is in his search for this nowadays. And in both editions the world of the clan is a sort of homeland of solidarity through likeness, in which 'religion penetrates the whole of life' (1893a: 194 / 1902b: 154). In the actual text it is the *lieu d'élection* – literally, the chosen or the favoured site – of such solidarity. Yet given the term's religious undertones and all the interest in ancient Israel, it might seem an allusion to a 'chosen land' of this solidarity.

In any case, it leads on to a radical claim. It isn't religion that explains the structure of worlds of the clan. It is the massive homogeneity built into their structure that explains 'the power and nature of the religious idea' (195 / 154).

But it is not until book 2 that the issue is discussed in any detail, while at the same time it is in an even more sweeping form. It is about the whole general abstract relation between 'consciousness' and 'structure', in which the thrust of Durkheim's argument can seem to be that 'consciousness' is not just embedded in 'structure' but entirely determined by it. If so, the argument runs straight into the objection that it is vacuous and circular, already assuming what it seeks to explain. On his very own account of worlds of the clan, 'consciousness' is integral to 'structure', built into it from the start. As in his paradigmatic case of ancient Israel, the clan consists of people 'descended, according to tradition, from a same ancestor', so that ideas of kinship are integral to relations of kinship and help to constitute the actual organization of this type of social world. Put another way, its social structure consists of a core set of ideas–relations, the set of ideas–relations to do with kinship, lineage and descent.

But this opens up another approach to what is at stake in his account. It means that structure, understood as a core of ideas–relations, can still help to shape and determine ideas in a wider domain of consciousness. A particular way to explore this is through his interest in attitudes to do with tradition. A general way is to examine his overall list of characteristics of a collective consciousness in worlds of the clan.

In the original introduction to his thesis, a brief yet clearly hostile reference that might puzzle the modern reader is to the 'solidarity of time' (1893a: 10). A once commonplace concept, it is a source of the nowadays more familiar idea of collective memory. It reappears in book 2 chapter 3, in a critical discussion that is part of yet further developments in a vast story of things. Roughly, the 'solidarity of time' is about feelings of attachment to a community that isn't just made up of present-day individuals. It stretches down through the past, to root the living in respectful memories of what they owe to the ancestral dead. Durkheim's critique is again evidence of his concern with solidarity as attachment in webs of ongoing contacts and relations. Appeal to the 'solidarity of time' is mere sentimentalism without these ongoing links, and the 'continuous contact of successive generations' (1893a: 327 / 1902b: 280).

He then gets on with what is in effect a sketch of a sociology of time, as frameworked and experienced in different sociohistorical worlds. A basic point is that the interlinkage of the generations tends to break down in modern society, with its mobile individuals, cult of youth, pursuit of the new, rapid change and whole general orientation towards the future. In contrast, the so-called 'solidarity of time' is above all an affair of worlds of the clan, with their webs of kin, respect for age, devotion to custom, settled horizons and whole general envelopment in the past (324–29 / 277–82).

Thus in worlds of the clan, a core structure of ideas and relations of kinship has further ramifications in a wider domain of consciousness. Not least, it helps to explain a whole general envelopment in the past and domination by forces of tradition. As this structure disappears, the authority of tradition 'necessarily diminishes' (323 / 277).

All the same, it doesn't add up to a general abstract story of how 'structure' determines 'consciousness'. On the contrary, the collective consciousness has an action and power of its own. Or any rate, this is the case if Durkheim is to be believed when he introduces it in book 1 as a set of ideas forming 'a definite system with a life of its own' (84 / 46). So a way to test his initial claim is to put together, from the thesis as whole, a list of his key elements of a clan-based society's collective consciousness:

1. It covers all of social life, with little room for individual difference;
2. It is detailed, specific and concrete, again with little room for difference through different interpretations of general abstract ideas;
3. It comes with a religious belief, intensely held and intolerant;
4. It runs on the authority of tradition, essentially accepted without question.

But although these form analytically distinguishable elements, it is because in practice they interact and reinforce one another that there is a final, overall characteristic:

5. It forms a system, with a life and power of its own.

It would nonetheless be a mistake to celebrate the relative freedom of action of this collective consciousness. It is embedded in a specific type of social organization, and 'this particular structure allows society to tighten its grip on the individual' (335 / 288). Put another way, structure and consciousness combine in a sort of overdetermination of life in worlds of the clan. While structure clamps down on individuality, the action of the collective consciousness ratchets up even further the overwhelming pressures to conform.

Indeed, a problem is where to find sources of change in all this closure. In the thesis, these weaken 'the force of tradition' (1893a: 337). In the new edition, they help to lift 'the collective yoke' (1902b: 290).

The Rise of the Division of Labour

Book 2 is where Durkheim aims to identify the causes of the rise of the division of labour, and so, in the process, the rise of modernity. Yet he sets himself something of a challenge, in the way he pictures a traditional world of closure that seems to make it impossible for his story even to get started. Like Houdini, he binds himself in chains only to effect a miraculous escape.

He rules out the division of labour's emergence on its own. An 'insurmountable obstacle' to this is not just the power of a traditional collective consciousness but the power of an underlying social organization (1893a: 282 / 1902b: 337). So if it isn't consciousness and it isn't structure and it isn't the division of labour's rise of its own accord, what is his source of the change? And does it matter?

He attempts to explain events in the remote past, but without a shred of evidence and through reliance on theory. On the one hand, then, his excursion into the empirically unknown mobilizes important sociological concepts and concerns. On the other, it is ineliminably speculative and leads down a sociological dead end.

A 'Break of Equilibrium'

Durkheim imagines a crisis in worlds of the clan that results in a transformation of their whole system, and that he accordingly calls a 'break of equilibrium'. He explains this crisis in terms of an explosion of their population, involving what he discusses as an increase in social mass and density. In turn, he sees this as the beginning of an unfolding series of causes and consequences. The increase in social mass and density leads to an intensification of the struggle for existence, which leads to a specialization of roles as a way to cope with the situation, which leads to the rise and development of the division of labour to become the dynamic of modern life. Finally, he insists that he has come up with a story in which everything happens mechanically, in a type of explanation that he accordingly calls mechanistic explanation. A question, then, is if it is anything of the kind.

Part of the trouble is that he operates with yet another dualism. Mechanistic explanation is opposed to what he understands as teleological explanation, in terms of pursuit of conscious aims, ends and ideals. But it turns out that his so-called mechanistic explanation in fact includes a teleological element, in including a role for ends and ideals. At the same time this is connected with how his explanation involves a complex of interacting elements in an overall process. It isn't just a mechanistic chain of causes and consequences, in which one leads on to another. Thus it isn't just because his account is an exercise in pure speculation that it leads down a sociological dead end. It is above all because he pictures a chain of causes and consequences in an attempt to pick out a beginning of this chain as a fundamental cause of everything.

True, he himself sees an interaction of elements in an overall process. 'If society, in becoming denser, determines the development of the division of labour, this in turn increases the density of society' (1893a: 287 / 1902b: 241). He still wants to claim it is the increase in social density that sets things in motion in the first place, while it is the division of labour that is the 'derived fact'.

Even then, the claim is not quite what it seems, since he distinguishes two aspects of social density. One is to do with the demographics of population size and concentration, which he calls 'material density'. The other is to do with webs of microsocial relations, which he calls 'moral or dynamic density' (283 / 238). The moral element of webs of microsocial relations is where he once again looks for solidarity. But this is not what triggers off his break of equilibrium. On the contrary, it is the purely material change of an increase in population that overcomes the otherwise 'insurmountable obstacle' of the clan's webs of microsocial relations, to open the way for the different webs of microsocial relations in a division of labour.

If it is asked how, here is his first line of reasoning. Members of the clan's homogeneous social world do the same things and have the same needs. Therefore an increase in their number intensifies 'the struggle for life', and people 'find themselves in competition everywhere' (294 / 248). Therefore a specialization of roles is a way to cope with the situation, in turn opening the way to the whole development of the division of labour itself. As a lengthy discussion explains, it is through different roles involving different needs that it is possible not only to limit conflict, but to cooperate and live together in 'the new conditions of existence' (294–305 / 248–59).

Here is his next line of reasoning. The emergence of the division of labour as a solution can occur 'only among members of an already constituted society' (305 / 259). This is because it depends on a deep-rooted moral commitment to one another, on a determination to stay together, and so, in his own words, on the strength of an already existing 'sentiment of solidarity' (306 / 260). Otherwise, events can take a very different course. And he lists the alternatives as 'emigration, colonization, resignation to a precarious, more contested existence, and finally the total elimination of the weakest through suicide or in other ways' (317 / 270–71).

In brief, Durkheim is concerned with a type of event that no doubt happened somewhere at some stage. But he never explains how his closed little communities of the clan, with all their forms of control, could just have had an explosion in population. He merely assumes this as a starting point, then uses a chain of deductive reasoning to 'prove' how it sets off a chain of causes and consequences, and writes:

> Everything happens mechanically. A break of equilibrium in the social mass gives rise to conflicts that can only be resolved by a more developed division of labour: this is the motor of progress. (299 / 253)

This clearly annoyed one of his thesis examiners, Emile Boutroux. In lectures later the same year, he is scathing in his criticism of an approach that he unmistakably identifies with Durkheim, if without actually naming him. It is all very well to explain 'the division of labour's development through increase in social density', and to see it as 'the necessary result of the struggle for life'. But there are other solutions to this – 'the simplest of which is eating one another'. So it just isn't the case that the division of labour is a 'mechanical' outcome of things. On the contrary, it depends on a pre-existing 'sympathy', which is why it is bound up with a more or less conscious end and ideal – 'the cessation of the struggle for life'. In short, 'the division of labour is a way, devised more or less intelligently, to realize this ideal' (Boutroux 1895: 131–32).

Thus the critique exploits key features of Durkheim's argument to show why – twice over – it isn't the type of explanation he claims it to be. The division of labour isn't a 'mechanical necessity', since there are alternative solutions to an intensification of the struggle for life. And it isn't a 'mechanical necessity', thanks to the decisive role of consciousness. It depends on a pre-existing sentiment of solidarity, which entails a more or less conscious end and ideal in the form of a commitment to a life together.

In sum, even his entirely speculative story of a long ago 'break of equilibrium' fails to come up with a clear case of mechanistic explanation. But if it is also asked about his account of things once the division of labour has taken hold, it is merely hopeless to try to represent it in terms of this type of explanation.

A Modern Dynamic

An overwhelming impression in reading Durkheim's thesis – and as suggested by the title itself – is that his dynamic of modern times is the division of labour. It just does not reduce to an affair of morphology and population size. It is nonetheless in a process of interacting elements that very much involve factors to do with morphology as well as structure and consciousness. So it may be eccentric to use a speculative story to pick out population growth as the 'first' and therefore the most fundamental of these. A question that remains is how it is possible to pick out any of the process's interacting elements as fundamental.

True, there is a case for insisting that 'the division of labour' is in practice a mix of all these elements. Even so, and in a need to approach things through analytical distinctions, it can be seen as a 'structural' affair of interlinkage in a core web of ideas–relations. In a way, then, the division of labour comes out as the work's dynamic of modern times because its 'function' is to generate solidarity. More basically, however, it comes out as this because what it actually generates is a whole problematic of how there can be a modern solidarity.

To recap some of the main reasons, one is that functional diversity entails moral diversity. Another is how this underlies a world of individualism, free thought and a multitude of disputes around a collective consciousness's abstract ideals. But also and not least, it involves a rise of mass society, mass markets and mass industry in which macrosocietal interconnectedness breaks up microsocial webs of relations.

Or to recap another main line of reasoning on the division of labour as a modern dynamic, it is how it is a source both of modern ideals and modern pathologies. But it isn't just that, despite Durkheim's own official appeal to 'abnormal' circumstances, his work implicates the division of labour in an internalist explanation of these pathologies. It is also that, despite his official insistence on a 'mechanistic' explanation, his work entails a sociology of action both in bringing in a role for ideals and in urging efforts at reform. Again, the trouble with his dualistic opposition between 'mechanistic' and 'teleological' explanation is that both these terms are inadequate. There is a need for a new term – 'dynamic' explanation? – to describe how the actual arguments of his thesis combine a sociology of structure and process with a sociology of action.

In any case, it is essential is to take on board his concern with *effort*. Indeed, this never comes to an end. Through its very action, it continues to generate new aims and aspirations in trying to realize an ideal. In the thesis:

> There will always be, between the furthest points we have attained and the goal that we tend towards, a field wide open to our efforts. (1893a: 385)

In the new edition there is extra emphasis: 'there is and there will always be' a field wide open to our efforts (1902b: 336).

Rethinking the 'Collective Consciousness'

Part of any overall assessment of Durkheim's thesis again involves the 'collective consciousness'. But it is merely untrue, and a recycling of mythology, to imagine he eventually abandoned the idea. He continued to draw on it, while also rethinking it, throughout his career. Yet given his own story of the rise of individualism, free thought and a multitude of disputes, is there any modern use for the notion of a collective consciousness at all?

Two Sources of Individuality
In introducing a 'collective consciousness', he explains:

> To simplify presentation of the argument, we assume the individual belongs to only one society. In fact, we form part of several groups and within us there are several collective consciousnesses; but this complication doesn't in any way change the relation we are in the process of establishing. (1893a: 113, n.1 / 1902b: 74, n.1)

It is important to keep in mind his readiness to simplify and exaggerate, to drive a message home. Thus he goes on to picture a time when the power of the collective consciousness is at a maximum, so that, as he adds with a flourish, 'at this moment our individuality is zero' (139 / 99–100). Or, even after several chapters developing and complicating the arguments of his thesis, he still remarks on and indeed emphasizes a time when the individual personality '*didn't exist*' (212 / 171).

A few pages later, it is made clear this is rhetorical talk. The individual personality always exists. It is because one of its sources is physical embodiedness, in turn one of the sources of psychic life and its realm of representations:

> This first basis of all individuality is inalienable and doesn't depend on the social world. (216 / 175)

The discussion then also makes clear his concern with the social world itself as the other and much more significant source of individuality. The message driven home by the earlier rhetoric is that everyone's character as an individual personality is above all 'the fruit of historical development' (217 / 176).

In any case it is *The Division of Labour* that makes a fundamental distinction between two sources of individuality, thanks to two sources of psychic life's realm of representations – the body, and the social world. The distinction then repeatedly turns up in later work, not least *The Elemental Forms*. But again it is merely untrue, and a recycling of mythology, just to associate it with later work.

Meanwhile, there is another point to make about the thesis itself. The way it represents a collective consciousness might make sense in the case of worlds of the clan, even though these always entail some sort of individuality. It runs into more serious trouble, once its evolutionary grand narrative moves on.

Collective Currents of Thought
It is instructive to strip the narrative down to essentials. In the beginning, there are almost no social sources of individuality. But a break of equilibrium sets in motion the dynamic of a division of labour and ceaseless processes of social change. So it might seem inevitable that this continuing change comes with continuing conflict at the heart of a social world. There is no possibility of a collective consciousness in the sense of a set of beliefs shared by almost everybody. It is functionalist nonsense to imagine a series of periods in which unanimity round one system of beliefs is magically followed by unanimity round a different system of beliefs.

Indeed, as Durkheim himself explains in his Latin thesis:

> The nature of societies contains opposites, which struggle with one another, just because it frees itself from an earlier form only little by little and moves little by little to one born out of this. (1892a: 68–69)

This links with a favourite Latin saying, often quoted in his work, on how god abandoned the world to men and their disputes. But it also links with a favourite classical example, the story of Socrates.

In the story as told in *The Rules*, Socrates was a criminal according to Athenian law, yet represented new tendencies that were stirring up. He 'helped to prepare the way for a new morality and faith, which the Athenians then needed since the traditions they had lived by were no longer in harmony with their conditions of existence' (1895a: 88–89). In lectures of 1898–99, Socrates was a deviant, condemned as immoral 'by most of his fellow citizens'. Yet in 'daring to shake off the yoke of traditional discipline', he represents one of humanity's 'great moral revolutions' (1925: 60–61, 103). In a text a few years later, it is now not just that 'Socrates expressed more faithfully than his judges the morality suited to the society of his time'. It is that he was part of a powerful collective 'current' of thought, representing how 'a new moral and religious faith had become necessary in Athens' (1906b: 93–94). What Durkheim emphasizes is at stake isn't merely an opposition between the individual and the collective, but an opposition between the collective and the collective itself:

> The very principle of rebellion is thus the same as the principle of conformism. It is the *true* nature of society that is conformed to in obeying traditional morality: it is the *true* nature of society that is conformed to when in revolt against the same morality. (95)

This spells out what is already a message of his subsidiary Latin thesis, as well as implicit in the narrative of his main thesis on the division of labour. There are different and conflicting tendencies inherent in the nature of a social world as a whole, involving what might now be discussed as different and conflicting collective currents of thought.

This opens up a number of questions for investigation. To what extent do these currents of thought spread everywhere, dividing individuals across all social classes and milieux? To what extent are they concentrated in particular groups as against others? But the key issue is what they are about. Durkheim repeatedly tends to see a basic struggle of forces of reaction and tradition against forces of the new and modern.

However, it is necessary to ask about different and conflicting currents of thought within modernity itself.

Indeed, this might give new life to his view of a collective consciousness as a set of shared ideas throughout a social world. In the case of modernity it is how opposing interpretations of shared general abstract ideals – freedom, equality, justice and so on – are an affair, not simply of individual disputes, but different collective currents of thought. In turn, it is to look for an overall collective change in the character and centre of gravity of disagreement round these ideals. Instead of arguments over 'equality' or whatever just staying the same, there is a move to a new collective framework of conflict, and so, in a way, to a new collective agenda.

A Changing and Developing Collective Agenda

Durkheim's narrative of evolutionary change is impossible to fit in with a 'functionalism' of different integrated self-maintaining systems that mysteriously and magically follow one another. Yet isn't it also far-fetched to see his narrative as a sociology of permanent crisis? So although it involves an account of permanent underlying forces for change, doesn't it also involve a sociology of long-term cycles? There are periods of relative stability and crystallization of a particular social order, but that inevitably – and, in a way, altogether 'normally' – break down in a crisis, in turn leading eventually on to what is again, in a way, the 'normality' of another period of a relative stabilization of things. Certainly, in the lectures on socialism that Durkheim gave in 1896, there is an expression of interest in a theory along these lines. It divides history into 'organic' and 'critical' periods. And he associates it with Saint-Simon's disciple, Saint-Armand Bazard. But as he comments: 'What escaped Bazard is that, the more one advances in history, the more one sees the characteristics of the critical period persist into the organic period' (1928: 313).

So this questions any simplistic idea of an 'organic' period of the future, which somehow manages to leave behind modernity's built-in forces of critical free thought, argument and dispute. Yet it isn't in resignation to a permanent crisis of going round and round in circles in the same old disagreements, without getting anywhere in them. Instead, it involves an idea of a changing and developing collective agenda. Indeed, it is this idea that helps to explain why 'there will always be, between the furthest points we have attained and the goal that we tend towards, a field wide open to our efforts'.

A way to explore things is through an issue that is central to book 1's concluding vision of a land of solidarity, but that then returns to haunt book 3 and the search for routes out of a world in crisis.

A 'Social Contract'

Durkheim begins book 1's concluding chapter by dismissing theories of a general social contract, which imagine how individuals might come to an agreement about an entire society and give it their consent. Instead, he emphasizes his concern with the actual legal institution of the contract, in which individuals enter into particular relationships and mutual commitments. He then goes on to attack theories that see the contract as an essentially private agreement between individuals themselves. On the contrary, it is an ineliminably social affair. This is because it is made within a framework that is formed and established in society, and that changes and develops through collective experience. So, it might be suggested, this core social element of the contract is why he sees it, in effect, as a social contract.

Or as he himself says: 'all in the contract is not contractual' (1893a: 230 / 1902b: 189). Spelling out the social, non-contractual element of the contract is then the business of a long discussion that follows (232–39 / 190–97).

An altogether basic concern is with the development, through collective experience, of standard or 'normal' forms of the contract. It is why he is so critical of theories of the contract as a private matter. These imagine that individuals are able to create – entirely on their own, and from scratch – an agreement that clearly and comprehensively covers the many different possible situations that can arise in a relationship. This is fantasy and taradiddle. Indeed, it is an invitation to a whole battleground of contractual uncertainty, in which individuals fight with one another over what they think they might have agreed to agree. It is a way, in fact, to destroy long-term relationships and undermine the everyday business of everyday cooperation in them. Thus, as he yet again insists, it is superficial just to see the contract as an exchange of goods and services. It is above all about relationships in a division of labour. Accordingly, the job of contractual law is to provide a stable basis of relationships and of cooperation within them – a job that is done through the development of standard forms of the contract, drawing on collective experience to crystallize a whole set of rights and obligations that cover a whole range of possible situations. So, as he also wants to emphasize, standard forms of the contract spell out the *implications* of a relationship that is initiated by individuals themselves. But it is once again fantasy and taradiddle to imagine the contract as having each individual's full, free, informed consent to all the detailed implications. Accordingly, it is because these implications are both the work of society and beyond fully informed individual consent that they constitute a non-contractual core of the contract.

Even so, a lot depends on whether or not present-day law's standard forms of the contract actually do the job that Durkheim asks of them. Thus his account also comes with worries and warnings. These are about 'unjust contracts', made 'with the support of society'. But he is especially concerned with them in the context of the changes, indeed 'the revolutions', in modern economic industrial life (236 / 194–95). And it is at precisely this point that he locates what, as already noted, is the main discussion in his thesis about the need for new occupational groups (238–39 / 196–97).

So, moving on to book 3, it is instructive to consider how Durkheim gets going with his description of a world in crisis:

> The working classes do not really choose the position they are placed in, but too often accept it, having no means to achieve any other, only under constraint and duress. (398 / 346)

An underlying message is to do with consent, not just in relation to this or that particular social role but an entire social order. While book 1 tries to bury the idea of a general social contract, in book 3 it stirs back to life again. It turns out that it is not so easy to dismiss classic canonical texts of the Enlightenment, such as Rousseau's *The Social Contract*. They symbolize modern aspirations to everyone's free consent as the basis of a social world's legitimacy. Thus book 1's official target is the idea of a world running on private individual contracts, which Durkheim associates with Herbert Spencer. But it is in a common rejection of the idea of a general social contract, as if it belongs to the rubbish of history. Accordingly, an actual though less obvious target nearer home is once again Alfred Fouillée, whose influential *Contemporary Social Science* attempts to revive the Enlightenment's idea of a social contract and to rework it for modern times. True, on this occasion, Durkheim at least mentions Fouillée by name (220 / 179). But the question is if, despite any desire to criticize a rival who was both alive and French, he himself ends up accepting the need to try to rework, rather than just to kill off, modern ideals of a society that has legitimacy because it is based on consent.

In book 1, it is just taken for granted that the contractual element of the contract is its free initiation by individuals. It is then brought out how there is also a non-contractual element, involving the vast set of rights and obligations that isn't realistically a matter of each individual's understanding and that is developed through law's articulation of collective experience. But in book 3 the landscape changes, bringing out warnings about the existing non-contractual framework of rights and obligations. However, it isn't simply that this framework is inadequate. It is part of an entire society in disrepair, lurching along in the class wars of a constrained division of labour and its unjust, indeed 'exploitative' contracts (432 / 379). So there is a switch of focus on to the whole idea of consent, in order to examine what was at first left in the background and taken for granted, the contract's contractual core as some sort of freely initiated agreement between individuals.

Thus Durkheim emphasizes the role of the contract in modern life, and wants to investigate what is at stake in the idea of consent itself. This involves him in three strategies. His main argument is about the dynamics of a division of labour increasingly bound up with modern aspirations to equality and justice, so that he goes on to formulate a definition of when, on this sociological basis, a contract has consent. Another argument is that his definition is in fact supported by the way consent is increasingly understood in general currents of opinion in society itself – in what sounds like an appeal to a collective consciousness, though now called 'the public consciousness' (429, 432 / 376, 379–80). Finally, he completes the picture with a sketch of the historical evolution of ideas about the contract, in which it has come to centre round consent (431–32 / 379–80).

A first comment, then, is how all this entails a picture in which 'consent' is not just a matter of individual ideas and representations but is above all a collective idea and representation, created, formed and developed in the whole business of social and collective life. Accordingly, far from just being an affair of individual agreements, it is the very idea of consent itself that lies at the social, non-contractual core of the modern contract.

The next comment is about Durkheim's effort to formulate a definition of when, nowadays, contracts have consent – 'the contract has full consent only if the services exchanged have an equivalent social value' (429 / 376). If his thesis really depends on such a vague abstract notion, it is in serious trouble. In effect, it leaves him with only two main routes out of the problem, which might be discussed as the 'escape-clause' and the 'civic' option.

The drawback with the escape-clause option is that it spells the end of his search for solidarity through the division of labour. It amounts to an appeal to a traditional collective consciousness, with detailed consensus round interrelated beliefs in freedom, equality and justice, rather than merely justice on its own. The only hope of rescuing the thesis is the civic option, but in a complex combination of ideas involving a collective consciousness, conflicting currents of thought, a developing agenda, webs of intermediate groups and their negotiation of a way through disputes to stay together in enacting reform.

So a final comment is to do with Durkheim's wavering between these alternatives. Certainly, he can seem tempted by the escape-clause option. In the conclusion to his thesis, however, he continues to insist that the main place to look for a modern solidarity isn't a collective consciousness, but webs of particular definite relations in a division of labour. In turn, his thesis points ahead to a follow-up work on webs of new intermediate occupational groups. It is in this overall context that the civic option – with its essentially republican discourse – can be seen as his consistent hope in a route to social and moral reform.

A World in Crisis

Book 3 is officially about the division of labour's 'abnormal forms', but is in practice about a modern world in crisis. It begins with a chapter on anomie, continues with a chapter on the constrained division of labour, and ends with a chapter on 'another', unnamed pathology. But there is a basic theme and concern running through all this.

The chapter on anomie starts with a key case as 'the antagonism between labour and capital' (1893a: 397 / 1902b: 345) – to go on to worry about forces of alienation at the heart of modern economic industrial life, but also how it consigns vast numbers to 'monotonous', 'degrading' work (415–16 / 363). The chapter on the constrained division of labour once again starts with its roots in 'class wars' (419 / 367) – to go on to worry about unjust exploitative contracts, but also how these are bound up with vast inequalities of wealth in which there are 'rich and poor at birth' (424, 430 / 372, 378). In sum, a basic theme is a breakdown of solidarity in the underlying tensions and overt conflicts of a class-divided society.

Turned round the other way, a basic theme is the ideal of a society that can overcome these problems, free things up and sweep away constraints. In going through and analysing Durkheim's account, it can be seen as involving three main types of constraint – 'aspirational', 'institutional' and 'structural' constraint.

Aspirational Constraint

There are two sides to aspirational constraint. One is to do with social forces that in various ways shape horizons and limit aspirations themselves, so that individuals and groups accept the position they are placed in. The other is to do with social forces that open up horizons and generate new aspirations, so that individuals and groups feel blocked and frustrated by whatever stands in the way of these. This is a situation of underlying tensions in which 'the working classes do not really choose the position they are placed in', but too often accept it 'only under constraint and duress' (398 / 346). It is also a situation making for overt conflicts in which 'the lower classes are not or are not any longer satisfied with the role laid down for them by custom', but 'aspire to functions forbidden them' in what become 'civil wars' (419 / 367).

Durkheim's approach to aspirational constraint is complicated, however, by a concern running through his work as a whole. This is a worry about the 'malaise' of an entirely unconstrained, socially deregulated formation of limitless horizons and aspirations to anything or everything. In *Suicide* it is a 'disease of the infinite', and in the case of anomie it is an 'infinity of desire' (1897a: 324). In his thesis, it is an underlying strand of a narrative in which the 'ever weakening' forces of a traditional collective consciousness manage for a while to suppress aspirations generated by a developing division of labour. There is then a critical time of 'danger'. The pressures keep mounting up, but, before anything new can be established, the old order constraining them gives way. 'At the very moment when the flood-tide becomes more violent, the dam that held it in check is breached' (1893a: 426 / 1902b: 374).

Even so, he is on the side of a new era, and campaigns for an ideal of equality that he formulates as 'equality in the external conditions of struggle' (426–27 / 374). To modern readers of his thesis, it could sound like a version of the nowadays familiar ideal of equal opportunity. But it is a mistake just to equate it with this. To readers at the time, a more or less obvious link is with the ideal of a career open to talents.

Institutional Constraint

Aspirational constraint works through both structural and institutional constraints. But while structural constraints are to do with the nature and range of social roles, institutional constraints are about the allocation of these roles. In essence, institutional constraints police who get which jobs in such a way that there isn't in fact a 'career open to talents'. Durkheim's account is concerned, then, with three basic forms of institutional constraint.

It starts with extreme cases of the use of 'violence' (422 / 370). It moves on to the continuing influence of caste-like 'prejudices', combining favouritism towards some with discrimination against others (423–24 / 371). But it is to lead up to what he sees as nowadays the most important factor of all in advantaging some while holding back others. This is the inequality of 'rich and poor at birth' – which has nothing to do with individual talent, but everything to do with the social institution of 'the hereditary transmission of wealth' (424 / 371–72).

However, it isn't a mere hangover from the past. On the contrary, it arises within the modern world itself. It involves an individualization of the inheritance of wealth, as against traditional collective forms. It needs to be tackled by a recollectivization of wealth through new oc-cupational groups – as in the argument of Durkheim's lecture just after handing in his thesis, and repeated in subsequent work.

Moreover, his concern with the injustice of private inherited for-tunes also comes with a worry about all vast inequalities of wealth. Thus it is fair enough to quote his remark that the division of labour 'implies an ever increasing inequality' (425 / 372). But it is misleading to do so, while leaving out and ignoring the entire argument that follows. This is in his main discussion of contracts that are unjust, and his main ex-planation of contracts that are unjust is that one class is exploited by another thanks to a vast inequality of wealth.

> One class of society is obliged to get acceptance of its services at any price in
> order to live, while the other can do without them thanks to the resources at its
> disposal, but that are not necessarily due to any social superiority. (430 / 378)

So although he undoubtedly associates a career open to talents with the legitimacy of wealth earned through these talents, this is in no way to sign a blank cheque for inequalities that recreate the exploitative con-tracts of a class divided society.

The reason is his consistent campaign for new occupational groups, as a road to a recollectivization of wealth but also to other vital reforms. These include the development of a social framework for an effective, morally legitimate regulation of economic life and negotiation towards justice in the contract. Not least, however, it is to renew microsocial webs of relations in an effort to begin to overcome the vast social gulfs and alienation at the root of present-day anomie. These vast social gulfs are inherently bound up with vast inequalities of wealth and power, and with his whole account of a world in crisis.

In sum, Durkheim's main modern institutional constraint isn't the violence and duress of a 'forced' division of labour – as in a misleading English translation of *la division du travail contrainte*. Nor is it the contin-uing power of caste-like 'prejudices' – a power that, thanks to his Jewish background, he encountered throughout his own life and career. Nor is it the transmission of forms of 'social capital' such as education – an issue discussed elsewhere in his writings, and nowadays often seen as a key to things. Instead, it is above all the combination of vast social gulfs, vast economic inequalities, the individual inheritance of wealth, and the lack of a framework for reform through occupational groups.

Even so, is the main source of aspirational constraint to be found in a whole formidable nexus of institutional constraints? Or is it instead to be found in structural constraints?

Structural Constraint

Structural constraint is about too many talented individuals and not enough suitable roles. It is why it isn't necessarily a big deal to clamour for the equal opportunity of equal life-chances. It might merely mean equal opportunity to get hold of one of the few appropriate jobs, while happily leaving others to rot in any of an entire range of dead-end situations.

Structural constraint is an issue throughout book 3's account of 'abnormal' forms of the division of labour. It surfaces, for instance, in the short final chapter on 'another' unnamed form. An explicit concern is with roles so divided up there is little or nothing to them and 'they do not offer sufficient content to the activity of individuals' (435 / 383). But the most obvious example is in the chapter on anomie. It ends with worries over modern mass industrial production and its deskilled degraded work, reducing the individual to 'a machine':

> Every day, he repeats the same movements with a monotonous regularity, but without interest in or understanding of them ... he is no more than a lifeless cog, which an external force sets in motion and always drives in the same direction and in the same fashion. Clearly, in whatever way one represents the moral ideal, it is impossible to remain indifferent to such a debasement of human nature. (416 / 363)

This leads straight on to the chapter on the constrained division of labour, which comes with yet further worries about the crushing of 'natural' abilities. True, it is especially in a concern with the institutional constraint of 'rich and poor at birth'. But an underlying concern is with structural constraint, and a squandering of people's talents in a scarcity of suitable roles.

There are two main ways of understanding his ideal of a 'spontaneous' division of labour, with its equality in 'external conditions of struggle'. One is to reduce it to the equal opportunity of equal life-chances. The other is that it is about developing and flourishing in a society that frees everyone to live up to their potential. It is this that is at stake in each of his two ways of defining the ideal.

In his first formulation, a spontaneous division of labour entails 'the free unfolding of the social force that each carries within them' (422 / 370). So this is about a society that frees everyone to develop in line with their potential, but in an unfolding of the 'social force' within them that entails a social shaping of potential into actual powers, abilities and talents.

In his second formulation, the spontaneous division of labour means that 'social inequalities exactly express natural inequalities' (423 / 370). So this is also about a society in which everyone can have a role in line with their abilities. But it focuses on natural potential in the raw, while there is no explicit indication of how equal or unequal its distribution might be. However, book 3 as a whole entails that it is equal enough to worry about a far-reaching structural constraint in which present-day jobs are so limited in content that they not only cramp 'the activity of individuals' but come with 'a debasement of human nature'.

In sum, the ideal set out in his thesis isn't about an equal opportunity that equalizes life-chances of imprisonment in such situations. It is about a society that frees everyone to develop, flourish and live up to their potential.

The Spontaneous Division of Labour and a Commonwealth of Persons

As Durkheim eventually reveals, 'the division of labour produces solidarity only if it is spontaneous and to the extent that it is spontaneous' (422 / 370). How, then, does his search for solidarity through a spontaneous division of labour entail a switch from a functionalist to a republican discourse, and a commitment to an ideal of a commonwealth of persons?

The functionalist discourse doesn't disappear. Although most obvious in book 1, it remains in evidence in book 3. A striking example is in the chapter on anomie, which ends in the passage about modern mass production and deskilled degraded work. The individual is reduced to a cog in a machine and is no longer:

> the living cell of a living organism, that vibrates in continuous contact with neighbouring cells, that acts upon them and responds to their action in turn, that expands, contracts, gives way and transforms according to needs and circumstances. (416 / 363)

It is nonetheless essential to take on board the next chapter on the constrained division of labour, which ends with a passage summarizing its argument. This is still in talk concerned with a 'harmony of functions', but in insistence that any modern harmony of functions depends on a modern 'need for justice' (434 / 382).

In other words, Durkheim continues to draw on a functionalist discourse as a core part of his thesis. But it simply can't deliver the goods on its own, and what is instead decisive is a republican discourse of freedom, equality and justice in a society of persons. Indeed, this is built into the work's whole argument from the outset. According to his own testimony, backed up by other independent evidence, it originated in the idea of the division of labour as the solution to a modern combination of solidarity and autonomy. That is, a general idea from the outset was of the division of labour as the solution to how there can be any modern solidarity at all, but which depends on reconciling it with autonomy. An interrelated point is how, at some stage in drafting his thesis, it came home to him that the division of labour's functional diversity inevitably comes with moral diversity, complete with individualism, free thought and disputes round abstract ideals such as justice. One of the inevitable implications of the argument itself is that it is impossible to make do with functionalist talk of social members as 'organs of an organism'. It is necessary to bring in a republican discourse, and terms such as the individual personality, the person, the citizen.

Thus, as already suggested, it is the functionalist view of social members as organs of an organism that is at the bottom of book 1's attack on a cult of the individual, in which attachment is not to society but 'to ourselves' (187 / 147). In the conclusion, in contrast, a cult of everyone's same status and dignity as a person is nowadays a moral 'rallying point' (450 / 396). True, it is still to insist the key to things is the division of labour. But it is to link this with everyone's development as a 'person' and accordingly as an 'autonomous source of action', since, with the division of labour, everyone develops as a distinct individual agent and 'the very materials of their consciousness have a personal character' (453–54 / 399).

Taken together, his arguments involve a problem to do with the relation between two sides of autonomy. In work such as *The Elemental Forms*, the emphasis is on sameness as a person rather than difference as a personality. It is the other way round in *The Division of Labour*, where an abstract universalizing ethic of the person is a moral rallying point, but is less important than developing and flourishing as an actual autonomous agent and a socially attached yet distinct individual personality. Here, however, what is significant is not so much *The Division of Labour*'s particular line on the issue, but how, more generally, it trumps functionalist discourse with republican concern with a society of persons.

A similar point can be made about the work's arguments over the issue of equality, complete with interlinkage with issues of freedom and justice. Again it is misleading simply to quote, out of context, the remark that the division of labour entails an increase of inequality. In the same paragraph in the same page, it is coupled with a remark on modern belief in an increase of 'equality between citizens', and on the need to understand this belief, since 'it cannot be pure illusion' (425 / 372). It then turns out that the division of labour's road to solidarity depends, not so much on the harmonization of roles among an organism's living vibrating cells, as on meeting aspirations to equality between citizens, opening careers to talents, ending exploitative contracts, tackling the huge inequalities created by the institution of individual inheritance, and working, through new intermediate groups, to build a morality founded on justice. Put another way, it requires an essentially republican solution to an essentially republican problem.

In sum, the work's ideal of a spontaneous division of labour is bound up with a republican ideal of a commonwealth of free autonomous persons, justice and solidarity. This is also why 'there will always be, between the furthest points we have attained and the goal that we tend towards, a field wide open to our efforts'. There is no shortage of issues – women's equality, gay rights, citizenship in religious, ethnic and cultural diversity – that involve all kinds of struggles in a complex moving agenda of a commonwealth of persons. But the problem that haunts *The Division of Labour* is a fundamentally class-divided society. Above all, it is what can be done about structural constraints generated by the present-day economic system – with its social gulfs and vast range of dead-end situations – in an effort to build a world of solidarity that frees everyone to live up to their potential.

A Road to Reform

In order to discuss *The Division of Labour* itself, a lot has already been said about the material for a companion follow-up volume. So a way to conclude investigations of the thesis is with the interlinked material on a road to reform. What are its main themes, and what are basic questions it raises?

Themes

Durkheim defended, from the outset of his career, an extensive modern role for the state. He opposed, from the outset of his career, a centralized monolithic state. In his Latin thesis, an authoritarian state attempting to rule over society is 'like a monster, in which only the head is alive, having absorbed all the energies of the body' (1892a: 39–40). Similarly, in *The Division of Labour*'s new preface, an authoritarian state attempting to rule over a mass of atomized individuals is a 'sociological monstrosity' (1902b: xxxii).

So it is important to understand his account of changes in the relation between the individual, social groups and the state. Part of the story is how the modern state helped to emancipate the individual from imprisonment in traditional community. Part of the story is also how there was a need to free modern commerce and industry from the control of the old guilds. But this organization was swept away without replacement, and the story brought up to date is about the need for powerful new intermediate groups between individual and state – separating while linking them, and with the status of public institutions. As in his conclusion to *Suicide*, envisaging a new form of the guild, 'it is essential that, instead of remaining a private group allowed by the law yet ignored by the state, it becomes a definite and recognized organ of our public life', but 'constituted outside of the state' (1897a: 436–37).

Another basic theme, then, is about new intermediate groups as occupational groups. A general argument is about the centrality of work in modern life, so that, again as emphasized in *Suicide*, the key form of decentralization away from the state is '*occupational decentralization*' (1897a: 449). But as in *The Division of Labour*'s new preface, it is above all in worry about a modern economic world characterized by 'a state of war, latent or acute' (1902b: iii). This reads like a reference to Marx's *Communist Manifesto* and its famous talk of a state of class war, latent or overt. In any case, it is the need to tackle a 'war' between workers and bosses – *ouvriers* and *patrons* – that drives Durkheim's campaign for new occupational groups.

Existing trade unions and employers' associations are separate and distinct, which is '*legitimate and necessary*', but they lack any adequate, continuing contact with one another, since they lack 'a common organization that links them' (1902b: vii). In outlining what is required 'in the existing state of industry', he outlines a structure involving both elected assemblies made up of representatives of employees and employers, and their own 'distinct, independent groups, since their interests are too often rival and antagonistic' (xxviii, n.2). But an essential point is the need, in the existing state of industry, to get going with a realistic, viable framework for reform through a type of self-governing common organization that is outside the state, though in interaction with it, and that is recognized as a key public institution.

Indeed, his concern with the importance of the status of a public body is why he so often talks of occupational 'corporations'. But he is even more concerned with the importance of the links, relations and attachments of a moral milieu, which is a reason for his continuing talk of occupational 'groups'. It is impossible to tackle a crisis rooted in a deep far-reaching moral malaise, without developing occupational life as a key moral milieu. This is just a basic repeated theme of his campaign for these new groups. It turns up in his thesis (1893a: 238–39 / 1902b: 196–97), in the lectures of 1896 on socialism (1928: 296), in the conclusion to *Suicide* (1897a: 436), in the lectures of 1898–1900 on occupational ethics (1950: 37), and again in *The Division of Labour*'s new preface (1902b: xxx).

Despite the social gulfs that are part of his account of a modern class war, he insists that occupational life continues to involve a common social milieu, which is also in its way a moral milieu. In the new preface, he suggests various ideas of building on this, through the occupational group's development as a centre of continuing education and recreation (1902b: xxxi). He also outlines ideas about its development as a centre of political life, already set out elsewhere and summarized in the new preface (xxxi–xxxiii). But his main ideas about developing a moral milieu are about the occupational group's core economic activities, and the cooperative joint effort of tackling problems to do with work itself.

In going through his various texts, it is possible to identify three main types of concern with these. One is with the many issues arising in the actual detailed activity of work – the nature, coordination and distribution of jobs, pay, hours, health and safety, etc. – in an emphasis on how it is not the state, but the occupational group that has both the information on the ground and the moral authority and legitimacy to deal with these. Another is to do with issues of social welfare – pensions, sickness benefits, insurance, mutual assistance – again with attacks on the danger of concentrating all this activity and power in the hands of the state, and insisting on a decentralization of welfare that involves occupational groups themselves. Finally, there is the issue of property and collective ownership.

This was tackled in the lecture of 1892 given just after handing in his thesis, but not published until 1921. It resurfaces in the lectures based on a manuscript of 1898–1900, but which was not published in full until 1950. It is not until *The Division of Labour*'s new preface that it is clearly brought out in a text appearing during his lifetime. Moreover, it is the issue he selects to conclude its overall argument. He first emphasizes the problems that won't disappear thanks to collective ownership, but that will continue to require occupational groups to deal with them. It is then to reaffirm the case, already made in the lecture room, for a reform that is a way to modern solidarity. It is a way to overcome present-day injustices, but without delivering individuals into the power of a monolithic state, since it is instead about a development through occupational groups of a decentralized collective ownership of social wealth (1902b: xxxiv–xxxvi).

Questions

It is now time to stand back, to try to identify basic questions in asking what to make of Durkheim's road to reform. A first question is to do with how, even in his call for a whole new web of intermediate groups, it is for a whole new web of intermediate groups of a single type. The point, here, is not just about his formal explicit arguments for the modern importance of occupational as against other groups, such as local groups. It is about an underlying implicit argument against a liberal pluralist picture of a flourishing civil society of all sorts of different kinds of groups and associations. A suggestion, then, is to do with his image of an authoritarian state as a 'monster', absorbing into itself all the energies of a wider civil society. So a question is if a liberal pluralist utopia is in fact an invitation to authoritarianism, thanks to a diffusion of civil society's energies among a mass of miscellaneous associations, which are no match for the power of a centralized state. Maybe what is instead required is a concentration of civil society's energies in a key type of intermediate group, with the status of a public institution, and strong enough to limit, check and interact on a mutually counterbalancing basis with the power of the state. A risk is highlighted by Durkheim's enthusiastic ideas on how occupational groups might develop to cover all sorts of aspects of life, more or less from the cradle to the grave. The risk, in other words, is to end up with the individual's reimprisonment in community. So a basic problem might be put this way. It is the possibility of an organization of civil society and its energies in a web of intermediate groups that can avoid capture and control by the state, while also avoiding the individual's reimprisonment in community.

Another, interrelated issue is to do with how Durkheim's campaign represents a disaffection with the failures and shortcomings of the existing, established system of parliamentary politics. Instead, and as in *The Division of Labour*'s new preface, he sees reform through intermediate groups as a way to draw the individual into 'the general torrent of social life' (1902b: xxxiii). More specifically, and as in his lectures of 1898–1900, they are a way towards an effective democratic public culture, through the development of effective forums of collective public argument. It is through such groups, rather than merely through the state, that information on the ground and collective currents of thought and experience can be articulated 'as clearly as possible', in processes of 'collective deliberation' in which they can be 'freely criticized and discussed' (1950: 105–6). The issue, however, is not only how this requires a voice for everyone as a citizen, in work or not, so that it seems necessary to look beyond his occupational groups. It is also that there is a need to make room, as in his example of Socrates, for the rebels of this world and for critics of the failures and shortcomings of whatever system might become established – again, there will always be a field wide open to our efforts. So another basic question is to do with reform towards a system that can claim legitimacy as a flourishing democratic public culture, yet that does not use this legitimacy to establish a complacent 'normality' and to turn a deaf ear to the voices of a rebellious politics.

All the same, occupational groups seem a crucial part of any reform and a democratization of economic life. So yet another basic problem might be put this way. It is the need, 'in the existing state of industry', to get going with a realistic, viable framework of reform, yet that avoids filling in too many details about what the reform ought to be, in a blue-print of the good society theorized and cobbled together 'in the silence of the study'. Again as in the lectures of 1898–1900, and in envisaging a collectivization of social wealth through occupational groups, it is emphasized it 'can only come about spontaneously, under the pressure of facts and of experience' (1950: 51). Or again, as in *The Division of Labour*'s new preface, it is emphasized that whatever the importance of a collectivization of wealth along these lines, it won't magically solve all the problems of modern economic life. But again in going through Durkheim's various texts, it can seem difficult or impossible to find anything directly on what to do about one of the most fundamental problems of all, the problem of structural constraint and the squandering of talent and potential in a vast range of dead-end situations. In fact, however, the basic key to the problem is his insistence on beginning to overcome social gulfs through a rebuilding of webs of microsocial contacts, links and relations. It is a fundamental, necessary condition of getting going a process of reform in which it is up to occupational groups themselves to get on with looking for ways to begin to tackle the problem, through job rotation, redefinition or whatever. On the one hand, then, it is a lack of faith in human creativity and imagination to insist, in advance, there is no solution. On the other, a key part of the expansion of roles is the actual participation and involvement, through occupational groups, in the democratization of economic life itself.

Even so, Durkheim's campaign for reform failed to get anywhere, and a final question remains. What is the point of discussing it at all? An answer is to free ourselves from mantras that there is no alternative, and that put human reason to sleep. In turn, this involves two things. One is critique of an existing 'order' that lives off modern aspirations and ideals, while systematically betraying them. The other is exploration of a road to reform that is a democratic, republican way of working towards something like the democratic, republican ideal of a commonwealth. It is one of the claims to a continuing attention of Durkheim's creation of a vast complex sociological landscape perhaps beyond his own as well as anybody else's full understanding, and centred round *The Division of Labour.*

CHAPTER 4

An Intellectual Crisis

How did Durkheim get to *The Elemental Forms*?[1] A draft can be found in lectures of 1906 and 1907, when he also wrote in a letter:

> It was only in 1895 that I had a clear sense of the key role played by religion in social life. It was in this year that, for the first time, I found a way to take a sociological approach to the study of religion. It was for me a revelation. (1907b: 404)

Yet wasn't this somewhat dramatic story of the past influenced by the present, and work on his new book itself? Or are we just to believe that, like a latter-day saint, he had a sudden and miraculous conversion on the road to Damascus?

In asking what happened, it is essential to check through the evidence that in the end counts – his actual sociological publications. There are various methods of doing this. But his new book is especially concerned with the positive, socially creative role of effervescence. So it is instructive to track its Durkheimian career.

Tracking 'Effervescence': 1890 to 1907

Durkheim's first use of the term 'effervescence' appears in 1896, and is clearly negative. But the idea appears in 1895 – the year of the 'revelation' – and is also negative. So a further complication is his sympathy towards it before 1895.

Early Sightings

Durkheim's first use of the idea can be traced to 1890, in his essay on the French Revolution. The Revolution's upsurge of idealism can be found 'in all creative eras, in all times of a new and audacious faith' (1890a: 224). So this is about effervescent times as mould-breaking, momentous times. It isn't about regular events in an established social calendar.

A second example is in his thesis. But it is more to do with regularly recurring events, since it is in his story of a collective consciousness's reaction to crime. This involves a discussion of how collective energies can reach a state of 'hyperexcitement' – a *surexcitation,* later to become one of his standard terms for effervescence – as in the case of 'large assemblies' (1893a: 106 / 1902b: 67).

But it is only in passing and as an illustrative example. He didn't develop it any further, just as he didn't do anything further with the Revolution as a case of creative times of a new faith. Indeed, these disappear from his thesis. *The Division of Labour* is overwhelmingly concerned with a solidarity based on everyday life's everyday relations. It has no real theoretical interest in special times of assembly, since it has no real theoretical need for them.

From the Year of the 'Revelation' to the Launch of the **Année sociologique**
What happened in 1895? In an article on modern social science, Durkheim mentions his new course on the sociology of religion:

> We have studied the different religions as they have existed and still exist, we
> have compared them, we have brought out their common characteristics and
> we have thus been able to identify what the religious phenomenon consists
> of objectively. It is to the *thing* defined in this way that we have applied our
> analysis. (1895e: 97)

How is this a 'revelation'? It invokes the scientific method of *The Rules,* based on his Latin thesis of 1892, which urged the study of religious facts as 'things'.

Concern with scientific method turns up in another article of 1895, on philosophical education. It is where he first uses an idea of effervescence in a clearly negative sense. He criticizes 'an abnormal hyperexcitement of energy' – *une surexcitation anormale de la vitalité* – to complain that modern philosophical culture, in its obsession just with the new, is in the grip of an 'unhealthy enthusiasm' (1895b: 405–6, 412).

It was also in 1895 that he began his course on socialism, and it is in a lecture of the following year that he first uses the term 'effervescence'. It is again in an unambiguously negative sense. But it isn't merely a malaise in philosophy. It is now a malaise throughout society itself. Moreover, he rejects a return to religion as a cure for this. Instead, he looks to new occupational groups to tackle a 'state of unruliness, effervescence and manic agitation' (1928: 297).

His conclusion to *Suicide* also rejects a return to religion. Once again he looks to new occupational groups to combat a state of anomie. But he now describes this in terms of the 'hyperexcited forces' of an 'unhealthy effervescence' – *forces surexcitées, effervescence maladive* (1897a: 408, 422).

In sum, it is only after 1895 that Durkheim takes a theoretically central interest in effervescence. But it is as a malaise. A way of trying to understand this is through development of the interest, in his thesis, in modern aspirations. It is concerned with the injustices that block a career open to talents, but also with an explosion of wants in a deregulation of desires. It is this that comes to the fore in his investigation of suicide, and modern scenes of a pathological 'effervescence'.

Yet it isn't the whole story. A rather different idea of effervescence turns up in a note on altruistic suicide. It is about the Revolution, and comments:

> In these times of internal struggles and collective enthusiasm, the individual personality had lost some of its value. The interests of country or of party took precedence over everything. The large number of executions arose, no doubt, from the same cause. Killing others came as easily as killing oneself. (1897a: 247, n.1)

Like his remark of 1890, this is about momentous times, except that it now seems so ambivalent about them.

It is also when he published his essay on rationalist empiricism, which also says something on effervescence:

> The particular moment at which a people sets out to change a system of ideas is a time when they can well believe, in an outburst of enthusiasm and youthful confidence, that the task is easy. But it does not take them long to experience all the difficulties, and the illusions they might have had only make their disenchantment more bitter. (1897f: 78–79)

There is nothing ambivalent about this, in its picture of an effervescence of hope that collapses in despair. In an obvious reading, it is again about the Revolution. But it could also be about the events that created the Third Republic. There is a striking similarity with Durkheim's recall of his own youthful 'enthusiasm' at these, quickly followed by 'disenchantment' (1898c: 276).

It is anyway important to ask about the year he wrote this. It is when he launched the first volume of the *Année sociologique*.

1898

To start his new journal, he led off with an article on an emotive, fundamental issue in human life, his essay on incest (1898a[ii]). At the same time he was preparing another lead article for the next issue, his essay on the definition of religious phenomena (1899a[ii]). Meanwhile, in other journals, he published 'Individual and Collective Representations' (1898b), as well as his essay on the Dreyfus Affair, 'Individualism and the Intellectuals' (1898c). He also began writing up his lectures on occupational and civic ethics, in the manuscript of 1898–1900.

There is little evidence in any of this of a change to a more positive line on effervescence. But there are signs of an intellectual crisis, involving different approaches to religion in different parts of his work.

Although both the essay on representations and the essay on religious phenomena see the realm of conceptual thought as a collective creation, neither of them hints at its creation through effervescence, as in *The Elemental Forms*. In fact, the essay on representations says nothing at all about effervescence. The essay on religious phenomena at least has a reference to it, but to reject any suggestion that 'extraordinarily intense forces' and 'energies' constitute a defining characteristic of religion (1899a[ii]: 19).

However, going through the material of this time turns up clues to something else. It is as if Durkheim inhabits separate intellectual worlds, in his contributions to the new journal and in his work elsewhere. His university lecture course on ethics continues with the campaign, not for a new religion, but for social and moral reform through occupational groups. The essay on representations not only has nothing to say about effervescence but also has nothing to say about the sacred. Even the essay on the Dreyfus Affair, in its very talk of a secular religion, is permeated through and through with the spirit of secular rationalism. After highlighting a new 'cult', it returns to familiar concerns with social and moral reform, concluding with the need for 'ways to organize economic life and introduce greater justice in contractual relations' (1898c: 277). Moreover, the 'cult' itself is a cult of the autonomy of reason and everyone's status as a person. It doesn't depend on the paraphernalia of ritual and symbolism, which are merely an 'external apparatus' and the 'superficial part' of religion (270). The world can seem very different in the pages of Durkheim's new journal, where ritual and symbolism are basic to religion, and where early elementary forms of religious life are basic to understanding continuing obscure roots of modern society.

In sum, tracking the career of effervescence is only one way to explore how Durkheim got from *The Division of Labour* to *The Elemental Forms*. But on the evidence so far, it wasn't in a sudden intellectual revolution. Indeed, whatever happened in 1895, a key date is the launch of his new journal in 1898. It is where he started to publish essays and reviews that prepared the ground for *The Elemental Forms*. At the same time it took him along lines of investigation that diverged from approaches elsewhere, to set up tensions in his work as a whole. Yet in the new journal itself there is a sense of confidence, rather than of any impending crisis.

1899–1907

A crisis came, however, with the publication of Spencer and Gillen's *The Native Tribes of Central Australia* in 1899. It was then, and only then, that Durkheim began to retheorize things in a way that sees times of collective creative effervescence as the key to religion, the sacred and society itself. But the breakthrough that matters isn't evident until his lectures of 1906 and 1907.

His essay on religious phenomena had already set up a distinction between 'two worlds' of the sacred and profane, yet while blocking the idea that effervescent energies have anything to do with this. His lectures, in contrast, see these 'two worlds' in terms of two times of the sacred and profane, the special times of collective effervescence as against ordinary times of the individual's routine concerns. Indeed, with Spencer and Gillen in mind, he insists that the rites at the heart of religious life in Australia take place only during these times of assembly, rather than outside them (1907f: 97).

So why might it solve an intellectual crisis to emphasize two times, rather than merely two worlds, of the sacred and profane? It is necessary to understand his core views in the early *Année sociologique*. It can then be seen how his theory was undermined at its very foundations by Spencer and Gillen's Australia, and how he attempted various ways to respond. His eventual solution, in the lecture course of 1906/1907, made possible the creation of *The Elemental Forms* itself.

The First Two Volumes of the *Année sociologique*: 1898 and 1899

Each volume consists of a preface, followed by two major essays, followed by over four hundred pages of reviews and shorter notices, divided into sections according to topic. So a number of points can be made straightaway.

Responsibility for the sections was distributed among the team that had been assembled. Some members were more peripheral than others. But Durkheim and Mauss formed the core.

The section on religion was given pride of place and entrusted to Mauss. Durkheim himself took charge of the sections on kinship, marriage, the family, crime and social organization. Put another way, the editor in chief and his closest collaborator ran the sections on two key groups of topics, religion and social organization.

Some statistics can help to bring out their role. Taking the first two volumes together, Durkheim and Mauss contributed in equal proportions to a third of all the material of all the subject sections – around 290 out of 880 pages. Counting only single-authored reviews of more than a page, they contributed a quarter of these – 38 by Durkheim, 32 by Mauss, making a total between them of 70 analyses of works in English, French, German and Italian.

So it is worth recording a 'brute fact', as part of a complex issue. Given Durkheim's own substantial personal contribution to the subject sections, his close collaboration with Mauss and his supervision of everything as editor, a 'brute fact' is the sheer scale and range of his acquaintance with up-to-date studies of different sociohistorical worlds. Year in year out, through his work for the journal, he accumulated a vast store of material.

Yet what did he do with it? Was his theory always in charge, whatever 'the facts'? Or did it interact with actual evidence and ethnographic sources? This is a reason for asking about the particular, yet crucial case of his response to Spencer and Gillen's Australia. However, it is necessary to identify not only what changed in his sociology but what remained constant. His new journal came, after all, with its own approach. He explains its editorial line in the prefaces to each of the first two volumes.

The Prefaces

The preface that introduces the whole project of the *Année sociologique* concedes a role for general theory, but only to stress that social science must develop through detailed research. This is what the journal is intended to encourage. It aims to cover a range of specialist fields, to review investigations that provide 'suggestive facts' or 'fertile perspectives' and to 'indicate to the reader what lessons come out of them for the sociologist' (1898a[i]: vi).

In a way it is a declaration of open-mindedness. It is just that it is a selective open-mindedness, along lines made clear in the preface to the second volume.

This insists on the need to understand religious, moral, legal and economic phenomena as 'social facts', by situating them 'within a specific social environment, within a definite type of society' (1899a[i]: ii). It also insists on a comparative method, to understand the institutions of a particular society in terms of similarities and differences with other societies. This is why a long discussion emphasizes that sociology, while drawing on other fields, must draw 'above all on history', so that it 'can engage in comparisons' (ii–v).

However, rather more is at stake. Durkheim responds to comments on the pre-eminence that had been given to the section on religion, and says it is because religion is 'the germ' of everything. It contains 'all the elements' that 'have given birth to the diverse manifestations of collective life' (iv).

Thus his argument is not just about the importance of religion. It is also about the importance of origins. It is concerned with an archaeology of social life and its genesis, in an approach that can be called the 'genetic' method. It is exemplified in his essay on incest. Early elementary forms of social life continue to have a deep-rooted influence on all the forms that develop out of them, even as these to some extent become free from them.

This is one of many reasons why it is nonsense to go on about Durkheim as a 'functionalist'. Although functionalist ideas constitute one of many strands in his sociology's overall web of concerns, he is not only explicit but scathing in his critique of any attempt to understand a social world just as a system of interacting factors in the present. 'This quick-fire method comes laden with illusions' – *cette méthode rapide est grosse d'illusions* – since to understand the present, 'it is indispensable to have studied the social forms of the most distant past' (v).

At the level of abstract statements of a theoretical, methodological line, it can all seem founded in the landscape of *The Division of Labour*, and its digging around in the early and elementary in order to understand the modern. But at a more concrete level involving his view of early elementary life itself, there are two main changes in this view between his thesis of 1893 and the essay launching his new journal in 1898.

In his thesis, ancient Israel is his key case of how, in the beginning, there are societies based on the clan and permeated by religion. In his new journal, Australia has become his key case of how, in the beginning, there are societies based on the clan and permeated by religion, and this religion is totemism.

In Search of Totemism

Durkheim's thesis has only a single brief mention of a work on Australia and says nothing about totemism. It is the new edition that inserts a reference to totemism (1902b: 273), while also deleting an earlier story of the evolution of religion.[2] This had become an embarrassment, since based on theories he now considered the rubbish of the ages. Why the change?

His letter of 1907 about a 'revelation' in 1895 talks of a special debt to William Robertson Smith. Yet there is reason to suspect he owed more to a work by someone else, James Frazer's *Totemism*. True, the two Scots were in close intellectual dialogue with one another. But Robertson Smith offered a biblical scholar's textually based, speculative theory of religion among peoples in the ancient Middle East. Frazer offered a clear, concise, highly accessible manual of up-to-date ethnographic 'facts' about the totemic clan in Australia and North America – in a word, a 'must' to put on a student reading list for a new course on the sociology of religion. Moreover, Durkheim himself might have noted with interest the challenge: 'No satisfactory explanation of the origin of totemism has yet been given' (Frazer 1887: 95). In any case, the first work after his 'revelation' that investigates religion is the essay he wrote to launch the *Année sociologique*. In this, the main reference that he approvingly cites again and again as a source of ethnographic information is Frazer's *Totemism.*

The essay on incest is an exercise in the genetic method's search for origins, above all to understand totemism in Australia as the early elementary form of social and religious life. This contrasts with the comparative method's prominence in the following year's article on the definition of religious phenomena. But the two essays are complementary. Looking for elementary forms of something that counts as religion entails a view of elemental forms of all religion.

The Essay on the Definition of Religious Phenomena

In negotiating a way through disputes in the contemporary literature, the essay tackles commonly used terms such as 'myth', 'ritual', 'symbolism' and 'the sacred'. In reworking these, it links myth with obligatory beliefs, ritual with obligatory practices, and symbolism with objects that constitute a concrete focus of the beliefs and practices. In the process, religion becomes an affair of obligatory beliefs and practices centred round sacred things. In an eventual definition, '*The phenomena called religious consist of obligatory beliefs connected with definite practices that are related to given objects in these beliefs*' (1899a[ii]: 22). But this abstract formula empties out meanings and concerns that drive the argument itself. To understand the essay, it is necessary to bring these back in.

It starts with a critique of rival theories, and first attacks views that identify religion with ideas of the 'supernatural' (4–7). Accordingly, a question is if accounts of belief in the 'supernatural' are so different from Durkheim's account of belief in a realm going over and beyond the ordinary world.

The next attack is on views that identify religion with belief in a god or gods. This continues a line of critique in his thesis, in using the example of Buddhism as a religion without deities (9–11). However, a new development is the use of totemism as another example. With belief in gods, the sacred is 'individualized' in a focus on particular beings. But this 'individualization' has not yet taken place in the early world of totemic religion. The totemic emblem is not a particular individual animal. It is the entire species, constituting 'a vast category of sacred things', so that the sacred 'remains diffused in a general class of things' (13–14).

A fly in the ointment is belief that the totemic species and the totemic clan share descent from an individual sacred ancestor. The essay just insists it is 'obvious' the idea arose at a later evolutionary stage. In contrast, *The Elemental Forms* incorporates it within the idea of an impersonal force. The point, then, is that the essay approaches the sacred just in terms of 'things', rather than in terms of a power or energy that constitutes the very source of the sacred and that transfers sacredness on to all manner of things. On the contrary, as already noted, it rejects the very idea of an extraordinary energy as an integral element of the sacred.

It remains significant thanks to its launch of the career of a universal dualism of the sacred and profane:

> All traditions inspire a very particular respect and this respect necessarily communicates itself to its objects, whatever they may be, real or ideal. It is why we feel the beings, which myths and dogmas teach us exist or that tell us their nature, have something august about them that sets them apart. The special way we come to learn to know them separates them from what we know through the ordinary processes of empirical representation. Here is the source of the division of things into sacred and profane that is the basis of all religious organization. (19)

Various points might be made about this birth of a sacred–profane dualism. One is how, with its stress on a necessary, obligatory respect for the august and set apart, it creates an impression of religion as an essentially negative affair of awe and reverence. In contrast, *The Elemental Forms* not only distinguishes a negative cult of the set apart and forbidden from a positive cult of coming together in communion, but makes coming together in communion the heart of religious life. So from this perspective, it is not just that the essay fails to distinguish negative and positive dimensions of religion. It is that its emphasis falls in entirely the wrong place.

Another point is to do with *The Division of Labour*'s idea of two sources of representations, in social life and in the individual's embodiedness. The essay now aligns a dualism of the sacred and profane with the dualism of representations. 'Sacred things are those with a representation that society itself brings about … Profane things, in contrast, are those that each of us constructs from sense-data and experience' (25–26). What might be noted about this?

It expresses a Durkheimian tendency just to equate the social with the sacred, and the individual with the profane. Yet the issue of the individual is also a source of complexity in his work. In his thesis, it is the division of labour's social dynamic that creates individualism and liberates us from the collective yoke. In the essay:

> From the beginning, besides the collective totem that the whole clan venerates, there are individual totems that each chooses as they wish and that are nonetheless the object of a genuine cult. (26)

Indeed, 'there are no forms of collective activity that are not individualized in this way' and individuals everywhere develop a personality of their own, 'however absorbed in society' (28). So this is a major change of tune, leading on to an argument in *The Elemental Forms* that has far-reaching implications for his whole effort to insist that the collective is somehow prior to the individual.

A final point is how his essay unconsciously generates a paradox, eventually made explicit in *The Elemental Forms*. In theory, he sets up a dualism of the sacred and profane. In practice, his arguments spread sacredness throughout the entire realm of social life in worlds of the clan, to leave nothing in them profane. In his thesis, religion at first permeates everything. In his new journal, it is the same, as in reviews written in the same period as the essay. 'At this time religion extends to everything' (1898a[iv][2]: 329). Or again, 'at this time there is nothing to which religion does not extend its empire' (1899a[iv][10]: 317).

In sum, the essay is important in launching a dualism of the sacred and profane, as well as in introducing a major change of line to do with the individual. It is still a long way from the landscape of *The Elemental Forms*. It has not yet latched on to effervescence, or special collective times, or a vast impersonal force, or how there is both a negative and a positive cult, or a paradox at the very heart of the sacred.

The Reviews

A study of all of Durkheim's reviews would fill a volume. It remains essential to check through them to see what turns up. An example involves a work on peasant life in medieval Germany, and his interest in its account of festivals.

> A common characteristic of all these celebrations is the frenetic energy people gave themselves over to in them. It stopped only when one could do no more. Meals that went on all day, interrupted from time to time by occasionally bloody fights, dances that soon degenerated into every sort of unruliness – these were the ingredients of the folk festivals. The contrast with the laborious and monotonous existence of the everyday was then at its *maximum*. The scale of the oscillations social life passes through between workdays and holidays has gone on diminishing with civilization. (1899a[iv] [3]: 309)

So here is an account of ordinary versus effervescent times, like the one that *The Elemental Forms* bases on Spencer and Gillen's Australia and appearing just before Durkheim's encounter with their work. Yet despite his review's interest in the case, he didn't do anything with it in his social theory at this period.

The situation is different with the two reviews, already noted, insisting on early society's permeation by religion. These are reviews of Marxists – Ernest Grosse and Heinrich Cunow – who see a social organization that is more fundamental than the clan and that is not religious, and who are accordingly criticized as having 'completely misunderstood' things. The issue is discussed in vague abstract terms in Durkheims' review (1897e), in another journal, of another Marxist, Antonio Labriola. But it is examined in more revealing detail in the reviews in the *Année sociologique* itself.

Durkheim makes his way through disputes in the literature to identify the basic unit of social life in Australia. It is not a nuclear family. It is not a local territorial formation. It is not a tribe. It is the kindred who constitute a clan but also a totemic group, so that the clan is simultaneously the key social and religious group.

Kinship, then, is a central issue and his very first review for the new journal insists it is mistaken just to see it as biological descent and consanguinity. 'All kinship is social, since it essentially consists of legal and moral relations sanctioned by society. It is a social link or it is nothing' (1898a[iv][1]: 318).

He continues with this argument in the review that immediately follows and accordingly also given a prominent position, the review of Grosse. The author has 'completely misunderstood' the nature of the clan. It is not a mere aggregate of biologically related nuclear families. It is formed by individuals whose 'belief in their consanguinity arises solely from thinking they all have a same ancestor, always of a mythical nature'. In turn, 'the sign by which they recognize their kinship is that they have a same totem'. And the totem is 'above all the centre of religious life'. So when, in Australia, the child assumes the totem of the clan, 'it is not simply a name that he receives in this way, it is a religion, a whole set of beliefs and practices that govern his life' (1898a[iv][2]: 328–29).

So it is not surprising that in a subsequent review 'the name symbolizes the whole organization of the clan: it is a sacred thing' (1899a[iv] [11]: 319). Or again, kinship is 'essentially religious' (1899a[iv][13]: 323). But a basic development is how he fills out the case for society and religion's fusion in totemism. It is in bringing in all sorts of detailed practices through which the totem becomes an integral everyday part of 'the *habitus* of individuals, who do their best to reproduce it in tattoos, hairstyles, etc.' (1898a[iv][2]: 328–29). True, these practices were common knowledge in the literature and are listed in Frazer's manual on totemism. The point, though, is Durkheim's use of them to build up his picture of a world of the clan that runs on a whole socioreligious identity, embedded in the everyday *habitus* of a vast concrete symbolism of names, emblems, tattoos, hairstyles, etc.

A ghost at this Durkheimian feast – not just any Marxist ghost, but Cunow – is the case for maintaining that the fundamental unit in Australia is the local group, not the clan. Durkheim was particularly riled by Cunow's argument that the local group is the elementary form of society in Australia and the totemic clan is only a later development. He nonetheless confidently dismissed him, as someone else who had 'completely misunderstood' the situation (1899a[iv][10]: 317).

In sum, the reviews make their way through an ethnographic battleground of competing interpretations of Australia. But it is firm in the belief that in the beginning society and religion are inextricably fused in the totemic clan.

The Essay on the Prohibition of Incest

The essay sets out to explain rules against incest and looks for the taboo's origins in the early elementary world of the clan. Durkheim's basic assumption is about its origins in a rule of marrying out (exogamy). But it could equally well be seen as a rule of marrying in (endogamy). His model of early clan-based society is that it involves two exogamous classes of individuals who must each marry out into the other. But this entails endogamy within the group as a whole. Moreover, he equates the early clan with a local formation, occupying the same territory. As the clan grew in size, 'its population could no longer occupy the same space' (1898a[ii]: 6).

This is to try to explain the development of an actually existing situation, in which the same local group contains many different clans, and members of the same clan are scattered in many different places. Indeed, he goes so far as to describe it as a situation in which the clan is 'an amorphous group, a floating mass, without any very defined individuality, whose contours are above all not imprinted physically on the soil' (20).

This might seem an extraordinary statement, from someone so insistent on the clan as the building block of social life in Australia. But it is part of a long argument about a problem that 'has made for the despair of ethnologists' (13).

In brief, it is about systems in which a tribe is divided into sections. In turn, each section is divided into clans, tracing descent through the female line. But each section is also divided into marriage-classes, with individuals assigned to these according to parentage, sex and generation.

Accordingly, the rule of exogamy does not just require marriage to some-one from a different clan. It requires marriage to someone from a differ-ent clan in a different section and from a different specifically laid down marriage-class in a same generation. So the prize goes to whoever can explain the logic of these complex cases, 'in appearance bizarre' (16).

The starting point of Durkheim's own bid for the prize remains his own basic picture of Australia. So if we concentrate on this, it involves checking his three main references. One is the study mentioned in his thesis, Lorimer Fison and Alfred Howitt's *Kamilaroi and Kurnai* (1880), in which Fison wrote about the Kamilaroi people, Howitt about the Kur-nai. Another is Frazer's manual on totemism (1887). The most recent, on structures of kinship in Australia, is by Cunow (1894).

Cunow begins his book with an analysis of the structure exemplified by the Kamilaroi (1894: 1–24). This is the complex system just outlined, and to help with understanding it he constructs a diagram based on Fison's original account of the Kamilaroi but adapted in light of new information to show them as having only two sections. Durkheim, per-haps by coincidence, uses a diagram similar to Cunow's but gives the er-roneous impression of basing it on the original ethnography. It can't be, since this reports *four* sections (Fison and Howitt 1880: 43–45). In any case, he agrees with Cunow in seeing the Kamilaroi system as a later de-velopment of some earlier form of Australian society. But which form?

This is where the Kurnai assume a key role. Cunow goes through Howitt's material to show that among the Kurnai the fundamental unit is the local group and the totemic clan does not exist. Accordingly, they are best described as a society of 'totem-less local groups' (Cunow 1894: 56). So here is an examination of the evidence that threatens Durkheim's whole theory. However, he just ignores its account of the Kurnai as actu-ally observed and instead plays the evolutionary card to see 'vestiges of an ancient totemism' (1898a[ii]: 24). So if we check his reference, it is to how the Kurnai trace their descent from the ancestral 'mythic pair' Yeerung and Djeetgung – the names of two species of birds – to identify all Kurnai men with Yeerung, all Kurnai women with Djeetgung (Fison and Howitt 1880: 194, 235). This isn't very impressive as evidence of an ancient totemism. In the first place, 'myths of origin' are not necessarily accurate about what might have happened long ago (Cunow 1894: 59). But also, it doesn't make sense as a story of two totemic clans with a rule of exogamy requiring their intermarriage. The Yeerung are all men, the Djeetgung are all women. So wouldn't they have intermarried anyway?

What in any case is to be made of 'myths of origin', not among Aus-tralian peoples, but anthropological theorists? The Kurnai represent Aus-tralia's most 'primitive' social system of all, according to Cunow (1894:

140–44). The Kurnai aren't 'old-fashioned' but 'new-fashioned', and represent Australia's most advanced social system of all, according to Howitt (Fison and Howitt 1880: 234–35). Durkheim explicitly disagrees with Cunow, without explicit support for Howitt. But in terms of his own approach, the Kurnai and the Kamilaroi might be seen as disturbingly different cases of the same evolution. Either totemism is at most a 'vestige', as among the Kurnai. Or it flourishes, as among the Kamilaroi, yet the totemic group itself is merely an amorphous 'floating mass'.

True, he offers a couple of references about present-day Australian peoples among whom 'the cult of the totem is still the basis of social organization' (1898a[ii]: 24). But his main reference is a secondary work's further references, since it is Frazer's pocket guidebook to totemism. This suggests he had not yet gone through all the primary sources for himself. Indeed, compared with Cunow, he seems an amateur. Cunow works through the primary material on Australia in an effort at a systematic analysis of different types of organization among its societies. Of course, it comes with the limitations of the ethnography on offer. Even so, it could have been appropriately entitled *The Elementary Structures of Kinship*.

But it didn't budge Durkheim from his beliefs. It also remained as involved as he was in a general ambivalence among theorists and ethnographers over the meaning of 'Australia'. Is it about its present-day peoples, supposedly a living museum of the 'primitive', yet nonetheless as actually described in present-day studies? Or is it about the folk of a vanished land of the early and elementary, inaccessible to these studies, yet nonetheless motivating and driving them?

Like his contemporaries, Durkheim switches between the two meanings and it is often unclear what 'Australia' he has in mind. But at some point he became gripped by the idea – expressed in a work to become almost a Bible for him – that in the beginning there is totemism and it is 'both a religion and a social system':

> How in the origin of totemism these two sides were related to each other it is, in our ignorance of that origin, impossible to say with certainty. But on the whole the evidence points strongly to the conclusion that the two sides were originally inseparable. (Frazer 1887: 3)

Except for its uncertainty, this summarizes Durkheim's core view in his new journal. But it was already under a threat too serious for him to ignore.

Shock News from Australia

Spencer and Gillen's study was based on fieldwork in 1896–97, written up in 1898 and published early in 1899 in London, where its impact was immediate. According to the President of the Anthropological Institute, it is 'a work of exceptional merit' that has 'enriched the literature of anthropology' (Rudler 1899: 322). In a comment by the President of the Folk-Lore Society, 'I heartily join with reviewers elsewhere in expressing the gratitude of anthropologists for a work which must for a long while rank among those of the first importance' (Hartland 1899: 239). Two further examples might be given, each in its own way revealing. In one, the reviewer of a new book on ethnology regrets it is already out of date, since completed before publication of Spencer and Gillen's 'great work' (Crooke 1899: 185). In the other, a leading authority on totemism hails Spencer and Gillen's 'momentous discoveries', which constitute 'one of the most valuable contributions ever made to the early history of mankind' (Frazer 1899: 286, 281).

Frazer's patronage helps to explain this whole impact.[3] He had been in correspondence with Spencer since 1897. He then persuaded his friend and fellow Scot, the publisher George Macmillan, to take the work and to produce it in such a handsome edition. Not least, he organized the book's 'launch' at a meeting of the Anthropological Institute at the end of 1898, assembling the great and the good of anthropological England to tell them about the study's far-reaching significance. A paper was first given by Spencer, who had come all the way from Australia for the occasion. It was then followed with a paper by Frazer, explaining major changes in his own theory and reinforcing the message of the new ethnography's importance.

However, another reason for the impact is the impressive nature of Spencer and Gillen's fieldwork itself. Commentators remarked on their presence at sacred, hitherto unobserved ceremonies, the detail of their description of these as well as of other aspects of life, and, as part of this, their extensive pioneering use of photographs, of which around a hundred eventually appeared in the book. For example, the invaluable 'copious' use of photographs attracts attention in reviews in *Notes and Queries* (anon. 1899a: 338–39) and in the *Journal of the Anthropological Institute* (anon. 1899b: 330–32), which also reprints a selection of them. And while the first of these reviews emphasizes Spencer and Gillen's 'unique opportunities' of access, the second the 'detailed description' of ceremonies they attended, both of them point out that the authors are 'fully initiated members of the Arunta'. This wasn't altogether accurate, just as they didn't really know the language of the people they called the 'Arunta' and didn't live among them in a way that would nowadays count as participant observation. What is nonetheless relevant is that their fieldwork was seen as exceptional in the context of the time.

It is also only in the context of the time that it is possible to understand the impact of their actual news from Australia. As explained at the 'launch', the new research changed everything. It was with Frazer's blessing that his old theory of how totemism combined 'both a religious and a social aspect' was quoted only to be rejected in the paper by Spencer (1899: 275). As explained in the work itself, the unit of ordinary everyday life among the Arunta is not the so-called totemic clan, a term abandoned as 'misleading' (Spencer and Gillen 1899: 59). It is the group that along with its other roles is centrally involved in the regulation of marriage, in which 'the question of totem has nothing to do with the matter' (116). A general conclusion is that the Arunta represent an early way of life in which totemism isn't a social but a magicoreligious affair. In the beginning, *these two aspects are separate.*

However, the work's impact is perhaps best summarized by an independent, eminent reviewer, Sidney Hartland. It is indeed the institution, discussed in the literature as 'totemism', that is at stake:

> But it is totemism of a kind that turns our previous ideas on the subject topsy-turvy; and we shall have enough ado to reconstruct the theory so as to make it fit the newly discovered facts. (Hartland 1899: 238)

This was the shock news from Australia, which then made its way from London to Paris.

A Work 'Rich in Materials'

Durkheim had dismissed Cunow as having 'completely misunderstood' things. It was impossible to hand out the same treatment to Spencer and Gillen. His initial strategy, in collaboration with Mauss, was to praise their fieldwork while questioning their theory. Thus his nephew's review begins with how their book is one of the most important works of *descriptive* sociology he knows (Mauss 1900: 205). Or as his own review ends, it is 'rich in materials' (Durkheim 1900a[8]: 336). But it was after having gone through the new 'materials' in a determination to stick with old ideas. And it was above all in repeating old evolutionary arguments about what might have happened once upon a time in a vanished past. In contrast, his nephew concludes with a retheorization of Spencer and Gillen's account of life among the present-day Arunta:

> At the basis of all these cults and all these beliefs, there is not the narrow and very limited idea of the totem, but the idea of the sacred and of magical and religious action. (Mauss 1900: 215)

But in both reviews, something conspicuous by its absence is the idea, as in *The Elemental Forms*, of special effervescent times alternating with ordinary mundane times.

There is quite a good reason for this – the idea's absence in Spencer and Gillen. Nor does it appear among their English commentators. Of course, like them, Durkheim and Mauss latched on to the 'detailed description' of ceremonies. It was without working it up, however, into 'two times' of the sacred and profane.

Yet there is also a reason for surprise at this. Durkheim's review of Spencer and Gillen is immediately followed with a review of Franz Boas, on seasonal variations among the Kwakiutl people of North America. As his review brings out, life among the Kwakiutl alternates between two periods in which summer is a time of the ordinary and routine, while winter is a time of the sacred when they 'celebrate the great religious ceremonies' (1900a[9]: 336). So a puzzle is Durkheim's failure to do anything with such material, in looking for a way to tackle Spencer and Gillen. Perhaps it is because his eventual picture of 'two times' of the sacred and profane draws especially on their second work, published in 1904. Even then, it involves a somewhat imaginative rereading of what they in fact say. But this takes us to the story of the creation of *The Elemental Forms* itself.

CHAPTER 5

The Creation of *The Elemental Forms*

The creation of *The Elemental Forms* might be divided into three periods. The first is from 1900 to 1906, the year a draft of the work began to appear in lectures on religion. The central period is 1906/1907, the year of these lectures. The final period is from 1908 to 1911, the year the manuscript of the work was completed.

Re-exploring Australia: 1900 to 1906

Spencer and Gillen constitute by far the most frequent and important reference in the eventual work. But Durkheim's effort to absorb their news from Australia didn't lead in a straight direct line to this. It involved him in a number of alternative projects. One could have become *The Elementary Structures of Kinship*. Another could have become *The Elemental Forms of Thought*. The third became *The Elemental Forms of Religious Life*.

Towards The Elementary Structures of Kinship

It is 1900 that begins the road to *The Elemental Forms*, in that it is when Durkheim made public his first reaction to Spencer and Gillen, in a defensive review hanging on to his old picture of Australia. It is 1902 that is when, worried by the threat they represented, he published a long, still largely defensive response yet with stirrings of new ideas, in his essay on totemism. It is 1905 that is when the whole tone changes, in his essay on matrimonial organization in Australia. Inspired by their second work, it is also in the context of a new ethnography by Howitt that he later on gave a long review (1906a[19]). It is especially this essay, in its use of the new material to develop a key interest of Durkheim's, that suggests a project on elementary structures of kinship.

In any case it is in itself a formidable achievement, and exemplifies his rationalist empiricism. It is an effort to make sense of a mass of apparently bizarre, bewildering data, in search of an underlying logic of things.

In brief, it is about the following problem. As updated by Howitt, there were well-known kinship systems that have four marriage-classes, with alternating generations and with descent through the female line.

In contrast, Spencer and Gillen's Arunta have eight marriage-classes, also with alternating generations but with descent through the male line. Their new study shows that eight-class systems are widespread, as, in a typical example, among the Warramunga people. Indeed, Durkheim sifts through the material to claim these systems are even more common than Spencer and Gillen report, since some of the peoples they say have only four marriage-classes in fact have eight (1905a[i]: 125–31). He also digs around in accounts of a people they call the Tjingilli, but whom the ethnographer Robert Matthews had called the Chingalee. Although in both accounts they have eight marriage-classes going through the male line, Matthews reports the totem as going through the female line, which according to Durkheim fits in with other evidence (139–45). His detective work thus comes up with three variations of an eight-class system, represented by the Warramunga, the Tjingilli and the Arunta. Among the Warramunga, the marriage-class's descent is through the male line and the totem also descends through the father. Among the Tjingilli, the marriage-class's descent is again through the male line but the totem descends through the mother. Among the Arunta, the marriage-class's descent is once again through the male line but the totem descends through neither the father nor the mother and is instead through a spirit that enters her body at conception. So how is it possible to explain *both* the differences between eight-class and other systems *and* the variations within an eight-class system itself?

Durkheim's basic constant is the rule of exogamy, on the argument that it makes for the cohesion of each society by linking its segmental groups through a requirement of marriage between these and a ban against marriage within them. His key variable is change to descent through the male line, on the argument that in the beginning it was through the female line and taboos rooted in this do not just go away. However, his account could be redescribed in terms of 'harmonic' and 'disharmonic' systems. In 'harmonic' systems, descent is through the female line and there can be as many as four marriage-classes. In 'disharmonic' systems, descent through the male line requires marriage outside the father's group but religious taboos still come down against marriage within the mother's group. It is then impossible to marry anyone, even with four classes alternating between generations. It is necessary to double these to eight classes, while letting in the variations represented by the Warramunga, the Tjingilli and the Arunta.

But the fundamental point with which he concludes is the operation of 'a remarkable logic' that underlies all the systems, as if in 'a mathematical problem':

Is it not further proof that these classes and phratries are not simply social categories but are also logical categories, no doubt subject to a special logic, different from ours, but nonetheless with its own definite rules? (1905a[i]: 147)

Here, in a sentence, is the key to a vast ambitious project, which went on to acquire a life of its own.

Durkheim's English sympathizers included a bright young Cambridge anthropologist, Alfred Brown, later famous as Radcliffe-Brown. In making his career, he criticized the essay's inability to account for types of system he had newly discovered in western Australia and also announced his intention to write a full-scale work analysing and comparing the continent's kinship structures (Radcliffe-Brown 1913: 192). This never materialized, though he continued to publish articles on the issue (Radcliffe-Brown 1918, 1923, 1930–31). But with his appointment in 1926 to the first chair of anthropology in Australia, at Sydney, he helped to initiate a whole new wave of modern fieldwork studies.[1] In turn, these fed into a project that did in fact eventually materialize, Claude Lévi-Strauss's *The Elementary Structures of Kinship* (1949).

In many ways, of course, it belongs to a different anthropological world from Durkheim's essay. However, a shared interest is the issue of cohesion, so that the terminology of 'harmonic' and 'disharmonic' systems, suggested earlier on, comes from Lévi-Strauss. An even more basic shared interest involves Durkheim's search, as if in a mathematical problem, for an underlying logic in Australia's kinship systems, which might otherwise seem bizarre. In investigating these, his successor not only has a section on their 'algebraic study', but ends with how 'an internal logic directs the unconscious workings of the human mind, even in those of its creations which have long been considered the most arbitrary' (Lévi-Strauss [1949] 1969: 220).

Towards The Elemental Forms of Thought

It is above all the essay on primitive classification, published by Durkheim and Mauss in 1903, that suggests a project on elemental forms of thought. It ends with how its enquiry into the idea of a type can be extended to other 'fundamental ideas of the understanding', such as the categories of time, space and causality (Durkheim and Mauss 1903: 72). Thus it is concerned not only with differences between various general styles of thought, but with elemental forms of all thought. One is the effort in every society to theorize, 'to achieve understanding, to make intelligible the relations that exist between beings'. In turn, this entails an effort to systematize, 'to link ideas with one another, to unify knowledge'. At the same time it is an effort to totalize, to see how things 'together constitute a single whole' (66).

Indeed, the essay's very title indicates its interest in entire systems of classification, rather than merely in particular ideas of a class, type, species, category, etc. True, it announces a focus on 'primitive' classification. But the introduction in fact sets up a distinction between 'primitive' and 'modern' ways of classifying things, as part of a whole key thematic distinction between 'primitive' and 'modern' styles of thought. The essay is repeatedly quoted in another work by Lévi-Strauss, *The Savage Mind* (1962), and this is as much as anything about 'the modern mind', even or especially in challenging ideas of a logical chasm between 'their' way of thinking and 'ours'.

Around half of the essay is taken up with two sections on Australia. It then has a section on North America, followed by one on China. Thus Australia is again the main Durkheimian research site, but now in an archaeology of the human mind. It is where, in the beginning, social groups of kin are the model of logical ideas of kind. But it is also why China is crucial. The essay sees evidence of a survival of 'primitive' elements, yet maintains that Chinese classification is 'independent of all social organization' (Durkheim and Mauss 1903: 55).

So it is odd to go on as if the essay's argument is that, always and everywhere, systems of classification are modelled on structures of society. This misunderstands Australia's archaeological role as the beginning of things, ignores the line on China, and fails to grasp the entire approach in failing to pick up on the story of 'primitive' and 'modern' styles of thought.

This is about a move towards a modern world of secular scientific thought, increasingly free from social determination. Put another way, it is about leaving behind a primitive world of socially embedded thought, where 'the first logical categories were social categories', but in an imagination of logical groups that 'contrasts with their true nature' (67–68). On more detailed investigation, it involves a set of oppositions that might be summarized in the following way. Modern thought is abstract, rationalistic and analytical. Primitive thought is concrete, emotive and dialectical.

Thus a key remark is that primitive thought embeds classification in 'all sorts of foreign elements' (6). Yet what are these 'foreign' elements, and how are they increasingly left behind and eliminated? The essay associates modern thought with 'abstract' classifications that lack concrete 'imagery', with principles based on science rather than on folklore, myth or 'religious beliefs', and with 'concepts' in the form of 'pure ideas', stripped of all extraneous layers of meaning and emotion, not least 'religious emotion' (64–70). It also associates it with what is readily identifiable as analytical thought. In modern classification, things are divided up according to fixed definite properties and kept separate by clear-cut boundaries. In primitive classification, in contrast, boundaries are fluid. Things can cross over these, change their nature and merge with one another in various processes of metamorphosis, dynamic interaction and indeed a transcendent fusion of identities (2–6). So it is a style of thought that could perhaps be seen as dialectical thought.

In sum, the essay's project is not just about the categories. It is also about different general styles of thought, in an evolution rooted in common characteristics of all thought. It clearly comes out against notions of the 'savage mind' as illogical. True enough, given the nature of its set of oppositions, it is still embedded in views of 'their' mentality and 'ours'. But it is possible to draw on these oppositions to investigate ways in which 'our' thought is in fact variously concrete, emotive or dialectical. It is also possible to ask about the grounds of the very ideal of the abstract, rationalistic and analytical. But understanding the essay itself requires recognition of its commitment to this ideal, as part of its line on enlightenment.

Towards The Elemental Forms of Religious Life

Perhaps Durkheim was already planning a great work on religion, when he launched the *Année sociologique*. If so, a setback was the news from Spencer and Gillen's Australia, which ruled out a pioneering 'great work' that just rehashed his old picture of things. In any case, there is a basic point to be made in asking how he moved beyond his initial, essentially defensive response to their account.

What matters is evidence of a coming together of a set of ideas in a new theoretical system, as in *The Elemental Forms* itself, but already in the lectures of 1906/1907. A methodological mistake is merely to hail the first sign or sighting of a particular idea. It is nonetheless necessary to try to track the career of particular ideas, as part of asking how and when they come together in a new theoretical whole. One of them is reconceptualization of the sacred in terms of an impersonal force, energy or power. Another is introduction of the idea of a positive cult, made up of rites of communion at the heart of religious life. In turn, this links with a new stress on the importance of assembly and effervescence. But a key to everything is a move from two worlds to two times of the sacred and profane.

Some of these ideas begin to turn up in the essay on totemism (1902a[i]). They include a move towards reconceptualization of the sacred in terms of forces, rather than just 'things'. Thus there had been widespread interest in Spencer and Gillen's account of sacred objects called *churingas*. Now, in Durkheim's essay, these sacred material things are containers of 'guardian forces' (93). Indeed, it is to see the churinga as the pre-eminently sacred thing and concrete focus of 'mysterious forces' (118). But it is not to claim any clear-cut belief about them. On the contrary, the Arunta have no doubt only 'a confused representation' of these 'religious forces' (87).

A problem, which Durkheim fails to mention but which no doubt helps to explain the Arunta's 'confused representations', is that it is difficult to find any report of belief in such 'forces' in Spencer and Gillen. The problem, put another way, is how Durkheim himself came up with the idea, since it doesn't come from his ethnographic source. However, he wasn't the only one to interpret the data along these lines. In a talk of 1899, published in 1900, the Oxford anthropologist Robert Marett had created something of a sensation by criticizing established theories and arguing that the way to make sense of early religion was through the notion of an essentially impersonal force, power or energy.

Another idea stirring up in the essay is the idea of a positive cult. Like others, Durkheim was impressed by Spencer and Gillen's account of rites of communion. But it had a particular personal impact on him, in that he goes out of his way to thank Spencer and Gillen for 'a very great service':

> Up until the present, in fact, we regarded totemism as little more than a system of wholly negative practices, that is, of prohibitions ... We were therefore unaware of how it could be made up of positive elements. From now on, this ignorance is at an end. (1902a[i]: 116)

Spencer and Gillen gave especially detailed descriptions of two kinds of ceremony, involving rites of initiation and a rite called the *intichiuma*. But their account of the intichiuma aroused special interest. It was widely seen as the first empirical proof of Robertson Smith's theory that the rite of sacrifice began as a rite of communion. Their discovery was 'striking testimony to the genius and accuracy of the late Professor Robertson Smith's scientific imagination', in a comment by one of the great and the good of anthropological England, Frank Jevons (1899: 379). In Durkheim's case, it was also their account of the intichiuma that especially fed into the development of his ideas. In general it was to see it as a 'positive' rather then merely 'negative' rite, as a coming together in communion at the heart of religious life. More specifically, it was to see it as a rite that re-energizes sacred forces. It centres round belief in 'a substance at once material and mystical', which constitutes the identity of the totemic group. It is a sort of vital principle, within themselves as well as within their totemic species, which makes them the same. And the rite is about the need for 'periodically renewing' this vital principle (1902a[i]: 114).

Even so, his essay is only a limited breakthrough. For example, it fails to address the paradox of a dualism of the sacred and profane in which there can be nothing left that is profane thanks to the spread everywhere of what have now become sacred 'forces'. Indeed, in responding to Spencer and Gillen's separation of religious from social life, it just insists that 'the environment in which the Arunta live is saturated with religiosity' (87).

Or again, it comes with numerous references to 'assemblies' (108, 109, 110, 120). However, it isn't to see two times of the sacred and profane. Instead, it is still in a variation of old evolutionary concerns. Thanks to a long-term change, totemic ritual is no longer 'an assembly of the clan, but an assembly of the tribe' (120). In sum, although his essay comes with germs of new ideas, it is in an overall argument in which his old core view of Australia is repeated again and again (88–89, 94, 107, 113, 115, 116, 119).

What happened afterwards? A further development can be dated to 1904. It involves an essay by Mauss, and is once more to do with the idea of an impersonal force. As already noted, a problem for Durkheim was the lack of evidence of such a belief in Spencer and Gillen. However, his nephew came up with a reference in their work to an evil magical force called *arungquiltha* (Mauss 1904: 326). True, it wasn't anything like a general religious belief in an impersonal force. But in a highly significant move, the essay linked it with just such a belief, the ethnographically well-documented Melanesian idea of a force called *mana* (368–89).

However, the ideas of *arungquiltha* and *mana* were similarly connected at just the same time by Marett (1904: 60–61). This followed on from his earlier, influential paper on the religious notion of an impersonal force. It led in turn to a perhaps even more influential paper entitled 'The Conception of Mana' (Marett 1908). The reason for its significance is that it converted an idea associated with the regional ethnography of Melanesia into a general anthropological term for a whole type of belief, found in a whole range of societies. In sum, Marett and Mauss were heading in the same direction, towards the conversion of 'mana' into a general, comparative term for religious belief in some sort of impersonal force. It is their work's joint impact on the anthropology of the time that constitutes the context of Durkheim's own use of 'mana' in this way in *The Elemental Forms*.

The next, crucial developments are to do with the ideas of effervescence and of two times of the sacred and profane. In lectures that Durkheim gave around 1905, the French Revolution's 'effervescence was immensely creative of new ideas' (1938: vol. 2, 169). In a review of the same year, again about the Revolution:

> The effervescence and collective enthusiasm that characterized this creative
> era necessarily came to take on, thanks to their very intensity, a religious
> character. (1905a[ii][2]: 382)

True enough, this is about the effervescence of historically momentous
times, rather than an established social calendar's periodic times. But
these two aspects of effervescence become interwoven in the eventual
overall theory of *The Elemental Forms*. Momentous, foundational times
are embedded in a social world's collective memory, and recalled and
revitalized in the rites of a calendar's periodic times.

Moreover, the nature and structure of calendars had just been explored in detail in an essay on the collective representation of time by
Mauss's close colleague, Henri Hubert (1905). It is also one of the concerns in an essay on seasonal variations among the Eskimo by Mauss
himself (1906). Of course, Durkheim had long ago come across clear-cut
cases of periodic times of the sacred and profane in his review of 1899
about festivals in medieval Germany and in his review of 1900 about seasonal variations in North America. It is just that he hadn't done anything
with them. But the intellectual context had now changed, thanks to the
collaborative work of his group as a whole, and his nephew's essay is
where the idea of two times of the sacred and profane at last surfaces as
a central theoretical Durkheimian concern. While summer, among the
Eskimo, is a time of individualistic dispersal and the ordinary mundane
business of life, winter is a time of non-stop religion and 'a season when
the society, strongly concentrated, is in a continuous state of effervescence' (Mauss 1906: 125).

There are two main reasons why the idea of two times of the sacred and profane is a key to understanding the creation of *The Elemental
Forms*. It is a way to tackle the *internally* generated paradox to do with
Durkheim's dualism of the sacred and profane. It locates the source of
the sacred's intense contagious energies in special times, while erect-
ing barriers to their spread everywhere and complete permeation of
everything in ordinary routine times. But also and not least, it is a way
to tackle the *externally* generated problem of Spencer and Gillen's news
from Australia. It makes it possible to concede that the totemic group
might lack importance in ordinary everyday times. But it can now be
triumphantly asserted that it remains the centre of socioreligious life
thanks to its pre-eminent role in the great communal rites and effervescent energies of special times.

The Lectures on Religion: 1906/1907

Durkheim's lectures were published in the *Revue de philosophie*, based on notes taken by Paul Fontana. Their significance is still not widely appreciated, although it has been suggested for some time that they constitute an early version of *The Elemental Forms*.[2] There are various ways of setting out to establish this. A method adopted so far could be called 'strategic', since it looks for a coming together of ideas in a whole theory. Another method is 'textual', since it looks for give-away terms, phrases, sentences or passages, which first appear in a draft and are then just repeated in an eventual work or involve only minor variations. A general approach is 'analytical', in a concern with individual arguments and how far they are the same. But a quite specific test is 'structural', examining the order of presentation of material in an overall architecture.

Table 1.5.1 Structure of Lectures of 1906/1907 and *The Elemental Forms*

The Lectures[1]		*The Elemental Forms*
		Introduction
65–70	definition of religion	Book 1 ch.1
71–75	critique of rival theories: animism	ch.2
76–77	naturism	ch.3
78	in the beginning there is totemism	ch.4
79–88	description of its specific features	Book 2 chs.1–4
88–91	critique of rival explanations	ch.5
	Centrepiece	
91–93	**notion of an impersonal force (mana)**	**ch.6**
93–102	**'god' is society; effervescence; two times of sacred and profane; symbolism; origins of conceptual thought**	**ch.7**
103–109	**universal idea of the soul**	**ch.8**
109–111	ideas of various spiritual beings	ch.9
112–118	the negative cult	Book 3 ch.1
118–122	the positive cult: sacrifice	ch.2
		more on rites, chs.3,4,5
		Conclusion

1. 'Religion: Origins' (1907f), in continuous pagination of Durkheim 1975, vol. 2.

The structures of the lecture course and of the eventual work are more or less identical (see table 1.5.1). This in itself is enough to indicate that one was a draft of the other. The main differences involve either the insertion or the addition of further material, as with the extra three chapters on rites. But there wasn't any radical change in the order of presentation of topics.

It is especially important to ask about structure in terms of a centre-piece. Material is arranged so as to lead up to this, which is in turn filled out in more detail by everything that comes afterwards. So it is again highly significant that the architecture of the lectures involves exactly the same centrepiece as the one in the eventual work, which comes in book 2 chapters 6 to 8, with its core as chapter 7.

The first of these chapters reveals an underlying impersonal force or 'mana'. The core chapter is where ideas about this impersonal force, effervescence, two times of the sacred and profane, 'god' as a metaphor of society, symbolism, and the origin of conceptual thought – each with earlier sources – come together in a new theoretical whole. It is then rounded off with a chapter on the soul, explaining how the relation between 'god' and the soul is a religious symbolism of the relation between society, the individual and the person.

A very general point about the lectures and the eventual work is how they involve the same fundamental project, of digging around in the elementary in search of the elemental. A particular key give-away term that first appears in the lectures and is then repeated in the book is about a search for the 'eternal' in religion (1907f: 122 / 1912a: 609).

However, it is not until book 2 that the reader really arrives in Durkheimian Australia. The preliminary business that takes up book 1 is concerned with the definition of religion itself and with a critique of rival theories, preparing the way for the announcement that in the beginning there is totemism. On the one hand, then, going through the lectures in detail would be almost like going through the whole of the eventual work. On the other, a solution to the problem is to compare the two texts through a focus on the preliminary business of the definition of religion and a critique of rival theories. This was largely unaffected by the insertion or addition of new material. It also clears the way for a focus on the landscape of Durkheimian Australia in *The Elemental Forms* itself.

The Definition of Religion

The lectures recycle some of the material in the essay on the definition of religious phenomena, but also make important changes. They continue to insist on a dualism of the sacred and profane. However, it is in a more explicit emphasis on how the sacred is set apart not just in the sense that it is forbidden but that it is in a league apart – in another, incommensurable, categorically different realm altogether. And it is in a use of two particular give-away expressions, first appearing in the lectures, then repeated in the eventual work. The difference between the sacred and profane is so great that it constitutes a 'radical heterogeneity'. Indeed, they are separated by 'a logical chasm' – *une vide logique* (1907f: 69 / 1912a: 55).

Yet however extraordinary the realm of the sacred, a nineteenth-century riddle is the difference within it between religion and magic. A solution suggested in the essay is that religion is obligatory, while magic is optional (1899a[ii]: 21, n.2). But the problem had become more urgent thanks to the impact of Spencer and Gillen's Australia and how, under the influence of Frazer, they pictured its world of the sacred as a world of magic. In an effort to meet the challenge, Durkheim's solution in the lectures and again in the eventual work is to rethink things so that religion, in contrast with magic, is an affair of the shared beliefs and practices of a whole community constituting 'a church'. In another give-away expression, first surfacing in the lectures and repeated in the work, there is no church of magic (1907f: 70 / 1912a: 61).

A change is how he gives greater emphasis to this by inserting the term 'church' into the work's very definition of religion. It is one of the reasons why it is of interest to note the career of his definitions (see table 1.5.2).

A question is why he continues to define the sacred in terms of 'things', when he had long converted to the view that the source of the sacred is a vast incommensurable force, energy or power such as 'mana'.

Table 1.5.2 Durkheim's Definitions of Religion

The Essay[1]	The Lectures[2]	The Work[3]
The phenomena called religious consist of obligatory beliefs connected with definite practices that are related to given objects in these beliefs.	[Religion] is a system of beliefs and practices relative to sacred things – beliefs and practices common to a definite collectivity.	A religion is a solidary system of beliefs and practices relative to sacred things – that is, set apart, forbidden – beliefs and practices that unite in a same moral community, called a Church, all those who adhere to them.

1. Essay on the definition of religious phenomena (1899a[ii]: 22)
2. Lectures on religion (1907f: 70)
3. *The Elemental Forms* (1912a: 65)

Another question is why, in contrast with the lectures, the eventual work inserts a highly ambivalent reference to the sacred as 'set apart, forbidden'. This invites complete confusion between what is 'set apart' since it is in an incommensurable league apart and what is 'set apart' since it is forbidden. In the process it also invites the entirely erroneous impression that religion is a mere negative affair of the forbidden. On the contrary, the heart of religious life is coming together in communion with a power that is set apart since in a league apart.

An official Durkheimian answer to these questions is that the job of a definition is to identify phenomena for further investigation through an initial external 'sign' (1907f: 69 / 1912a: 55), such as, in this case, 'things' that are 'forbidden'.

An alternative answer is to do with the art of how to structure an unfolding, increasingly complex argument, not least the art of how to set the scene for revelations brought out later on in a centrepiece. In any case, a guaranteed way to misunderstand Durkheim is just to latch on to his initial definitions, when, on the contrary, these should in no circumstances be read as a definitive theoretical statement.

The Critique of Rival Theories

The critique first appears in the lectures, was then written up as a separate article, and was in turn incorporated, through this, in the eventual work. So it is in a series of three different versions (1907f; 1909c; 1912a). But it is in the same basic argument. Yet what is the significance of its sustained, consistent effort to deconstruct 'animism' and 'naturism'? At first sight, nowadays, it might merely seem an engagement with the corpse of long dead and buried nineteenth-century ideas.

In all three versions, 'animism' and 'naturism' represent ideal-types of a general approach. One looks for religion's origins in beliefs about individual spiritual beings, the other in awe at forces of nature. But both of them come out as psychologism. One homes in on an inner world of dreams, the other on sentiments of an external, mysterious universe.

Durkheim does not use the term 'psychologism' himself. But it helps to sum up the whole philosophical attitude he opposes. Its theories attempt to explain the realm of the sacred by deriving it from empiricist psychology and a world of what he variously calls 'sense-data', 'impressions' and 'immediate experience'. Put another way, they try to derive the sacred from the profane. In his lecture course, they 'try to extract the idea of the sacred from things given in immediate experience and that first present themselves as purely profane' (1907f: 77). In his article and again in the eventual work, they assume it is 'the nature of either man or the universe that is where to look for the seeds of the great opposition that divides the profane from the sacred' (1909c: 162 / 1912a: 123). In all versions of his critique, to attempt to cross this divide is to attempt the impossible. So, we might say, these theories make a category mistake. They fail to understand the categorial difference – indeed, the 'logical chasm' – between the profane and the sacred.

In all versions of his critique, moreover, this links with another failure. Any theory of religion must explain why it is universal and has survived so long. This is difficult to do, if it just comes out as nonsense. Yet it is how it comes out in psychologistic theories that try to get from immediate experience to the realm of religion. In his lecture course, these end up seeing religion only as a 'living dream', a 'system of hallucinatory, false ideas', a 'pure and simple illusion', or, in a word, a 'phantasmagoria' (1907f: 77, 99). In his article and again in the eventual work, he repeats the argument complete with give-away talk about the reduction of religion to a 'living dream', 'hallucinatory representations', a 'tissue of illusions', or, in word, a 'phantasmagoria' (1909c: 27, 162 / 1912a: 97, 124).

In all versions of his critique, then, he concludes with the same point. In his lecture course, the sacred constitutes a '*sui generis*' realm of its own, so that it must have as its basis 'a reality with a nature of its own' (1907f: 77). In his article and again in the eventual work, neither the human individual nor the material physical world are sacred in themselves, so that religion must have a basis in 'another reality' (1909c: 162 / 1912a: 124).

So in sum – whether in a methodology of science or an art of argument – the preliminary business of his critique is to get us to ask ourselves the question: what is this reality? He is then ready to take us on a search for the answer.

It is true that he had long ago disclosed, in the pages of his journal, the secret of the eventual destination of this apparent mystery tour. The totemic system in Australia reveals how the basic, continuing, eternal forms of religious life are bound up with the reality that is society. But this was before Spencer and Gillen's shock news reached Paris. The story of his whole imaginative transfiguration of their Australia is something to be left till later.

Writing Up *The Elemental Forms:* 1908 to 1911

Durkheim had already got down to writing 'my book' by 1908, as he refers to it in letters of that year.[3] On the basis of this and other evidence, it is possible to put together a rough picture of the creation of *The Elemental Forms* from a draft, through worked-up versions, to the manuscript's final revision and completion (see table 1.5.3).

Table 1.5.3 The Creation of *The Elemental Forms*

1906–1907	draft	Book 1, Book 2, Book 3: chs. 1–2
1908–1909	worked up version	Introduction, Book 1
1909–1910	worked up version	Book 2
1910–1911	worked up version	Book 3, Conclusion
1911	final revision and completion	

During this time, however, there was further shock news from Australia. It came in a series of ethnographic studies by Carl Strehlow, challenging Spencer and Gillen's account of the Arunta as in all sorts of ways inaccurate and mistaken. So it is of interest to ask how Durkheim coped with the news, while writing up ideas he had already crystallized. Indeed, it is a way to date completion of *The Elemental Forms*. Strehlow's latest study came out in 1911, and Durkheim says he is unable to discuss it since his manuscript was ready to go to press (1912a: 130, n.1).

Another development involves a change of plan, expanding on his material to do with the categories and conceptual thought. The idea is discussed in one of his letters of 1908, in which he refers to his new work as *The Elemental Forms of Thought and Religious Practice* (1975: vol.2, 467). In articles of the following year it was publicly announced, instead, as *The Elemental Forms of Thought and Religious Life* (1909c: 1, n.1; 1909d: 733, n.1). At some unknown point afterwards, it returned to its roots in his lecture course. This had been called *Religion: Origins*. In a more elaborate version of its title, but following the same format of accessing the elemental through the elementary, the work was published as *The Elemental Forms of Religious Life: The Totemic System in Australia*.

More Shock News from Australia

The news from Strehlow's Australia, which started to come through in 1907, created a stir for a number of reasons. It involved a study of the Arunta, made ethnographically famous by Spencer and Gillen. But it redescribed them as the Aranda, in a set of detailed attacks on Spencer and Gillen's general competence and reliability. However, an important background factor was perhaps not so much that Strehlow was a German, but that he was a missionary, who had come to do God's work in Australia. Accordingly, his own account was attacked in turn. For example, he relied on 'Christianized' informants who served up to him what they thought he wanted to hear. Or he never actually observed, since he refused to attend, 'heathen' ceremonies.[4] What, though, was Durkheim's response?

A basic pattern emerges, in going through the references to Strehlow in *The Elemental Forms*. Most of them are to his studies published in 1907 and 1908, and are concentrated in book 2. Only a few are to his study published in 1910, and tend to come in book 3. So this in itself helps to indicate when these books were written up. But it also indicates different approaches to the new material.

Book 2 draws on this in a number of key cases, which all use Strehlow in positive ways. The chapter in search of a vast impersonal yet nonetheless godlike force – difficult to find in the godless Spencer and Gillen – now mobilizes Strehlow for more helpful support (1912a: 281–83). The chapter on the soul goes over their contradictory ethnographic reports to argue that at a fundamental level both of them confirm the work's theory of the soul as an emanation of a vast force (353–67). Finally, Strehlow is also recruited over the hotly disputed issue of belief in a 'high god' and used to back Durkheim's view of its internal evolution within Australia itself (410, 415).

Book 3, in contrast, has little time for Strehlow and relies overwhelmingly on Spencer and Gillen. An explanation can be found in the chapter on sacrifice. Strehlow's report of rites and ceremonies must be treated with caution since he did not observe them himself, unlike Spencer and Gillen. And his report, though published after the chapter had been written, contains nothing that requires major revision (475, n.1). But in a way this summarizes the pattern throughout *The Elemental Forms*. It draws on or disregards Strehlow in line with ideas already established in the lecture course's draft.

More on the Categories and Elemental Forms of Thought

Nor was there any radical change in structure, even in all the expansion of material on 'elemental forms of thought'. It was instead incorporated in the lecture course's pre-existing architecture. This was done either by inserting a section within a chapter or adding it at the end: for example, the chapter on the soul ends with an account of the idea of the person. Indeed, it was never Durkheim's intention to write a whole separate part of the work on 'religious life' and another whole separate part on issues to do with 'elemental forms of thought'. His idea was to weave these in as a theme running through it. As he himself explains in his letter of 1908, his plan is to discuss them 'along the way and in the course of the book' (1975: vol. 2, 467).

Moreover, as the letter also shows, it involved an interest in general forms of thought and not just in particular categories. True, the eventual work includes a variety of these. But a key overarching concern is with what was not, in fact, usually listed as a category – the whole general notion of a force, power or energy.

His lecture course's centrepiece had already discussed this as a basic form of thought, while at the same time linking it with the particular, conventional philosophical category of causality (1907f: 93). In the eventual work, the elemental concept of a force keeps its place of honour in the centrepiece. But causality is in a way demoted to book 3, as one of a number of expressions of a force, power or energy. Indeed, it ends up as a tailpiece to the weakest chapter, on something weird and wonderful that he calls the 'mimetic rite'. In any case, given his whole core theory, it is hardly an architectural accident that book 3's discussion of categories begins with the category of time, to emphasize a periodic upsurge of energy that revitalizes social life in rites of communion. Nor is it an accident that causality is followed up with concern with creativity – not a routinely listed philosophical category, to be sure, yet central to his concern with the creation and recreation of social life through the effervescent energies not only of periodic but historically momentous times. In sum, book 3 elaborates the centrepiece's notion of a vast, many-sided, protean power by interlinking its different expressions in time, causality and creativity. This is not something that happens in the lectures. It is a new development, generated in writing up *The Elemental Forms* itself.

But again, it is not just in a focus on conventional philosophical categories. It is about a birth, through collective effervescent times, of a whole realm of logical and conceptual thought. This comes in the lecture course's centrepiece, and keeps its pride of place in the centrepiece of *The Elemental Forms*. It involves development of the interest, in the essay on primitive classification, in different overall styles of thought. But if anything, it is even more emphatic in its rejection of a 'gulf' between the modern and the primitive. 'Our logic was born from this logic' and 'they are made with the same essential elements' (1912a: 340–42).[5]

In Quest of the 'Eternal'

There can be little doubt that Durkheim became drawn into and absorbed in anthropological investigation as of interest in itself. An example is the effort to understand complex kinship structures, in his intellectually formidable essay trying to crack the 'mathematics' and discover the underlying logic of matrimonial organization in Australia. But there can also be little doubt that an overall project was to dig around in the elementary in search of the elemental, to see, not least, how different styles of thought 'are made with the same essential elements'.

When his lectures on *Religion: Origins* introduce the earliest religion as totemism, he emphasizes straightaway that his aim is not to dwell on what is 'archaic' about its ideas. It is to bring out 'what, in these, can help to explain the religious evolution of humanity and to understand the nature of religion in general' (1907f: 78). Or again, in his conclusion, it is a quest for the 'eternal' in religion.

The story is the same in his article that, with various revisions, became the introduction to the eventual work. He emphasizes straightaway that his aim is not to study an 'archaic' religion merely to say what is odd and peculiar about it. It is how best 'to get to understand the religious nature of man, that is, to disclose to us an essential, permanent aspect of humanity' (1909d: 733 / 1912a: 2). Or again, it is in an effort to penetrate beyond the complexity of different beliefs and practices, to reveal 'the essential, permanent elements of what is eternal and human in religion' (737 / 6). In his article, this is a search for '*homo religiosus*' (1909d: 738). In the work, it is changed to a search for 'the fundamental states, characteristic of the religious mentality in general' (1912a: 7). But the message remains the same.

Another example involves a possible misprint. A change from *religieuse* to *religieuses* entails a change from 'thought and religious practice' to 'religious thought and practice'. But again Durkheim's basic message remains the same:

The Article	The Elemental Forms
What we would like to do is to find a way to arrive at the causes, always in existence and effective, that underlie the most essential forms of thought and religious practice. (1909d: 741)	What we would like to do is to find a way to detect the causes, always present, that underlie the most essential forms of religious thought and practice. (1912a: 11)

Despite what may have been a misprint, he could hardly have been clearer about the grandiose nature of his ambitions.

CHAPTER 6

In Quest of the Sacred: *The Elemental Forms*

Durkheim's work generates many questions. But they could be boiled down to two. One is to do with what, in the end, he identifies as elemental forms of religious and social life. The other is to do with his use of ethnographic material, its role in the construction of his theory, and if this really depended on a trip to Australia.

An idea has already been given of the overall architecture of *The Elemental Forms*, including the build-up of preliminary material in book 1. So it is now possible to concentrate on the rest of the work, starting with book 2 chapters 1–4, as the effective point of arrival in Durkheim's Australia.

Arrival in Australia

Durkheim gives this group of chapters the title, 'Beliefs Specifically Totemic'. But apart from the issue of whether or not they are in fact specifically totemic, they don't just involve beliefs. On the contrary, his account continuously interweaves beliefs with practices and also raises other questions.

A Falsification of the Ethnography?

The account begins with an authoritative announcement:

> At the basis of most Australian tribes, we find a group that holds a preponderant place in collective life: it is the clan. (1912a: 142)

Yet there is something odd about this. It is one of the few places where Durkheim fails to mention Spencer and Gillen to support a key ethnographic claim. The reason, of course, is their rejection of any such claim.

Another sign of something odd going on is in a footnote, which says that social organization has 'only secondary interest for our subject' (151, n.9). This is to explain why it is not examined in detail. An extreme example is how his analysis of complex systems in the essay on matrimonial organization gets only a single mention in a note (153, n.1). In general, he compresses his previous work on elementary structures of kinship into a few pages (148–55). The result is a picture of Australia that might as well have been taken from Frazer's old manual, and as if Spencer and Gillen hadn't changed anything.

They had separated the sacred from the social. Reuniting these is an essential function of the chapters that introduce the innocent reader to Durkheim's Australia. This means interweaving religious with social life, far from downgrading it to a 'secondary interest'. Indeed, in summarizing his opening account, he says he has shown that totemism is a religion 'inseparable from social organization based on clans' (238).

So a criticism is he has done no such thing. But in any case it is important to ask how Spencer and Gillen themselves viewed his use of their work. While preparing *The Northern Tribes of Central Australia*, Spencer received a letter from Frazer drawing his attention to Durkheim's essay on totemism. In writing back, he says the essay is 'full of misconceptions' and he is going to add a footnote to the new study to deal with one of the many points on which Durkheim is 'quite astray' (Spencer, letter of 1903, in Marett and Penniman 1932: 84–85). The footnote duly appeared, although in fact it covers a whole set of points about social organization. But in general it is on the lines: 'The difference between the actual state of affairs and the erroneous supposition of M. Durkheim is fundamental' (Spencer and Gillen 1904: 121, n.1).

Durkheim in turn replied in a note in his essay on matrimonial organization, which he insists 'confirms' his earlier views (1905a[i]: 131, n.2). But Spencer could not have been entirely impressed:

> Sometime I must certainly have a go at Durkheim ... He does not I think deliberately distort things in order to make them fit in with any theory of his own. He simply does not understand matters. (Spencer, letter of 1906, in Mulvaney and Calaby 1985: 394)

However, he never had his 'go at Durkheim' or at least never appears to have publicly commented on *The Elemental Forms*. His old friend, Gillen, died the year it came out, while he himself was on an expedition to northern Australia.[1] In a later study he updated their fieldwork on the Arunta (Spencer 1927). But here he concentrates his fire on Strehlow, his rival ethnographer, while saying nothing about Durkheim or his theories.

To return, then, to *The Elemental Forms* itself, a feature of its introductory account of Australia is how in contrast with Durkheim's earlier essays it fails to come out into the open over key differences with Spencer and Gillen. A mystery, though, is why he adopted a strategy of cover-up and camouflage. He had found a way round Spencer and Gillen he could quite easily have brought out into the open. Indeed, it is the underlying argument that drives his account. Thanks to the totemic group's centrality in religious life, it is also central in social life.

This locates the clan within a web of groups in a wider society, in which the cults of each clan are 'elements of a same religion' and 'totemic religion is the complex system formed by their union' (1912a: 220–22). The clinch argument, however, is the clan's key role in the great religious rites of special collective times, which are not just an affair of the clan itself but involve assemblies of a whole wider society (221).

This might or might not be the case in a 'real' Australia, as described with total accuracy by a magically infallible ideal observer. A humbler empirical point is that it is a fair enough theoretical reinterpretation of Australia as described in Spencer and Gillen's ethnography.

Put another way, Durkheim's opening account is *neither* an accurate representation *nor* a hopeless falsification of the ethnographic reference that is the most important in the entire work. It is an imaginative theoretical reconstruction, perhaps best described as a transfiguration of Spencer and Gillen's Australia.

Totemism as a Religion

Durkheim's opening guide to Australia has other functions, besides secretly reuniting the social and sacred sides of things, separated by Spencer and Gillen. Its main official job is to show that early elementary 'totemism' is indeed a religion, and in the process to pick out its specific, distinctive characteristics as a religion. At the same time it has two other roles. One is to show step by step how the sacred spreads everywhere, thus setting up the paradox that it leaves nothing profane, and that is on the agenda for tackling later on. The other is to keep raising the question of the source of all this sacredness, again on the agenda for tackling later on. Like the author of a detective work, he helpfully provides a trail of clues in leading up to his eventual revelation of a vast impersonal force in the form of a totemic 'principle'. But it is only in rereading them afterwards that it is possible to appreciate the full import of his slipped-in references to a sacred 'principle'.

So what is his argument that totemism is a religion? It gets going in book 2 chapter 1 with a number of basic points. The first is how the totemic clan usually takes its name from a species of animal or plant, with which the clan's members believe they share a common ancestry and have a special kinship (1912a: 143–48). The next point is that 'the totem is not merely a name; it is an emblem' (158). It involves symbols of a collective identity that he variously discusses as 'totemic representations', 'totemic designs, 'totemic images', 'totemic marks', and that are reproduced not only on objects and on bodily costume but on the body itself. The third and main point is how the totem is not only a name and an emblem but a sacred thing. Indeed, these symbols of a collective totemic identity constitute the paradigmatic case of sacred things:

> They are used in the course of religious ceremonies; they form part of the liturgy; it is therefore the case that the totem, at the same time that it is a collective badge, has a religious character. And in fact, it is in relation to it that things are classed as sacred and profane. It is the very type of sacred things. (167)

So in fact it is also a paradigmatic case – in what is billed as an analysis of 'beliefs' – of a whole intertwining of belief, symbolism and ritual.

Indeed, he is especially concerned with a set of three examples that especially involve ritual and that are based on Spencer and Gillen's report of three types of sacred object, the *churinga*, the *nurtunja* and the *waninga*. But he explains that a key difference is how churingas are enduring ritual objects with enduring prestige, stored for safekeeping in sacred places when not in use. Nurtunjas and waningas are temporary, constructed for particular ritual occasions without being preserved afterwards. So how are these different types of ritual things all sacred things? He assumes it must be because they share a same source of sacredness, and locates it, for now, in the designs of the totemic emblem itself (167–77).

Book 2 chapter 2 extends the sacred from this ritual–symbolic core to other things and beings, and starts with animals or plants of the totemic species itself. But in the process he mentions belief in a 'principle' that resides within these, and that requires treatment of them with caution and respect (182). So this is the first clue to the eventual revelation of the source of sacredness as some sort of vast elemental force. Yet it is easy to miss, in a long discussion in which he focuses on taboos surrounding the totemic species to compare them with taboos surrounding the totemic emblem. These are 'more numerous, more severe, more strictly imperative' (188). In a formula taken word for word from his earlier lecture course, he emphasizes that '*the images of the totemic being are more sacred than the totemic being itself*' (189; c.f. 1907f: 82).

The details of his discussion make clear a number of points, which a number of commentators misunderstand and misrepresent. In his dualism of the sacred and profane, sacredness is a matter of degree, the 'profane' refers to the everyday, and things can switch between the two categories. Animals and plants of the totemic species are to some extent sacred some of the time. But in most situations and most of the time they belong to ordinary life. Churingas are permanent, pre-eminently sacred things, and he writes lyrically about their storage in deep far-off caverns that are like 'a temple, at the threshold of which all the bustle of profane life starts to die away' (188).

It is also clear that what is at stake isn't just belief but ritual. It is only 'exceptionally' that the totemic animal or plant is involved in this. In contrast, it is the type of exclusively sacred thing such as the churinga that has 'the leading role' in 'the ceremonies of the cult' (189).

It is in this context that he proceeds to extend the sphere of the sacred still further, to include the human beings who have a leading role in ritual in that they actually perform it. But it is in a specific concern with them as totemic groups. And this interweaves belief back in. For it is in an effort to understand belief in an identity in which the individual is *both* a human in the usual sense of the term *and* an animal or plant of the totemic species. So it leads to another long discussion. Now, however, it is not about taboos that surround human/totemic beings to function as signs of their sacredness. It is about myths that surround human/totemic beings to function as expressions of some more fundamental belief in a sacred identity. This is belief in a 'sacred principle' residing within the human body and the same as that which resides within the totemic species (196).

So here is the second clue to the source of sacredness as a vast elemental force. But although perhaps easier to notice, it can again be lost in all the detailed concerns of the discussion as a whole (190–96). Sacredness is not just generally diffused throughout the body but is especially concentrated in particular bodily parts – blood, hair, the penis's foreskin and so on – each with a role and importance in particular rites. And he then goes on to work in still further material (196–97). This is still to do with how sacredness is not just equally spread and diffused. But it is now to bring out how, for example, it is more concentrated in men, who dominate the ceremonies, rather than in women, and is also more concentrated in the old rather than in the young and ritually uninitiated.

Book 2 chapter 3 completes his set of developing arguments, in that it extends the sphere of the sacred to reach everywhere. Totemism is a religion since it forms a 'whole representation of the world' and a 'cosmology' (200, 222). To take one of his examples, it is not just that human individuals of the white cockatoo clan are themselves in some way white cockatoos. The same applies to all the other things and beings grouped with them, so that, for instance, the sun is also a white cockatoo. Similarly, in the case of the black cockatoo clan and how the human individuals belonging to it are black cockatoos, the moon is also a black cockatoo. It is a 'solidary system' in which all those grouped together – humans, animals, plants, objects – 'participate' in its nature and 'sympathetically vibrate' with one another. So he is not referring to a mere lifeless abstract analytical logic when he describes participation in this sympathetically vibrating whole and says, 'A same principle animates and unifies it: it is the totem' (213).

Here is a third clue to the source of sacredness as an elemental force. But it can be overlooked, in the more spectacular news of a spread of sacredness to the entire universe:

> since there is nothing known that is not classed in a clan and under a totem, there is also nothing that does not receive, in varying degrees, some reflection of religiosity. (219)

Yet this is the news that not only ratchets up the riddle of how anything can be left profane, but underlines the question of what can be a same source of sacredness in a whole cosmos of apparently altogether different things.

In sum, Durkheim's opening account in effect argues that totemism is a religion because it involves beliefs *and* practices that centre round a core of symbolic sacred things, and because it extends this further afield to an entire sacred universe. At the same time he lays a trail of clues about the source of all this sacredness in a notion of an underlying, impersonal force. Turned the other way round, his opening account's explicit claim is that what is specific and distinctive about early elementary totemism is how it forms a religion without ideas of individual spiritual beings or gods.

A Slippery Business

Just as Durkheim concludes his introductory guide to Australia by saying he has shown totemism is a religion 'inseparable from social organization based on clans', he also says he has shown it does not involve ideas of individual 'spiritual beings' (238). This is fundamental to his whole interest in digging around in the origins of religion to insist it is essentially a collective, impersonal affair. But it can seem another exercise in obfuscation, cover-up and camouflage, built into the very way that he plans book 2's story of things and that exactly follows the plan laid out, earlier on, in his lecture course.

After the opening chapters, introducing an early elementary land of collective rather than individualistic religion, the centrepiece drives this message home with its account of a vast impersonal force in the form of the 'totemic principle' or 'mana'. But it is soon followed with a chapter on belief in the soul, revealed as 'mana individualized'. And this is followed with another chapter on belief in individual spiritual beings, including belief in 'high gods'. It turns out, in other words, that religion in Australia all along comes with individualistic beliefs in souls, spirits and gods. This is a reason, merely in reading the work itself and without any check on its ethnographic sources, that his introductory picture can seem an exercise in camouflage. So one question is why he decided to adopt and indeed, in writing up his lecture course, to stick with a plan of argument that is less than straightforward. But a more fundamental question is why, in the end, he still maintains his study shows the roots of religion are social and collective.

On the one hand, it is certainly the case that his arguments continue to invoke an evolutionism in which religious notions that are essentially collective and impersonal come first in time, then help to generate a development of more individualistic beliefs. This is especially evident in book 2 chapter 9 – the book's final chapter – and its story of an internal evolution of Australian religious ideas towards belief in an individual deity. This is their 'logical outcome and highest form' (415). It is also a religious symbolism of how webs of relations extend far beyond the clan, so that each of the variously named high gods is a 'personification of tribal unity' (421). Or they even tend to merge into a notion of single god to express an even wider identity, in a sort of 'internationalism' (422).[2]

On the other hand, however, Durkheim clearly comes out against total reliance on evolutionary stories of a move from the collective to the individualistic. Book 2 chapter 5 follows up the opening account of Australia with yet another critique of rival theories. This includes an attack on a theory called 'pre-animism', emphasizing notions of an impersonal force or energy and put forward by Marett (1900). According to Durkheim, 'pre-animism' imagines an early era of religion in which there were no beliefs in individual spiritual beings and only notions of an impersonal force, and he rejects any such view (1912a: 289, n.4). But this interpretation of 'pre-animism' had been rejected by the term's own originator. It is instead about the relative importance of notions of an impersonal power or energy, however variously and simultaneously combined with beliefs in individual spiritual beings – as made clear in his introduction to an influential, well-known collection of essays (Marett 1909: x). Durkheim's criticism was out of date and out of touch. Yet it still means that he explicitly rejects any simplistic evolutionism, in which in the beginning the only religious ideas are collective and impersonal. His message, in other words, is that collective, impersonal notions remain more fundamental than individualistic beliefs, since they are still in some sense 'prior' to these, even though *not* prior to them in time.

This becomes especially evident in book 2 chapter 8, where the individual's soul is an emanation of an impersonal force in the form of the totemic 'principle':

This principle is immanent in each of the members of the clan. But, in penetrating inside individuals, it is inevitable that it is itself individualized. Because the consciousnesses, of which it thus becomes an integral element, differ from one another, it is differentiated in their image; because each has its own character, it takes on, in each, a distinct character. (1912a: 356)

That is, there is a simultaneous process of internalization/individualization, in which there are always individualistic expressions of collective notions in the very internalization of these as beliefs.

A first main comment is how this undermines and explodes the initial claim about what is specific to totemism as a religion. Part of the background is how Frazer's old manual had made a distinction that remained widely accepted in the literature, and this is a distinction between collective, individual and sexual totems. Durkheim's opening account overwhelmingly concentrates on the collective totem. But book 2 chapter 4 rounds off the picture with a brief coverage of individual and sexual totems, and indeed begins with the announcement: 'There is no religion that does not have an individual aspect' (223). But there are two things that are odd about its discussion of individual totemism in Australia and insistence this does not involve belief in spiritual beings. It is padded out with a lot of material on North America, since it transpires that among many or most of the peoples of Australia itself the institution of individual totemism is 'entirely unknown' (233). It also transpires, in book 2 chapter 9, that in the Australian case it is bound up after all with belief in souls, spirits and ancestral personalities (399–402). So whatever is specific to totemism in Durkheim's early elementary Australia, it isn't and can't be that it doesn't come with belief in an individualistic sacred world of ancestors, souls, spirits and gods. All of these are not only eventually described in book 2, but are seen as integrally linked with totemism. In explaining them as individualistic emanations of a collective force, he explains them as *individualistic emanations of the totemic 'principle' itself.*

In the end, then, the question that matters has nothing to do with what might or might not be 'specific to totemism' – one of the great red herrings of *The Elemental Forms.* Instead it is why, although his chapter on the soul brings out a process of *simultaneous* internalization/individualization, he still maintains that individualistic beliefs are only 'secondary formations', while the collective is 'essential', 'fundamental', 'at the basis of totemism' and 'consequently of religious thought in general' (343). After all, as he himself insists, it can't be because the collective comes first and is prior in time. And he suggests it is prior in a 'logical' sense (382). But he says this in passing, and never spells out what it might mean.

In practice, his claim that religion's roots are social doesn't depend on philosophical theorizing but on building up a picture of Australia in which religion centres round beliefs, symbols, rituals and special effervescent sacred times that are overwhelmingly collective. A lot therefore depends on the work's centrepiece, which begins in book 2 chapter 6 with an account of a vast elemental force.

The 'Totemic Principle'

What exactly is the 'totemic principle'? There are three main ways in which, at the start of the chapter, it is described (269–72). In its very first characterization, it is impersonal – an 'anonymous, impersonal force'. Next, it is simultaneously immanent/transcendent – immanent, since 'embodied' within all sacred things; transcendent, since going beyond all of these and 'not identified with any of them'. Finally, it is a one-and-manifold energy, force or power – an 'energy, diffused throughout all sorts of heterogeneous beings', which is both 'a material force' and 'a moral power'. In sum, it is a vast immanent/transcendent one-and-manifold power. So it is not surprising, given these theological attributes, that he also talks of it as the 'totemic god'. Only, as he says:

> it is an impersonal god, without name, without history, immanent in the world, diffused in a numberless multitude of things. (269)

A Hidden God

It is significant that it doesn't have a name, and he talks of ideas that are 'confused' (272), while his lectures talk of the confused and 'hidden' (1907f: 92). But there is another reason for seeing a hidden god. This is his difficulty in finding evidence of it. He even seems to manufacture evidence.

His introductory guide to Australia had provided a trail of clues about an underlying force, and the first of these comes with a long list of references (1912a: 182, n.1, n.2). But on checking them through, it is hard to find reports of belief in such a force. There is simply a description of how people talk of the totemic species as 'bone of their bone and flesh of their flesh' (Fison and Howitt 1880: 169). Or there is simply a description of a belief that individuals eating a forbidden animal will fall sick and might die (Howitt 1904: 769). Or, in yet another example, there is simply a description of how food restrictions 'seem to be done away with in the instance of very old men; they may eat anything, but this only when they are really very old and their hair is turning white' (Spencer and Gillen 1904: 167–68).

Durkheim might well have been convinced in *reading into* these reports an underlying force that in his view makes sense of what they describe. But he fails to make this clear. Instead, he creates the misleading impression of solid ethnographic 'facts', by citing the reports as if they actually record what he reads into them. Indeed, this is one of the main patterns that emerges from checking through all his many references to his most important source, Spencer and Gillen.

There are also other problems with his use of their material in the chapter on the 'totemic principle' itself. He picks out their report of the particular evil influence *arungquiltha*, and argues a way round how it doesn't add up to a vast sacred force at the heart of totemic religion (1912a: 281–83). But he overlooks another difficulty. In their report, *arungquiltha* has no connection with totemic beliefs and practices at all (Spencer and Gillen 1899: 548–52).

In contrast, they report the sacred objects called *churingas* as intimately bound up with totemic belief and ritual. So perhaps these are a concrete material focus of a vast anonymous force – except that they describe in great detail how churingas are bound up with belief about individual ancestral figures to do with mythical times of the *alcheringa*. Undaunted, Durkheim sees evidence of an impersonal force in the very meaning of *churinga*:

> Spencer and Gillen say this term designates 'all that is secret or sacred. It is applied both to an object and to the quality it possesses'. It is almost the definition of mana. (1912a: 283, n.4)

In fact they don't talk of it as 'designating all that is secret or sacred', but just as 'implying something sacred or secret' (Spencer and Gillen 1899: 648). In any case, it is a triumph of hope to see almost a definition of mana. They never mention a notion of a general impersonal force, just as they never refer to the idea of mana.

Mana
Durkheim nonetheless wants to situate their ethnography within a wider comparative discussion (1912a: 273–79). This draws on the new anthropology of the 1900s, pioneered by Marett and Mauss, and converting 'mana' to a generalized anthropological term for a whole type of belief in a whole range of societies. So in wondering how it might throw light on religion in Australia, a way to explore *The Elemental Forms* on the issue is through Marett.

In looking around for a term to describe religious belief in an elemental force or energy, he had at first suggested borrowing from a Greek word for power to call it 'teratism' (Marett 1900: 13). The term never caught on, and what took hold was the generalized use of 'mana'. Yet this could be seen as ironic. He had aimed to distinguish a range of cases, varying from the purely impersonal to the thoroughly individualistic, and had identified 'mana' as a case in which notions of an impersonal power are inextricably bound up with ideas of individual spiritual entities (27).

But even or especially in going on to generalize it beyond Melanesia, he still insists that one of its characteristics is a combination of the impersonal and the individual. Mana is above all a protean, many-sided power. So, as he puts it, '*mana* is always *mana*', a power that can vary in its particular manifestations and in its degrees of intensity, 'but never in essence' (Marett 1908: 137–38). Its mix of the impersonal and the individual is part of this. Yet as a whole it is impersonal. It centres round religion's collective forms, even while leaving a place for individuality and its future evolution. This is 'the ambiguity that lies sleeping in *mana*' (140–41).

An example with a key role in the development of his ideas has to do with Australia and an object known in the literature as the 'bull-roarer'. As he explains in a popular textbook on anthropology, the bull-roarer is 'a slat of wood on the end of a string, which when whirled round produces a rather unearthly humming sound' (Marett 1914: 125). But at the time of his original essay, the bull-roarer had been acclaimed as evidence of Australian belief in God, thanks to its association with a being that seemed divine and was even addressed, according to some reports, as 'Our Father'. An aim, then, was to deflate this fevered theological speculation. It is instead the humble material inanimate object, the bull-roarer, which lies at the source of ideas of a great religious power. 'Its thunderous booming must have been eminently awe-inspiring to the first inventors, or rather discoverers, of the instrument' (Marett 1900: 17–18).

He concedes its wonder-working effect is reinforced by layers of ritual, symbolism and mythology built up round it. But these don't get to the bottom of the religious notion of an elemental power. And although he elaborates on the issue in various places elsewhere, it is spelt out in plain terms in his textbook on anthropology. In brief, anthropology can't just be content with a description of ways of life encrusted in traditional practices and folklore. It involves a search for their hidden, underlying sources. The discipline's basis is the development of detailed ethnographic studies. Yet it is possible to get only so far with these, in an effort 'to disclose the hidden motives, the spiritual sources, of the beliefs that underlie and sustain the customary practices' (Marett 1914: 227). Although people everywhere reflect on their world to understand and make sense it, it is through ideas that often have the air of mythology but that in any case are not the only possible explanations. And when it comes to choosing between these, the anthropologist 'may just as well endeavour to do it for himself' (228).

Put another way, it is essential to try to understand a social world's own stories, accounts and explanations. But it is legitimate to try to construct an alternative story, even though it depends on *inferences* from such data about obscure underlying notions and forces. So it is not a knock-down, fatal criticism of Durkheim's search for mana in Australia that it had little basis in available ethnographic reports. What counts is going through the material in a detective work's piecing together of various clues in an overall retheorization of things. Thus although his introductory guide to Australia helps to prepare the ground for the chapter on a totemic 'principle', his boldest inference about a hidden god is still to come.

This is in his next chapter, at the core of the work and its whole new theory. It describes an extraordinary effervescent energy created in special times of the sacred, alternating with ordinary times of the mundane, and it is this extraordinary collective energy that gives birth to 'the religious idea' (1912a: 313).

His inference, then, is that it is impossible for explosions of all this energy to take place without also generating notions of a vast power itself. And perhaps he is right. At any rate, it is a fair enough inference to draw from the ethnography if it in fact describes such extraordinary scenes.

God, Society and Effervescent Sacred Times

Durkheim reveals god as society in book 2 chapter 7, the core of the entire work, but immediately followed by his chapter on the soul, complete with maybe his most convincing inference of all about an underlying impersonal force. A way to cope with everything going on is to divide discussion of his core chapter into two parts – starting as he starts with the sections leading up to effervescent sacred times, then moving on to his concern with a general theory of symbolism and conceptual thought.

Specifics: The Clue of the Emblem

He begins with what he has already argued is the main sacred thing, the totemic emblem. So this emblem has got to be where to look for the main material embodiment of a sacred force. Yet it is also the emblem of the key group in early elementary society. So is it not both 'the symbol of the god and of the society'? This in turn suggests that the god of the clan must be the clan itself, but transfigured and represented symbolically (1912a: 294–95).

Generalities: 'God and Society'

His next move is to back up this specific if less than cast-iron inference about the totemic emblem in Australia with a discussion of 'God and Society' everywhere (295–307). But in fact it is addressed to a readership with a Judaeo-Christian understanding of 'God'. So it mobilizes familiar theological attributes, to see *both* god *and* society as constituting a vast immanent/transcendent one-and-manifold power, and accordingly to infer that god is in practice a religious symbolism and transfiguration of society.

The comparison is particularly structured round the many-sidedness of a power that combines negative with positive dimensions. He begins with a distant forbidding authority that commands respect, to go on to emphasize joining with it in communion. So this helps to prepare the way for his account of periodic rhythms of life, in which times of everyday rules and routines alternate with times of uplift, coming together and communion. Meanwhile, though, he especially works in a concern with historically momentous times. Thus he talks of the 'superabundance of forces', 'hyperactivity' and 'effervescence' characteristic of 'revolutionary or creative eras' (300–1). And he gives various illustrations. But the case he picks out is the French Revolution. Its energies generated a new secular religion, complete with its altars, festivals and system of sacred things. Yet also and not least, it constitutes an actual historical example in which:

> society and its essential ideas became the object of a genuine cult, directly and without transfiguration of any sort. (306)

Really? A superabundant, hyperactive, volcanic upsurge of energy might seem a guarantee of transfiguration. But the business, for now, is the account he proceeds to give of rhythms of collective life in Australia.

Two Times of the Sacred and Profane

He relies almost entirely on a single reference to Spencer and Gillen.

Spencer and Gillen	Durkheim
From the moment of [a boy's] initiation, however, his life is sharply marked out in two parts. He has first of all what we may speak of as the ordinary life, common to all the men and women, and associated with the procuring of food and the performance of corrobborees,	The life of Australian societies alternates between two different phases (see Spencer and Gillen, *Northern Tribes of Central Australia*, p. 33) ... These two phases contrast in the sharpest way with one another. In the first, economic activity predominates... The state of

the peaceful monotony of this part of his life being broken every now and again by the excitement of a fight. On the other hand, he has what gradually becomes of greater and greater importance to him, and that is the portion of his life devoted to matters of a sacred or secret nature. As he grows older he takes an increasing share in these, until finally this side of his life occupies by far the greater part of his thoughts. (1904: 33)

dispersion in which society finds itself at this time results in a life that is unvarying, listless and dull. But when a corroboree takes place, everything changes ... There are transports of enthusiasm. (1912a: 307–8)

Durkheim clearly isn't saying quite the same as Spencer and Gillen. But it might boil down to a difference of perspective in interrelated concerns. In his case, it is with a social calendar and an external division of life into two times. In their case, it is with men's increasing absorption in an internal world of thought on the sacred.

The trouble is that in searching through their ethnography it is hard to find any report of a fixed calendar, establishing two clear-cut periods, requiring performance of ceremonies during one of these, and laying down when each of them should take place. Indeed, there is little interest in the issue of a social calendar at all. Durkheim's key idea of two times of the sacred and profane again appears to involve a transfiguration of Spencer and Gillen's Australia. Its essential ethnographic basis is their description of the rites themselves.

'Scenes of the Wildest Excitement'

It is commonplace to suspect Durkheim of exaggeration in his account of effervescence in Australia. But perhaps it is because his critics have not read what he read.[3] On the whole, he is quite faithful to Spencer and Gillen:

Spencer and Gillen

The smoke, the blazing torches, the showers of sparks falling in all directions and the mass of dancing, yelling men with their bodies grotesquely bedaubed, formed together a genuinely wild and savage scene of which it is impossible to convey any adequate idea in words. (1904: 391)

Durkheim

'The smoke, the blazing torches, the rain of sparks, the mass of dancing, yelling men, all this', Spencer and Gillen say, 'formed a scene of wildness, an idea of which it is impossible to give in words.' (1912a: 312)

Here, if anything, he tones down the original text. But also, on occasion, he touches it up. This is what happens in his showcase passage on effervescence (1912a: 310–11) – or what happens at the end. Otherwise, it is almost word for word from Spencer and Gillen (1904: 237–38).

They describe a ritual concerned with an ancestral snake, Wollunqua. Its main phase began on the fourth day. But at night, 'amidst a scene of the wildest excitement, fires were lighted all around the ceremonial ground, making the white trunks of the gum-trees and the surrounding scrub stand out in strong contrast to the darkness beyond'. There was dancing, swaying, chanting, a great clanging of boomerangs and shrieking – *'Yrssh! yrssh! yrssh!'* – around a mound linked with the snake. After a climax, activity continued on and off until morning, when the mound was destroyed in a furious attack. Then, as we read:

Spencer and Gillen	Durkheim
The fires died down, and for a short time there was silence. Very soon, however, the whole camp was astir. (1904: 238)	The fires died down, and there was a profound silence. (1912a: 311)

It is obvious that the change in some way transforms the original account. Yet in what way? Doesn't it help to capture the whole dramatic atmospherics in the rite's creation of a sense of the sacred? Even if literally false, isn't it artistically true?

Collective Effervescence

Part of the issue is again to do with the role of art in science, not least the art of argument. But it is also to do with the role of art in the rites themselves, as described by Spencer and Gillen and in turn by Durkheim. What, after all, helps to generate effervescence? Although it is a term he himself does not use, or might never have wanted to use, it can be suggested that his account of effervescence is about a whole fusion of energies in a 'total aesthetics'.

In introducing his showcase passage, he says it is to bring out how effervescence involves a 'total physical and mental high' – a *surexcitation de toute la vie physique et mentale* (1912a: 310). A task, then, is to go through and analyse his account, to identify the various elements that interact with one another to make for 'total' bodily-mental highs. But his discussion of these elements is distributed between books 2 and 3, not just concentrated in his account of effervescence in the centrepiece itself.

Thus the centrepiece's concerns are with the elements of assembly and symbolism, and it is not until book 3 that art is explicitly woven into the picture. For example, the centrepiece's interest in the role and impact of totemic emblems in effervescent assembly focuses on their symbolism rather than their art, although, as in the case of the churingas, this is something discussed at length by Spencer and Gillen. The role and power of art is nonetheless clearly implicit in Durkheim's many references at this point to song, chant, dance, bodily decoration and costume, and the atmospherics of ceremonies held 'at night, among shadows pierced here and there by the light of fires' (310). Indeed, he talks of 'a sort of electricity' generated by assembly itself (308). But on analysis of books 2 and 3 as a whole, the 'electricity' created in the total bodily-mental highs of effervescence is created in a total aesthetic fusion of the energies of assembly, symbolism and art.

Meanwhile, let us return to his inference about scenes of an extraordinary explosion of collective energies that generate notions of a vast power itself. On the one hand, then, it may well be a fair enough inference to draw from the extraordinary scenes that are in fact described in his main ethnographic source. On the other, what he actually says at this point is that they generate 'the religious idea' (313). Although this includes the notion of a vast power, it can also be interpreted as concerned with the notion of the sacred itself.

The extraordinary energies of collective effervescent times do not just create and construct god, but an entire realm of the sacred, in a symbolic process in which, once got going, god and sacred things create and construct each other. It isn't a simplistic one-way affair in which – as in orthodox theology or devotional altar paintings – god radiates sacredness out on to a lowly surrounding multitude. Durkheim's subversive message is that a humanly created world of sacred things radiates sacredness back on to god. It is a dynamic in which god, the faithful, altar paintings, saints and other iconic things and beings all interactingly sacralize one another.

But on any interpretation it is a hopeless misunderstanding to debate if, in *The Elemental Forms*, it is society that makes religion or religion that makes society. Instead it is how, in the very same process, the energies of times of effervescence create both society and the sacred. In other words it involves a process that generates society but also transfigures it, in simultaneously generating the sacred. So is it just a story about 'Australia'? Does it not imply the inevitability of every social world's transfiguration?

God, Society and Symbolism

What, roughly, does Durkheim mean by 'transfiguration'? A clue is in his course on moral education. He talks of penetrating the fog of religious symbolism to see an underlying reality in bare, naked, rational language. This transparent language is his baseline, in terms of which symbol-laden discourses are transfigurative. So here is a way to summarize a core argument of *The Elemental Forms.* Symbols help to express society, for the very good reason that they help to construct it. Yet it is in effervescent energies that sweep far beyond any expression of social life in bare transparent language. They create but also transfigure society, through a vast symbolism.

Three Cases

This still sees religious symbolism as a way to understand society. So why worry if it is transfigurative? But Durkheim prepares the ground for a general theory of symbolism with three cases that might well give cause for concern.

In one, 'the totemic emblem is like the visible body of the god' (1912a: 316). Yet this is not just to do with how a concrete image represents an abstract religious idea and is merely a convenient aid to understanding. He is instead concerned with an image that has a key role in ritual, that turns up everywhere and that is reproduced in all sorts of shapes and forms. It is embedded in consciousnesses as an extraordinarily powerful focus of thought, feeling and action. Indeed, it is so powerful that it overshadows the abstract idea and 'takes its place' (315). But he omits to mention that what he describes has a familiar, quite unflattering name. An image that takes the place of god amounts to *idolatry.*

In a closely related case, 'the totem is the flag of the clan' (315). This is not just about symbols of a social identity. It is about symbols that are so sacred that they again take the place of what they represent. His paradigmatic case is the soldier ready to die for the flag, a supersacred thing that is neither just a bit of cloth nor just a reference to an idea of country. He uses the same example in an article published after the chapter's completion but now gives it a name, *fetishism.* Indeed, as he writes, 'there is no living faith, however secular, that does not have its fetishes' (1911b: 127).

Another case rounds off the picture. It is how religion is 'a sort of delirium', only, as he emphasizes, a '*well-founded*' delirium (1912a: 324). This involves his long-running claim that religion isn't pure illusion and is based on something real. But it is now in the context of a theory of effervescent energies that create total bodily-mental highs, in a word, *delirium.* Yet he just repeats his old standard arguments in writing:

> Religion thus acquires a sense and a reasonableness that the most intransigent rationalist cannot fail to recognize. (322)

Really? You don't have to be a hardline secular rationalist to worry about a transfiguration of society that comes complete with idolatry, fetishism and delirium.

A General Theory
However, he has still to lay out his general theory of symbolism, which has a number of different implications. Here is its main claim:

> In all its aspects and at all moments of its history, social life is made possible only thanks to a vast symbolism. (331)

One reason is to do with collective memory. Enduring, concrete symbols act as reminders of social ideals and sentiments stirred up in special times, helping to keep them alive during ordinary times (330–31). The main reason is to do with effervescent times themselves. It is above all in the energies of these times that symbols acquire the shared meanings that make possible *both* communication *and* communion – thus making possible both the realm of conceptual thought and the realm of society itself.

Without communication, how can there be communion? Yet without communion, how can there be communication? His solution could nowadays be seen as a sociological version of a 'big bang' theory of the origins of the universe, in the way he imagines an explosion of energies in a creative effervescence. He assumes as his argument's background his showcase passage on effervescence, with its scenes, in fires ablaze at night, of dancing, swaying and chanting in unison, and ending in a profound silence. These are the scenes in which symbols get going with shared meanings. Thus 'individual consciousnesses are by themselves closed to one another and can communicate only through signs that come to translate their internal states' (329). This is how symbols can act as 'material intermediaries', linking the world of internal states with the realm of collective representations (330). But it requires the extraordinary energies of effervescence to kick-start the process and convert mere sense-data into symbols with shared meanings, in turn making possible more abstract ideas of 'god', etc.

What are the implications? Just as a big bang theory is difficult to comprehend within the framework of classic science and philosophy, so is the attempt to break the logical logjam of no communion without communication, yet no communication without communion. Indeed, there is a difficulty for his own classic philosophy of a logical chasm that separates two categorially different worlds. The energies of total bodily-mental highs cross over the chasm to get, via the material intermediary of the symbol, from the world of sense-data to a realm of ideas. He himself seems well aware of this implication. In leading up to the theory he says that, 'as we are about to show', it is necessary 'to anchor ideas in the material things that symbolize them' – but at once adds that 'the role of matter is here reduced to a minimum' (326). It is understandable that he is anxious to reduce its role to a minimum. His critique of rival explanations of religion had accused them of an empiricism in which, in attempting to get from the world of the profane to the categorially different realm of the sacred, they attempt the logically impossible. Yet here he is, at the core of *The Elemental Forms,* going about the logically impossible. But what this embarrasses is his tendency to extreme formulations of a profane–sacred dualism, rather than his theory of symbolism itself.

In any case, there is another implication. He introduces his theory with how the emblem is a symbol that does not just express, but creates and constitutes an idea of a collective identity (329). He goes on to emphasize how the energies of collective effervescence do not just express, but change and transform individual inner states, in the very way they create shared meanings round the material symbol. Thus symbols come to communicate the ideas of abstract collective representations, for the very good reason that 'they have helped to form them' (330).

An error, then, is to assume the symbol is merely a label stuck on to already existing ideas. On the contrary, the symbol's concrete meanings are an 'integral part' of ideas (331). If we expand on his initial example, the flag is an integral part of the abstract idea of a nation, the cross is bound up with the whole idea of Christianity, while iconic images of liberty feed into the idea of liberty itself. Indeed, he himself sums up by saying social life depends on 'a vast symbolism'. And throughout the discussion itself, he gives the impression that his theory of symbolism applies to *all* collective representations. So in that they are an affair of such representations, a radical implication is that there are no such things as purely abstract ideas, concepts or categories.

Perhaps Durkheim wants to skip over this, just as he wants to play down the element of materialism in his theory. But his sociology of the symbol entails at least scepticism and doubt about the very idea of purely abstract ideas. So it is important to recall his concern with the symbol, in going on to the picture of a realm of conceptual thought that follows, and that ends the chapter as a whole.

Styles of Thought

An overall interest is in general styles of thought, but as varieties of universal forms of thought. In practice, however, Durkheim focuses on the relation between modern science and primitive religion. 'Our logic was born from this logic' (340). There isn't a 'gulf' between them, and in-

stead 'they are made up of the same essential elements, although une-
qually and differently developed' (342). So along with the universalities,
what are the differences?

It was suggested, in discussing the essay on primitive classification,
that it is concerned with differences in which modern thought is abstract,
analytical and rationalistic, while primitive thought is concrete, dialectical
and emotive. But Durkheim now adds a new dimension. Like modern science, primitive religion uses the same basic universal logical operations
of linking and distinguishing. A difference is the style of making links
and distinctions. Modern scientific thought is 'nuanced', while primitive
thought 'seeks extremes': 'when it makes links, it sees a total identity;
when it makes distinctions, it sees a total opposition' (342).

An irony is how this could perhaps describe Durkheim's own
thought and his attraction, in dualistic oppositions, to extremes. In any
case, a 'nuanced' approach is to differentiate styles of thought according to a set of dimensions in which, for example, some tend to be more
concrete while others are more abstract. Indeed, given his concern with
the symbol and the scepticism it implies about pure abstract ideas, it
seems appropriate to focus on the concrete–abstract dimension as a way
to follow through his account.

A more concrete style of religion tends to centre round the imagery
of a vast, elaborate, ritually enacted symbolism. A more abstract style
of religion tends to centre round an idea of the vast immanent/trans-
cendent one-and-manifold power that is god, in emphasis on bare, naked belief. It is the first, more 'Catholic' style of religion that is accused
of idolatry and fetishism by adherents of the other, more 'Protestant'
style – in its turn attacked as too individualistic and too intellectual to
constitute the community of a living faith. But given Durkheim's views,
a basic point is that *all* varieties of religion transfigure society, whether
it is mainly through a concrete ritual-symbolic imagery or an abstract
theological belief.

However, there is the question of a modern 'secular' religion, or
rather, varieties of secular religion. In *The Elemental Forms*, the model
associated with the French Revolution is more concrete and 'Catholic',
thanks to its whole new ritual and symbolism. In the essay on the Dreyfus
Affair, the model associated with a cult of the individual is more abstract
and 'Protestant', in its hostility to the mere external apparatus of ritual
and symbolism. So a problem with the Revolution's model is how, even
if giving up on 'god', it can seem a guarantee of transfiguration thanks
to its resurrected paraphernalia of altars, festivals and sacred things. A
problem with a mere secular philosophical cult of the individual is if
it can ever constitute the community of a living faith at all. Into the

bargain, it can still come complete with transfiguration. This is because Durkheim makes a distinction, in his article of around the same time as *The Elemental Forms*, between 'concepts' and 'ideals of value'. The role of concepts is to 'express the realities to which they apply'. The role of ideals is to 'transfigure the realities with which they are concerned' (1911b: 140). In sum, it could be said that the theoretical landscape of *The Elemental Forms* points to the social world's inevitable transfiguration in one way or another. The only task, then, is to sort out which varieties of society run on which varieties of transfiguration.

A drawback with this interpretation of the work is how it ignores the author, and his clearly stated belief in the possibility of a society 'without transfiguration of any sort'. This links, moreover, with an overall set of attitudes involving his belief in the power of the concept, in 'rational' language and in 'enlightened' consciousness. Thus it is significant that he chooses to conclude the work's core chapter with a discussion of the realm of conceptual thought, complete with a message of progress from primitive to modern scientific thought. Another clue is how it leads straight on to the chapter on the soul, revealing this as the origin of the concept of the person and again coming with a message of progress from obscure religious talk of god and the soul towards an enlightened secular society of persons.

The Soul

Durkheim's account of the soul involves him in a major theoretical statement of the relation between society and the individual. More precisely, it involves him in a major theoretical statement of the relation between society, the individual and the person. But it is once again embedded in his analysis of religious symbolism in Australia, and needs to be approached through this analysis.

The Soul in Australia
He introduces his account with the universalist claim that every religion comes with belief in a soul (1912a: 343). In getting on with the case of Australia, his first move is to identify the notion of the soul with a notion of an inner 'life principle' that animates the body (344). So although the soul is in some way distinct and independent from the body, his next move is to warn against any simplistic soul–body dualism. On the contrary, the soul is united with the body 'through the closest ties' (347). At death, however, it departs the body for 'the land of souls' (350). Or at least this is a moment in its career. A key belief is in a continuing series of reincarnations in which souls re-enter the bodies of new generations.

In turn, Durkheim's key interpretation of the belief involves a dualism within the soul itself. One of its elements is individual, while the other is common to all souls. So, as we might put it, an impersonal soul-stuff is part of every soul. As he himself puts it, 'the soul is none other than the totemic principle, incarnated in each individual' (355–56). Or again, the soul is '*mana* individualized' (378).

How does this compare with Spencer and Gillen? They never mention 'the soul'. Still, some of Durkheim's references are accurate enough. Others are misleading or merely erroneous. An example is his picture of a 'land of souls'. Citing Spencer and Gillen, he says the Arunta imagine this as a place where rivers never run dry and the sun always shines (350). In fact, their report of places with 'streams of running water and perpetual sunshine' is about haunts of spirits called *iruntarinia* (Spencer and Gillen 1899: 513, 524). A dead person's spirit has a different name and goes somewhere else. This is made clear in their original account, though revised in a number of details in a later work. For example, it renames the alcheringa the *alchera*.

In brief, when an ancestor of the time of the alchera died, he left behind his churinga along with a 'spirit part' of his being, identified in the later work as the *kuruna*. At the place where the ancestor descended into the earth, there arose a rock or tree called the *nanja*, and there issued from this another form of the ancestor's spirit, called the *arumburinga*. It is the kuruna that enters a woman to reincarnate itself in her child, while its independently existing counterpart, the arumburinga, takes a general interest in the new individual's career. On death, the individual's kuruna becomes a spirit called the *ulthana*. This watches over the grave until the final mourning ceremony has been completed. It then departs, returning to live alongside its arumburinga and to resume the form of a kuruna that can be reborn. In the original account, it returns to the nanja rock or tree. In the later work it is to where the churingas are stored, now named the *pertalchera*. But in both versions these are nearby, closely associated places, which together constitute a centre of sacred life (Spencer and Gillen 1899: 512–15; Spencer 1927: 421–23).

It is in no way like Durkheim's picturesque, far-off 'land of souls'. Each nanja–pertalchera cluster is part of a set of specific sacred places situated throughout the landscape, each forming a specific locus of a whole way of thinking about birth, life and death. Moreover, these sacred places and this way of thinking are embedded in a cosmology about a world formed through the individual ancestral beings of the time of the alchera. Although Durkheim gives readers at least some idea of this cosmology, he nonetheless creates the overwhelming impression of a world formed through an impersonal force. In effect, he 'mana-izes' the alchera.

Yet it is in making perhaps his most convincing inference that there must be a hidden god, involving an impersonal force and soul-stuff. The cosmology of the alchera is about a sense of identity in which individuals feel linked with one another as members of a same community of the dead, the living and the not yet born. Belief that the soul comes from somewhere before birth and lives on after death is a religious symbolism of this community. So, as he emphasizes, society exists only in and through individuals. Yet it precedes as well as survives each individual, to be renewed in every generation (1912a: 384–85). More specifically, it is an identity constructed through kinship. But it is in no way a merely biological kinship. It is a spiritual kinship. It is through souls that stem from the ancestors of the alchera and that are re-embodied in each new generation. It is the cosmology itself that entails an impersonal soul-stuff, common to all souls and linking the souls of every past, present and future individual. Or as he himself says, it entails a 'mystical form of germinative plasma', transmitted from one generation to another and creating the clan's 'spiritual unity' across time (385).

The Dualism of the Soul

Thus a key dualism in Durkheim's account isn't a soul–body dualism at all. It is a dualism within the soul itself, and how it combines both individual and impersonal collective elements. In part, this involves another case of his reimagination of Spencer and Gillen's Australia. But it also involves some of his most fundamental, general theoretical concerns.

In insisting on a dualism within the soul itself, he goes so far as to remark, at one point, that it is an affair of 'contradictory' elements (356). On the one hand, the soul is an inner life principle at the core of the individual's whole spiritual, moral being. It is an integral constituent of the individual personality. On the other, it is also independent and draws on forces from outside and over and beyond the individual, and so from some sort of external, transcendent source. Yet this is not just a cue to link everything with the external transcendent power that is god/society. True enough, he talks about the soul as 'a spark of the divinity', to link the energies inside everyone with the forces of religious, moral and intellectual life (375–77). But a basic theoretical lesson of his dualism inside the soul is what it brings out about his very idea of society itself.

Society, like 'god', is simultaneously immanent/transcendent. It is absurd to picture it as a merely external transcendent force, entirely outside and over and beyond the individual. As he yet again insists, 'society can exist only in and through individuals' (356). The dualism of the soul's individual–impersonal elements is the other side of a dualism of society, in which it is both an external transcendent force and an inner immanent energy, active within the lives of individuals.

In turn, this links with his view of a process of simultaneous internalization/individualization. In Australia, the totemic principle is 'immanent in each of the members of the clan', but, 'in penetrating inside individuals, it is inevitable that it is itself individualized' (356). More generally:

> The impersonal forces that arise from the collectivity cannot take form without becoming embodied in individual consciousnesses, where they are themselves individualized. Nor, in reality, is it in two different processes, but in two different aspects of one and the same process. (382)

As already discussed, this generates the problem of why he maintains the collective is still somehow prior, when it isn't prior in time. But it also involves other issues, to do with what is at stake in individualization itself.

One of its aspects is shared collective belief in individual sacred beings. Another aspect, however, is everyone's own particular ways of understanding a collective belief. These could be their own particular interpretations of a collective belief in individual spirits, souls, gods and so on. But Durkheim is above all interested, as in the following passage, in a process of internalization that entails everyone's own individualistic interpretation of collective ideals themselves:

> Each of us puts our own imprint on them; this is how everyone has their personal way of thinking about the beliefs of their Church, the rules of common morality, the fundamental notions that serve as a framework of conceptual thought. ([1914a] 2005: 43)

This is in his essay on the dualism of human nature. It is often treated as if a unique source of his ideas on the subject. In fact, it was written in an effort to explain a theme of *The Elemental Forms*, in turn with roots in *The Division of Labour*.

A Dualism of Human Nature?

Durkheim's account of effervescence involves a sort of spontaneous combustion, in which individual internal states are transformed in the very creation of communication between them through the 'material intermediary' and shared meanings of the symbol. What he now wants to explain is why it is always the case – even in extraordinary collective effervescent energies – that when individuals internalize collective currents of thought they inevitably understand them in their own particular ways. As he puts it: 'there must be a factor of individuation'. As he at once claims: 'it is the body that plays this role' (1912a: 386).

Yet how, exactly? His thesis on the division of labour had distinguished two quite different types and sources of representations – one to do with the material world of the embodied individual, the other to do with the realm of society. His essay on the definition of religious phenomena had taken a further step – identifying the divide between material and social sources of representations with the logical chasm between the profane and the sacred. But he concludes his core chapter of *The Elemental Forms* by emphasizing the nuanced style of modern scientific thought, and his chapter on the soul follows this up by beginning with a warning against any simplistic body–soul dualism. It then goes on, however, to sweep the warning aside. Apparently, ideas about the body and soul constitute a religious symbolism of a fundamental dualism of human nature in which 'we really are made up of two beings', the 'sensate being and the spiritual being' (377), and in which the soul has little or nothing to do with individuation but 'it is the body that plays this role' (386). There are many ways to question such a picture of things, yet not least through his own sociology.

Part of the picture is the claim that 'the soul is always considered a sacred thing', as 'opposed to the body, which in itself is profane' (375). Yet *The Elemental Forms* is full of cases in which the body and parts of the body are sacred things. True, in the claim's smallprint it is the body 'in itself' that is profane. It still creates the impression of just the sort of simplistic dualism he had warned against.

Moreover, it also sweeps aside his whole account of effervescence and sociology of the symbol. The physical, sensate individual has an ineliminable, crucial role in the uplift of total bodily-mental highs. The physical, sensate individual at the same time helps to make social life possible, thanks to a vast symbolism that acts as a material intermediary between the world of sense-data and the realm of conceptual thought. Thus it just is not the case that, in *The Elemental Forms*, the embodied individual is always a force getting in the way of society. At the heart of the work, embodiedness is an artery of collective life.

But also, it is sociologically incoherent to finger embodiedness as the sole source of individuation. Or at least this is the message of Durkheim himself in his thesis on the division of labour. It is one thing to recognize embodiedness as a first, inalienable basis of individuality. It is another to rely on this essentially permanent basis of variation as the main or only way to explain increasing variation. The author of the chapter on the soul comes to his sociological senses when, at the end, he refers to his thesis to bring back in how 'society itself is an important source of individual differentiation' (390, n.1).

True, this is in a footnote and his conclusion highlights something else. But it is not the issue of how to explain individuation. It is simply to drive home a point about 'the fact of individuation' (390). Yet it is the issue of how to explain individuality that helps to generate all his fuss about a 'dualism of human nature'. So in the end it can seem so much hot air, giving vent to his rage against some forms of individualism while suppressing his support for others. In any case the chapter finishes on a calmer note, to insist on a basic 'fact' about society, the individual and the person. It is a mistake to equate the person with the individual, since, instead, the person is about what 'we have in common' (389).

Reason, Autonomy and a Society of Persons

In Durkheim's Australia, the clan's impersonal soul-stuff is about a collective identity across time, but is also to do with a 'spiritual principle' that is the same in everyone and 'in and through which consciousnesses commune' (386). In the modern case of the person, this impersonal spiritual soul-stuff is none other than reason. Thus he draws approvingly on Kant, to write:

> Reason is that which is most impersonal in us. For reason is not my reason; it is human reason in general. It is the power the mind has to rise above the particular, the contingent, the individual, and to think in terms of the universal. (387–88)

Indeed, the Kantian references in the argument are so important that a way to explore what is going on is through a Kantian reading of Durkheim himself.

A start can be made by returning to why he maintains that the collective is prior to the individual though not prior in time, and to his remark that it is prior in a 'logical' sense. A Kantian reading of the remark – in line with the passage just quoted – is that reason constitutes a logically prior impersonal framework of basic categories and operations of thought, which is assumed in individual reasoning, which makes this possible, and through which individual reasoners commune.

All the same, one of the issues at stake is that one of the things common to everyone as a person is their individuality, in reasoning and universalizing in their own ways in terms of a shared logical, conceptual and moral framework. In fact, in *The Division of Labour*, it is almost as if it is individual difference that makes everyone identical as a person. What is stressed is how the person is 'an autonomous source of action', thanks to a social process of individuation in which everyone thinks in their own way and 'the very materials of their consciousness have a personal character' (1893a: 453–54 / 1902b: 399–400). In contrast, in *The Elemental Forms* what is emphasized is the impersonal, and it is almost as if it is forgotten that the impersonal and general necessarily entail a key active role of individual reasoning to interpret them.

So again on a Kantian reading, *The Division of Labour* and *The Elemental Forms* involve their own distinctive versions of the ideal of a 'kingdom of ends' and its union of autonomous persons. However, there is a more fundamental difference. Both of them see autonomy as something 'progressive', in that it develops in history. But in the beginning, in *The Division of Labour*, it does not exist at all, while in the beginning, in *The Elemental Forms*, there is already a kernel of a society of autonomous persons.

In the beginning, in *The Division of Labour*, society has such control over the individual that it amounts to control of a heteronomous 'thing'. In the beginning, in *The Elemental Forms*, there is already the kernel of a 'relative autonomy' (1912a: 388). But it is thanks to society itself. For it is thanks to the collective creation of a realm of conceptual thought, which helps to free the individual from domination by the senses and the material, physical world. Indeed, 'the only way to liberate ourselves from physical forces is by opposing them with collective forces', in turn a way to a developing autonomy in which 'we are all the more a person the more we are emancipated from the senses, and the more we are capable of thinking and acting through concepts' (389).

A number of comments might be made, but again especially to do with a 'dualism of human nature'. There is an obvious similarity between Durkheim's dualism of the sensate/the conceptual and a Kantian dualism of the sensate/the intelligible. Yet it is also obvious that he is against any Kantian identification of the intelligible with a mysteriously pre-existing conceptual framework. It is precisely a project of *The Elemental Forms* to look for origins of the realm of conceptual thought in the sociohistorical world itself. Indeed, this might be why he limits himself to a brief passing remark about the 'logical' priority of the collective and impersonal. Any further elaboration can come too close for comfort to a Kantian view of the logical priority of a framework that must somehow exist as a given, necessary to get on with reasoning in the sociohistorical world and making it possible. In any case, it is precisely his own actual account of this conceptual realm's sociohistorical creation – involving the bodily-mental highs of effervescence and the material intermediary of a vast symbolism – which helps to make his 'dualism of human nature' incoherent.

But instead of just approaching it literally and criticizing it as an illusion, perhaps it can be understood as a metaphorical expression of real underlying concerns in his work. One of the candidates is his worry over anomie, and his belief in an anchorage in rules that constrain individual desires. So maybe his dualism's underlying message is that society helps to free the individual from passions that 'enslave' (389), but which is also why it imposes pain and suffering and indeed, as in his essay, does 'violence to some of our most tyrannical inclinations' ([1914a] 2005: 44). Yet, like passions that enslave, this seems a clear reference to Kantian talk of the tyranny of desire. In sum, it is possible to understand his dualism as an expression of deep-rooted Kantian, 'Protestant' and puritanical tendencies running throughout his work. He never fully converted to all the embodied emotiveness of coming together in communion, despite the theoretical role of effervescence in *The Elemental Forms*, or despite his efforts to defend what some would condemn as idolatry, fetishism and the paraphernalia of ritual and symbolism. In a word, he never fully converted to 'Catholicism'.

It might seem odd to see an ambivalence between 'Protestant' and 'Catholic' tendencies in the writings of a secular intellectual from a Jewish background. But it is a way to try to sum up different currents of thought in his work as a whole.

Elemental Forms of Religious Practice

Book 3 can be seen as recalling one of the work's earlier, projected titles, *The Elemental Forms of Thought and Religious Practice*. It is especially where various discussions of basic forms of thought are incorporated, along the way, in an account of basic forms of religious practice. In any case, it consists of five chapters that are arranged according to the following plan. The first chapter gets going with rites of the negative cult, and how an essential aspect of religion is to do with barriers that separate the sacred from the profane. The three central chapters concentrate on rites of the positive cult, and how religion is above all a coming together in communion. The final chapter is about a rite that expresses an ambiguity built into the sacred. A route into the account is to begin with this final chapter, then to work up to the whole central concern with religion as communion with the divine and with one another.

The Piacular Rite and the Ambiguity of the Sacred

There are many ways in which Durkheim might be seen as original in his effort to identify, analyse and explain a special type of rite, to do with times of stress. But at least one way is that he gave it a name, and made it famous in the literature as the 'piacular' rite. In choosing this name, he picks out two of the various meanings of the Latin term *piaculum* – a broad meaning to do with misfortune, and a core meaning to do with expiation or atonement (1912a: 557). Thus the rite has two basic jobs. It is about the collective expression of a whole ambiguous mix of emotions

– distress, fear, anxiety, anger, resentment – stirred up in times of misfortune. But it is also about a process of healing, of overcoming these emotions to renew confidence in life through solidarity and communion.

> Communion in grief is still communion and every communion of consciousnesses, whatever the elements at work in it, increases social vitality. (574)

It is the combination of these two jobs in an overall social process that underlies the rite's specific character, and its expression of an ambiguity in the sacred itself. Yet what exactly is this ambiguity?

The sacred is about out of the ordinary forces. In familiar religious terms, they are forces of good and evil. In Durkheim's account, it involves variations in the same basic opposition – 'the pure and the impure, the saintly and the sacrilegious, the divine and the demonic' (586). But let us just stick with it as the divine and demonic. It is then not very difficult to see how the ambiguity of the sacred might refer to a power struggle between clearly defined antagonistic forces. It is perhaps more difficult to see it as to do with a religious world in which the energies of the sacred can switch over and transform into one another. According to circumstances, the divine can become dangerous and demonic, while the demonic can become divine and a force for the good. Put another way, it is a religious world of belief in the same power's opposite effects in different contexts. And in fact, this is what he characterizes as 'the ambiguity of the sacred' (588).

It might help with understanding the ambiguity to recall conventional theological talk – not least in times of grief, stress or disaster – that good can come of evil, or that the Lord works in mysterious ways, or indeed is a power beyond human comprehension. For Durkheim, however, 'god' is not beyond human comprehension. His general key to what is often discussed as the problem of theodicy and human suffering is the many-sidedness of society itself. 'It is the unity and diversity of social life that at the same time generates the unity and diversity of sacred things and beings' (591).

But his unity and diversity of social life includes the ordinary and profane, not just the sacred. Indeed, it is contact between the sacred and profane in the wrong circumstances that constitutes some of his most important cases of an ambiguity in which the same power has opposite effects and the divine is so dangerous it is as good as the demonic. So a way to understand the ambiguity is not just through book 3's final chapter, on the piacular rite, but also its first chapter, on negative rites that fence off the sacred and regulate contact with the profane.

At the same time the ambiguity of the sacred links with a paradox of the sacred, in which it is so powerful it can spread everywhere to leave nothing profane. What, then, could be the underlying social point and purpose of limiting this power, to safeguard a life that is ordinary, routine, workaday and mundane?

The Negative Cult and the Paradox of the Sacred

Durkheim begins the chapter with rites that separate the sacred and profane through negative prohibitions, and says it is why he calls this system of rites 'the negative cult' (1912a: 428). He goes over various detailed examples of how they divide the sacred from the profane, to boil it down to a division in terms of space and time. But it is the division in terms of time that comes across as more significant. This is because he leads up to how it is generally the case that 'acts characteristic of ordinary life are forbidden, when those of religious life are going on' (437). It is especially the ordinary everyday business of work that is suspended during sacred times, since 'work is the pre-eminent form of profane activity' (438).

In any case a key 'characteristic' of the sacred is its concentration in particular places and times (441). But a puzzle is then why, if this is a mark of the sacred, so, in 'a sort of contradiction', is its power to spread everywhere (454). How it is 'eminently contagious' and can spread everywhere was explained by 'the theory of religious forces we proposed' (463). So, to recall a theory he does not feel a need at this point to repeat, it is not just about two worlds but two times of the sacred and profane, in a creation and recreation of society through moments of extraordinary effervescent energies. Yet how is it possible, beyond these moments, to sustain these energies? So perhaps he is quietly putting together a story that solves the 'contradiction' of the sacred. The ordinary, pre-eminently mundane activity of work has got to go on most of the time, but necessarily interrupted by upsurges of effervescence that can only last some of the time.

Yet will this do as a solution? The work's very first chapter comes with a clue. He talks of a 'logical chasm' separating the sacred from the profane, but at once adds they must somehow be interlinked, since otherwise the sacred would be good for nothing (55). What, then, is it good for? The work's very last chapter reveals, five hundred pages later, the whole point of religion:

> In all its forms, its object is to lift man above himself and make him live a higher life than he would lead if he just obeyed his individual impulses. (592)

So how does religion make for uplift all the time, even during long stretches of everyday routine, rather than just in limited, effervescent moments? More specifically, how can a dour, puritanical, negative cult spell uplift?

In brief, it doesn't, if merely to clamp down on any contact between the sacred and profane. And this is the impression he gives at the start of his chapter on negative rites. But it lends drama to his news that, after all, they have 'a positive action of the highest importance' (441). The negative cult is 'the condition of access to the positive cult' (442). It transforms ordinary individuals, changing them so that they have the qualities required to enter into communion with the sacred.

It helps with understanding his argument to distinguish between a rite's 'mode of action' and its 'rationale of action'. In his start-up cases of the negative rite, its mode of action is the prohibition and its rationale of action is to separate the profane from the sacred. In his switch of focus on to its positive role, its mode of action is still the prohibition but now its rationale is to join the profane with the sacred. Indeed, it is part of what he eventually explains is a general lesson. The same ritual action can do different jobs, while the same job can be done by different ritual actions (552). Moreover, this picture of ritual changing around and flexibility links with crossovers between the categories of the sacred and profane, as well as with an ambiguity in which the same energy can have different effects and the same effect can flow from different energies. The last thing Durkheim describes is a religious world of a fixed, neat and tidy, immutable order. Put another way, and in line with an earlier suggestion, it is a religious world characterized less by an analytical and more by a dialectical style of thought.

But to return to the case of the prohibition, how is it that it can have such different uses and, instead of fencing off the sacred, can open the way to the sacred? He sees an answer in asceticism, and so in a form of the negative rite that could be called the 'ascetic rite'. In the process, he links the prohibition with religious practices that variously involve abstinence, privation, pain and suffering, and in general maintains that suffering is an 'essential element' of religion (445). Thus the ascetic rite helps to access the sacred since it is 'a necessary school in which man shapes and steels himself, and acquires the qualities of disinterestedness and endurance without which there is no religion' (451–52). That is, the ascetic rite's mode of action is suffering, while its rationale is to teach qualities that are part of self-discipline, in turn an indispensable part of uplift to a higher life.

Accordingly, he sees it as an essential element of rites of initiation, helping to launch the individual's career as a full participant in a society's realm of sacred life. But he also discusses what he calls a 'systematic asceticism', which is not for everyone or part of a standard religious career. It is a full-time asceticism, practised by monks, hermits and other holy men and women who 'acquire a special sanctity through fasts, vigils, retreat and silence, in sum through privations, more than by acts of positive piety (offerings, sacrifices, prayers, etc.)' (445). So on the one hand, it is precisely through a systematically negative mode of action that its rationale is a specially close communion with the divine. On the other, it is not for everyone and is not at all like the uplift and communion of the great religious rites described in his account of the positive cult. But it also involves him in a brief remark, of considerable interest, about the role of extremism in uplift. 'It is necessary that an elite sets the goal too high, so that the crowd does not set it too low' (452). Translated in terms of his own theory, and in a way that he himself does not make explicit, it is a key to the 'contradiction' of the sacred and to its underlying social point and purpose: life in ordinary everyday times would aim too low, without the idealism of effervescent times that sets sights so high.

In order to create, construct and constitute a vision of a social world, there is a need to separate out this activity and to protect idealism from ordinary everyday life, with its inevitable compromises. But things also work the other way, in a need to get on with the mundane business of life, complete with its compromises, and to protect it from an idealism that 'sets the goal too high'. Yet without any impact on ordinary life, the ideal, like the sacred, would be good for nothing. To influence and spread on to ordinary times that nonetheless remain and have to remain separate from it, idealism, like sacredness, requires the energies generated in special effervescent times. Everyday symbols and everyday memories – as well as the everyday school of hard knocks – might do their bit. But everyday uplift is above all based in the special moments of inspiration and idealism that involve, in religious terms, a positive cult's moments of communion with the divine.

The Positive Cult: The Core Elemental Rites of Religion

Durkheim's account of the positive cult draws on various ethnographic sources, though overwhelmingly on Spencer and Gillen's material, especially their account of ceremonies of the *intichiuma*. And it is in a radical reanalysis of their overall material that breaks it up into a number of basic elemental rites. He talks of these as sacrifice, the mimetic rite and the representative or commemorative rite. But it makes more sense to rework his three great rites of religion as *sacrifice, prayer* and *sacred drama*, while continuing to see them all as rites of communion.

Sacrifice

In Spencer and Gillen's ethnography, the ceremony of the intichiuma is concerned with the renewal and reproduction of the totemic species, and involves a ritual in which some of the totemic species is eaten by members of the totemic group, then shared out with others. But they never describe this meal in religious terms – not even as a meal of communion, let alone as a form of sacrifice – and they eventually make clear why, since they see it as a 'magical ceremony' (Spencer and Gillen 1904: 309, 318).

Yet in a common response to their news from Australia, the intichiuma was at once hailed as evidence of Robertson Smith's theory of sacrifice. This located the roots of sacrifice, not in the offering of gifts to a sacred being, but in the communion of a meal in which the faithful eat the sacred being itself. So a challenge for Durkheim was how, instead of merely repeating common interpretations, to say something new. His main strategy involved the radical reanalysis of things in terms of a set of basic rites. But in the process it also involved an attack on Robertson Smith, while paying oily tributes to his 'revolution' in the theory of sacrifice (1912a: 480). Durkheim massages and manipulates the material on the intichiuma in an effort to show it is simultaneously both a meal of communion and an offering of gifts. So, contrary to Robertson Smith, these two elements are part of sacrifice from the very beginning.

All the same, this is still within a standard framework of ideas and disputes about the rite's mode of action. But he goes on to make a more original claim about its underlying rationale. It is a crucial case of how the 'rhythm of religious life' is bound up with the 'rhythm of social life':

> Society cannot revive the sentiment it has of itself unless it assembles. But it cannot remain in session forever. The demands of life do not permit it to remain in an indefinite state of congregation; so it disperses, to reassemble once again when, once again, it feels the need. These are the necessary alternations to which the regular alternation of sacred and profane times responds. (499)

So it is simultaneously a key to the paradox of the sacred, to two times rather than merely two worlds of the sacred and profane, but also and not least to the social sources, in the rhythms of social life's energies, of the category of time itself.

Prayer

What happens in the next chapter? It is significant that Durkheim wrote up his account of the 'mimetic rite' in 1910. This is because Mauss's study of prayer appeared in 1909. It is impossible that he was unfamiliar with his nephew's work, which uses the same ethnographic sources on Australia to see them, in a well-known dispute of the time, as evidence of an early basic form of prayer. Yet Durkheim's chapter makes no reference to this dispute or how the material on his so-called mimetic rite can instead be interpreted – in fact was interpreted, by his own nephew – as prayer. What is going on?

In a way there is a very good reason why his chapter never mentions prayer. Having already attacked Robertson Smith, his next big target is Frazer. But it is above all in a whole bigger wrangle over magic and religion and which of them gave birth to science.

Just as a common line on magic and its practices saw a basic type as 'mimetic' magic, imitating a hoped-for event, Durkheim's line on religion and its practices sees a basic type as the 'mimetic' rite, imitating a hoped-for event. He first goes through the Australian ethnography to collect miscellaneous examples of acts that imitate the totemic species and its renewal, and to glue these together as an entire type of rite (501–8). Next, this helps to show that in the beginning there is religion (508–18). Finally, it also helps with showing how it is the religious idea of a force that gave birth to the category of causality, and so how it wasn't magic but religion that gave birth to science (518–28). Yet given his desire to look for and find a 'mimetic rite' that opens the door to this Aladdin's cave of revelations, it might be wondered if there is something magical about his discovery itself and if it is not so much a piece of science as a piece of science fiction.

It is true enough that Spencer and Gillen have numerous references to an evocation of the totemic species and its renewal through imitative imagery. But they also have numerous references to its evocation in a variety of other ways. These include abstract symbolic designs, with 'no attempt at any resemblance to the objects which they are supposed to indicate' (Spencer and Gillen 1899: 180). Moreover, at most stages of most ceremonies, a key element impossible to reduce to imitation is the rhythmic chanting, in a special sacred language, of poetic, stylized, formulaic verses. Indeed, the language can be so special and so sacred that, even if there is an idea of its general symbolic significance, its actual formulas are unintelligible: 'the words have no meaning known to the natives, and have been handed down from the Alcheringa' (Spencer and Gillen 1904: 286). In any case, something they report again and again is a chant's repetition again and again (e.g., Spencer and Gillen 1899: 173, 181, 196; 1904: 234, 235, 310). Durkheim could hardly have failed to notice this, yet fails to pick out and distinguish a 'repetitive rite'. So why pick out and distinguish a 'mimetic rite'? It is only a particular ingredient of a whole complex mode of ritual action that evokes a hoped-for event. And in an analysis of the Australian material undoubtedly known to Durkheim, it is a mode of action clearly and cogently identified as prayer (Mauss [1909] 2003: 88–96).

It seems all the more to do with prayer, in going on to explore Durkheim's explanation of the rite's rationale. Among his account's usual quota of misleading references, he selects a comment from one of his sources that 'the ceremonies represent animals' as if this is obviously just about imitative representation (1912a: 504) and at the same time omits how the same source says they involve 'prayers' that the animals 'may again appear in the same numbers' (Schulze 1891: 243). Similarly, he omits the report in his main ethnographic source that the rites involve 'invitations' to the totemic species to reproduce and multiply (Spencer and Gillen 1899: 172, 184, 186). In general, in order to play up a symbolism that is imitative, he plays down or ignores all the evidence of a symbolism that is not. Yet his argument about the power of concrete imitative imagery can be extended to the power of other forms of concrete symbolic action.

He sees the rite as a way the faithful express a key collective concern, on which 'they concentrate the forces of their attention and of their will'. But the way to concentrate these forces of attention is through concrete collective symbolic action, 'to say the thing wished to come about, to call for it, to evoke it' (1912a: 512). So isn't this like prayer? It might be insisted that prayer must always include a petition or request. Yet Durkheim still does not mention prayer even in mentioning how the faithful meet together 'to request from their gods an outcome that is their fervent wish' (513). In any case, and like other rites, prayer can come in different forms, whether in a call to god, imitative imagery, mantra-like chants repeated again and again, or indeed a special sacred language that people no longer understand. Underlying these different modes of action, the same rationale is how the very expression of key collective concerns helps to create and keep up hope, in turn a way not only to express but to generate and sustain solidarity itself.

In sum, the work's early version had concluded with the claim, in discussing sacrifice: 'the profound moral efficacy of the rite determines belief in its physical efficacy, which is illusory' (1907f: 122). The final version repeats this claim, though now in discussing what sounds like prayer: 'the moral efficacy of the rite, which is real, has driven belief in its physical efficacy, which is imaginary' (1912a: 513). But it is now also in turning to a rite of special sociological significance, in that it comes without mysterious ideas about its 'physical' efficacy and is instead understood by the faithful themselves in essentially social and moral terms.

Sacred Drama

A ceremony described in the work's main source is introduced as 'representing' episodes in the career of mythic ancestors, and also as 'commemorative' in its recall of their history (Spencer and Gillen 1904: 297). So perhaps this gave birth to the 'representative or commemorative' rite announced in *The Elemental Forms*. Moreover, just as Spencer and Gillen talk of the ceremony's 'performances', Durkheim also talks of them in these terms, indeed as 'dramas' and 'dramatic representations' (1912a: 531, 534, 537, 543). Accordingly, to capture concern with such performances and what they represent and commemorate, they can be discussed as sacred drama and its enactment of sacred myth.

Sacred drama is of particular interest to Durkheim. He sees it as helping to clinch his whole theory of religion as a social and moral affair. As just mentioned, he identifies it as a core religious rite that the faithful themselves understand in social and moral terms, with little or no involvement of belief in its physical efficacy. This is why it has 'exceptional importance' (541). And for good measure, he adds examples of other, minor rituals that 'obviously cannot have physical effects of any sort' (542).

The situation is more complex with his cases of sacred drama itself. He concedes they might come with at least some element of belief in physical efficacy, while doing his best to minimize its role. So a way to proceed is just to concentrate on the case in which the actual available ethnographic evidence appears to come down more or less convincingly on his side. Spencer and Gillen describe it in detail and at length in a chapter on a set of ceremonies among the Warramunga, and to do with the great ancestral snake Wollunqua.

As they at once report on these ceremonies, 'there is no idea associated with them of securing the increase of the Wollunqua' (Spencer and Gillen 1904: 227). They then suggest the real underlying purpose is to control and placate the snake. But they emphasize it is their own interpretation: 'the natives have no very definite idea in regard to this, merely saying that it pleases the Wollunqua when they are performed and displeases him when they are not' (227–28). In other words, they have no hard evidence of belief in the rite as anything other than as actually described in detail in their own account – namely, a way to enact, recall and bring to life a sacred history. So the way is in turn open to Durkheim to insist:

> Here, then, is a whole set of ceremonies that are solely intended to arouse certain ideas and sentiments, to connect the present with the past, the individual with the collectivity. In fact, not only can they serve no other ends, but the faithful themselves ask nothing more from them. (1912a: 541)

Yet it is one thing to bring out the faithful's own understanding of the rite in social and moral terms. It is another to see this as clinching his theory of religion as a social and moral affair.

The great religious rites of sacrifice, prayer and sacred drama are rites of communion both with one another and with 'god'. Accordingly there is more at stake than belief in either 'physical' or 'moral' efficacy. It is belief in the very reality of the force – personal or impersonal – that is 'god'. The rites can involve any of various ways to mobilize this power in human lives, to help with any of various spiritual, moral, social or physical concerns. But if sacrifice and prayer camouflage from the faithful the cult's real underlying Durkheimian function, it isn't merely thanks to a physical efficacy he sees as imaginary. It is above all due to the 'god' he sees as imaginary. Nor can sacred drama make clear this function. It is also shot through with belief in 'god'.

It is still special. It is a form of communion with one another and with 'god' that is less a way to do something about particular practical concerns, more a way to think about, explore, express, construct and affirm a whole human–divine relationship. That is, it is less a practical and more an existential rite, thanks to the essence of sacred drama as the enactment of sacred myth.

Enacting myth is a way to think about the human situation, not simply a way to tell a story. As Durkheim puts this, myth is 'an ethic and a cosmology at the same time as a history'. It is how a society represents 'man and the world' (536). And the point of a collective dramatic performance is not just to bring myth to life. It is to keep it alive. Continuing new collective enactments 'revitalize the most essential elements of the collective consciousness' and 'impress it more deeply on minds' (536–37). But also, there is clearly more to myth's enactment as drama than symbolism, and he is at last ready to focus his attention on art.

True, it is in a relatively brief as well as a somewhat general and abstract account, more or less leaving out all the material on art in Spencer and Gillen. Thus each of their studies concludes with a long discussion of the nature and role of art in Australian culture (Spencer and Gillen 1899: 567–635; 1904: 696–743). At the same time it is an interest that runs through their ethnography as a whole, as, for example, in discussing the art and symbolism of the designs of the churingas, of bodily decorations and of ground drawings, but also and not least in discussing the rite to do with the ancestral snake Wollunqua. Indeed, it is thanks to the skill, scale and power of the art and symbolism mobilized in its performance that they pick it out as special. 'It is not possible to convey in words anything like an adequate idea of this series of ceremonies, which were the most impressive of any that we witnessed' (Spencer and Gillen 1904: 247).

Still, they did a good enough job for one of the scenes they describe to turn up as Durkheim's star case of effervescence in the centrepiece of *The Elemental Forms*. It is also the overall rite that becomes his star case of sacred drama, picked out as of 'exceptional importance'. But it is thanks to its importance for his own social theory. It isn't, in contrast with Spencer and Gillen, in any particular interest in the art and aesthetic achievements of Australian peoples themselves. It is almost as if this champion of science felt compelled to say at least something about art, in an effort to round off his social theory as a whole.

Art – The Joker in *The Elemental Forms?*

While religion gave birth to science, it also gave birth to art (1912a: 544). Thus art is not a mere external ornament of the cult but is rooted in the sacred itself, and 'there is a poetry inherent in all religion' (546). In general, then, these ideas are bound up with Durkheim's concern with the sacred as a vast elemental force. In one of its forms, it generated science and concepts of causality. In another, it generated art and 'free combinations of thought and action' (545).

However, a particular key to his story of art is the idea of a free creative *surplus*, and a particular example helps to bring out what is at stake:

> A recipe for error, in setting out to understand the rites, is to believe in having to assign each action an exact aim and definite rationale. Some have no purpose ... There are scenes of jumping, whirling, dancing, shouting, singing, without it always being possible to give a meaning to this agitation. (545)

This involves what we might discuss as *pure aesthetics*, to do with what he himself calls 'pure' art (546). It is about the creation and enjoyment of art for its own sake, in energies that sweep far beyond symbolism and the use of art merely as a vehicle of social, sacred meanings. Yet he insists there is always some sort of underlying meaning, if not in each and every action, at least in what is created as a whole. So we might discuss this symbolic, message-bearing function of art as *practical aesthetics*. In effect, then, his account entails a total aesthetics in which – although in different ways in different cases – there is always a combination of practical aesthetic concern with meaning and pure aesthetic interest in the art itself.

To take an example, how might this apply to his brief reference to poetry? A bottom line is that it is impossible to render poetry as prose, precisely because it is not a mere matter of meaning. On the one hand, it mobilizes pure aesthetic elements such as rhythm, rhyme, repetition and sheer enjoyment in the sounds of words and patterns of words. Yet on the other, these also entail a practical aesthetic empowerment of the meanings of the words themselves, a practical aesthetic power they would lose if translated into prose. An extreme case in point, which Durkheim could have used instead of just a brief abstract reference to 'poetry', involves Spencer and Gillen's report of verses chanted in a special sacred language, which is untranslatable since unintelligible.

To return to his own actual argument, it is concerned with distinguishing two basic types of event during special collective times. One is the hard-core religious rite such as sacred drama. The other is more secular, such as the corroboree, the carnival, the festival or the game. But it is to make the point that they always combine, in their different ways, the same elements. However laden with practical aesthetic meaning and symbolism, the religious rite also comes with a pure aesthetic enjoyment in the art itself. Even in all the pure aesthetic playfulness of the game, it still secretes a practical aesthetic seriousness of underlying social, sacred meanings.

So far, so good – except that he also lays false trails. Art is 'superfluous' and a 'luxury', yet at the same time it is a 'necessity' (545–46). Or, let us just say, it is a *superfluous necessity*. This is straightforward enough, in that he is talking about it as a 'luxury' compared with the grind of everyday toil, yet which is precisely why it is a 'necessity', as a form of escape from the utilitarian routine business of work. Indeed, it fits in with his whole concern with times of effervescence, revitalizing us with fresh energies to see us through times of the profane, which he especially links with work. The problems with his account lie elsewhere.

He distinguishes the *vie sérieuse* – 'life in earnest' – from a 'life less tense, easier and freer' (546–47). But in the process he can seem just to identify art with a bit of light relief and entertainment. To the extent that he creates such an impression, it is nonsense. The *vie sérieuse* includes the sacred, complete with the poetry inherent in religion, while it is impossible to equate art's elements with overall types of event, as if there is no earnestness in the game or no play in sacred drama. As he concludes his account of art, the difference between such events is 'the different proportion in which these two elements are combined' (548).

In sum, there are various ways in which art can come out as the joker in *The Elemental Forms.* The least important is Durkheim's own apparent attempt to cast art as mere playfulness, and light relief from life in earnest. An almost ironic way is how, despite his dedication to science, he lays the basis of an original theory of art – as a total aesthetics in which symbolism is always fused with enjoyment in the art itself, in which the paradigmatic case of art is a combination of art forms in a participatory collective event such as sacred drama, and in which the fundamental criterion of aesthetics is creative energy and power. But the key way is how art can switch what the message of *The Elemental Forms* is all about, just as the joker in a card game can switch which suit trumps. This is again to do with the poetry inherent in religion and the paradoxical idea of art as a superfluous necessity.

How is art a surplus and why is it necessary?

> Although, as we have shown, religious thought is altogether different from a system of fictions, the realities to which it corresponds can nonetheless acquire religious expression only if the imagination transfigures them ... Because the intellectual forces that go into making it are intense and tumultuous, the task that just consists in expressing the real with the help of appropriate symbols is not enough to occupy them. A surplus remains generally available. (544–45)

On one reading, an elemental form of social life is its inevitable transfiguration, not just thanks to the sacred as 'god' but the sacred as poetry. On another, the underlying belief is the possibility of development towards a more enlightened and transparent world, with self-understanding through a bare, naked, rationally 'adequate' language. Taking both readings together, it is a critical, revelatory moment in the work's ambivalence and switching around between different sociologies. So perhaps, in the end, the fundamental question raised by *The Elemental Forms* is how to choose between its two sociologies.

CHAPTER 7

Transparence or Transfiguration?

This chapter attempts a number of things. One is to review the relation, in Durkheim's reimagination of Australia, between theory and 'facts'. Another is to rethink the issue of transparence and transfiguration. A final concern is with his own interpretation of his work, in launching and publicizing *The Elemental Forms*.

Durkheim's Australia

Durkheim claimed to be doing science. So it is absurd to discuss his theory without even asking about its relation with the 'facts'. A test case is his use of Spencer and Gillen. What then becomes clear is that it is also absurd just to assert he imposed a pre-existing theory on the 'facts', with no need to visit Australia or anywhere else.

Durkheim had no choice other than to attempt a response to Spencer and Gillen's Australia. It had a sensational impact in London, and undermined the old theory he had just set out in his new flagship journal of social science. Indeed, there is a gap of well over five years between their first ethnography in 1899 and the first draft of *The Elemental Forms* in 1906/1907. This was a time of experimentation, when he tried out a variety of responses involving a variety of projects, which could have given birth to three major works. Thus it is when he began to come up with ideas crucial to his creation of *The Elemental Forms*. But what counts – as at last happens in the first known version – is the coming together of a set of ideas in a whole new theoretical system. And it is abundantly evident that the need to revisit Spencer and Gillen's Australia was a major driving force and stimulus in the creation of this new theoretical system.

It is also clear that *The Elemental Forms* is not an entirely faithful and transparent representation of their Australia. In terms of detail, it is necessary to check all of Durkheim's mass of impressive-looking references to their material. What then emerges is that many are accurate enough, that many are just mistaken, that many are in various ways misleading, and that many things are left out despite their relevance to his argument. In terms of the bigger picture, it is necessary to evaluate his active, systematic search through the material to put together a whole theory. What then emerges is a story of his creative reimagination of Spencer and Gillen's Australia – or, in a word, its transfiguration.

Or rather, it is part of the story. For example, it was a development within his own theory that generated the 'contradiction' of a spread of sacredness leaving nothing profane. Or again, he owed a lot to Marett and Mauss on mana, in his search for a similarly elemental force in Australia. And in a way he never gave up on an old core view, so clearly expressed in Frazer's old manual, that in the beginning there is the socioreligious world of the totemic clan. Yet in order to preserve he transforms this view, above all through the idea not just of two worlds but two times of the sacred and profane. In sum, his creative retheorization of things involves both a transfiguration of Spencer and Gillen's Australia and a transfiguration of the old Durkheimian Australia.

Transfiguration and Transparence

It is not necessarily a criticism, but a way of understanding the nature of Durkheim's achievement, to describe *The Elemental Forms* as a work of transfiguration. True, he might not have appreciated this description. He consistently used the term to refer to a fog of mystification that obscures the real, far from making it transparent. Yet in his own time and milieu, the paradigmatic case of transfiguration had a very different meaning. Transfiguration *is* transparence.

This is the Transfiguration of Our Lord Jesus Christ, an event periodically re-enacted in sacred drama. In brief, Jesus was known to the world only in his outward profane form as a man, until – in an intense, stunning effervescence of light – his transfiguration made transparent his inner divine nature as the Son of God and as Christ. A general point, then, is how the drama is a case of the sacred as poetry, which unites a religious and an aesthetic version of transfiguration as transparence. More particularly, it combines the idea of 'bringing to light' with the oppositions 'outward' / 'inner' and 'the surface' / 'the underlying'. So there is an essential similarity with Durkheim's sociology as a new rationalism, digging around in an external surface world of 'facts' to bring to light an inner underlying logic at work in them.

Indeed, it could be argued it is a scientific version of transfiguration as transparence. The conceptual realm of theory transfigures actual social 'facts' in the effort to explain them and make transparent an underlying logic and reality. Thus it is possible to identify at least three different versions – the religious, the aesthetic and the scientific – of the same basic scheme in which transfiguration *is* transparence. Even so, can there be much doubt about which of these versions Durkheim would privilege as the way to enlightenment?

He divides his conclusion into four parts. In the first, he emphasizes the aspect of religion as action, and as the rites and practices of a cult. In the second, he emphasizes its aspect as belief, and as a whole way of thinking about the world. In the third and fourth sections, he expands on his theme of a religious birth of conceptual thought, but to emphasize it as a religious birth of science and enlightenment. Thus an unfolding overall argument is about religion as its own gravedigger. It sows the seeds of its own replacement by science across the entire domain of understanding, or, as he says, 'in everything that concerns the cognitive and intellectual functions' (1912a: 613).

Perhaps this can still leave an important place for religion as an affair of action, rather than ideas. Yet as he had also just said: 'A society can neither create nor recreate itself without, in the same action, creating an ideal' (603).

This is the context in which he goes on to discuss if his science of religion kills off religion itself:

> It is said that science denies religion in principle. But religion exists; it is a system of given facts; in a word, it is a reality. How could science deny a reality? Moreover, insofar as religion is action, insofar as it is a way to make men live, science cannot take its place, since if it expresses life, it does not create it … There is thus only a conflict on a limited front. (614)

An initial comment is that it is difficult to see how there can only be a 'limited' conflict, when his science of religion repeatedly claims that 'god' does not exist and is nothing other than a symbolic representation of society. There is a little more room for compatibility with belief in God's actuality if he had been content to claim that 'god', whatever else, is an important way to think about the social world. But the main comment is that he himself goes on to concede the impossibility of any radical divorce between religion as action and as belief. On the contrary, the faithful need to justify and make sense of religious action through a whole system of ideas, or, as he says, a 'theory' (615).

Thus he proceeds to recycle an old long-running argument. On the one hand, the demands of practical life are too urgent to wait around for the slow, laborious, forever incomplete business that is science, and rely on essentially speculative theories going beyond science itself. On the other, science continues to advance. Accordingly, with this advance, religion is a system of action and belief that must increasingly submit to the control and critique of science – a 'rival power' that becomes ever more extensive and effective, 'without it being possible to assign a limit to its future influence' (616).

In effect, Durkheim concludes *The Elemental Forms* with a restatement of his vision of science as part of a developing civic enlightenment. In general, as in the lectures on moral education, science is part of a story in which thought is liberator of the will. More specifically, as in the chapter on the soul, it is part of a developing emancipation thanks to thinking and acting through concepts. In other words, as in the essay on primitive classification, the style of thought that is privileged as the way to enlightenment isn't the poetry inherent in religion. It is the prosaic, abstract, analytical and conceptual style of thought exemplified by science.

So it is important to recall, at this point, how another long-running theme of his social science is a critique of modern malaise, in a campaign for reform through a new network of intermediate groups. The road to a society of persons does not just depend on appropriately enlightened styles of thought. It depends on the institution of effective public forums of debate and reasoning. These forums might come with an element of ritual. But they aren't mere ceremonies of solidarity. They entail a network of assemblies to address and tackle social issues through an effective process of collective argument. In turn, however, these could be seen as part of a much wider network of different kinds of assemblies, in a whole wider process of collective debate and reflection on the social world. A paradigmatic case is the debate and reflection – not just the ritual, and not just the entertainment – at the heart of drama.

Durkheim is original, not least, in laying the basis of a theory of total aesthetics. A limitation, however, is that in his approach to art he remains in the grip of deep-rooted philosophical prejudices, involving an intellectualism that privileges abstract conceptual thought and that consigns thinking symbolically to a lower form of life. Art, in his book, entails a mystificatory surplus that sweeps far beyond any language 'appropriate' to an earnest interest in understanding the world. Into the bargain, its exercise of the 'intellectual functions' is very much through the senses. Rather than a far-reaching reliance on concepts, it exploits the 'material intermediary' of the symbol. Its essential style of discourse isn't thin-textured and abstract, but thick-textured and concrete. Yet isn't this precisely why it can be a powerful and illuminating way to think about the human situation?

In sum, Durkheim's study of elemental forms of sacred and social life comes with arguments that point in different directions – to a sociology of developing enlightenment, and to a sociology of inevitable mystification. A basic source of the ambivalence is the argument about energies that create and constitute the social world, and in the process transfigure it. But what is also involved is the assumption that transfiguration spells mystification. So a way to open things up is to drop the assumption, and explore forms of transfiguration as transparence. This is also to drop the dogma of conceptual reason as the one and only path to enlightenment. Instead, it is about a sort of epistemological pluralism as a way to rescue ideals of enlightenment – specifically, ideals of civic enlightenment – but together with his entire vision of sociology as science.

He insists on the development of social science through specialization, which to some extent entails a secret knowledge limited to experts. However, opting for a theory of an inevitable mystification of social worlds seals its fate as an esoteric elitist knowledge, impossible to spread in a surrounding world itself. It sabotages his commitment to sociology as a form of enquiry with an indispensable role in public life – through critique, through reflection on ideals, and in a contribution to processes of collective argument that make for a society with self-understanding. But it is precisely as a *contribution* to a whole wider public culture, a culture that accords science respect yet that is necessarily diverse and that develops in a variety of ways. These include an indispensable role for art, on its own terms and in its own right, and as a reflection on the human situation through the particular and concrete. It isn't a substitute for thinking and theorizing through abstract conceptual discourse. But neither is it just an underprivileged, poor relation.

Durkheim on Durkheim

The Elemental Forms attracted a vast number of reviews, not least from a spread of Catholic, Protestant and secular writers, whose spread of responses has been analysed by W.S.F. Pickering (2008).[1] A current project is for the first time to collect together and make available for future research all the different yet widely scattered reviews. But to return to Durkheim himself, it is instructive to consider his own presentation of his work. In almost all of the known occasions in which he commented on it, he emphasized its concern with religion's 'dynamogenic' character. What does this mean, and how is it significant?

The 'Dynamogenic'
A history of the 'dynamogenic' has been sketched out elsewhere (Watts Miller 2005). In brief, the term got going in medicine in the early 1880s, to describe what increased an individual's energies – not least, sexual energies – as against what lowered and inhibited them. It then

spread to a range of domains, including avant garde art, to become a buzzword of the time. One of many who picked up on and repeated it was William James, notably in *The Varieties of Religious Experience*, published in 1902 and translated into French in 1906. In a recently redis-covered review of this translation, it is in turn repeated by Durkheim ([1907g(2)] 2010: 16). A minor mystery is that it never appears in *The Elemental Forms* itself, but is taken up in a sort of effervescence of the dynamogenic in his launch and publicization of his new book. What, though, is the significance of his use of the term?

A basic point is that it emphasizes the work's concern, not with the early and elementary, but the continuing and elemental. For ex-ample, it is the 'dynamogenic influence of religion that explains its permanence' (1913b: 27). Or again, the work is about a 'dynamogenic influence that religions have in all times exercised over men' ([1914a] 2005: 43). Put another way, the dynamogenic is a core element of re-ligion, indeed, *the* core element. As in a talk given in 1914: 'the char-acteristic of religion is the dynamogenic influence it exercises over consciousnesses. To explain religion is above all, therefore, to explain this influence' (1919: 309).

Another basic point is that the dynamogenic is clearly to do with the extraordinary increase and uplift of energies in his book's scenes of ef-fervescence. But how exactly does it picture these? The review he signed jointly with his nephew concludes with this characterization of religion:

> Although it has a speculative role to play, its principal function is dynamogenic. It gives the individual forces that allow him to transcend himself, to raise himself above his nature and to master it. Yet the only moral forces that are superior to those available to the individual, as such, are those coming from individuals in association. Here is why religious forces are, and can be, none other than collective forces. (Durkheim and Mauss 1913: 98)

This could at first read as if religion is less to do with belief, and above all an affair of action. But it straightaway homes in on 'moral forces', and it is hard to see how these can be disentangled from belief. In fact, in another discussion – the essay on the dualism of human nature – the 'moral forces' at 'the source of the dynamogenic influence that reli-gions have in all times exercised' are straightaway linked with 'ideals', and 'the great religious, moral and intellectual conceptions that soci-eties draw from their heart during periods of creative effervescence' ([1914a] 2005: 43).

In sum, an ambivalence at the heart of *The Elemental Forms* is the relation between action and belief, and remains an ambivalence at the heart of its launch as an affair of the dynamogenic. It is possible to select passages relating to either one side of things or to the other. But there are diminishing returns in trying to extract from the text a choice that is never finally made, and in arguing over whether it prioritizes 'action' or prioritizes 'belief'. At the same time it is a diversion from Durkheim's whole preoccupation with prioritizing the social. The dynamogenic energies through which religion lifts the individual up to another realm of action and belief are above all, in his book, collective energies.

The 'Dualism of Human Nature' Revisited

Durkheim was invited to give a paper on his new work to a meeting of philosophers in 1913. He chose as his theme the duality of human nature, while weaving into it the idea of the dynamogenic. The barrage of criticism he encountered may have been one of the factors prompting him to make another attempt to explain his views in his subsequent essay on the dualism. In particular, the meeting ended with a long heated exchange between himself and Jules Lachelier, and this clearly made something of an impression. For example, it was included in a philosophy textbook (Baruzi et al. 1926: 103–11), and picked out as a 'memorable dialogue' in the preface to a work by one of those who had been present, Léon Brunschvicg (1939: 1). But it could also be described as a dialogue of the deaf, with Lachelier insisting that religion is at core an individual affair, Durkheim insisting that it is collective, and ignoring his opponent in just repeating his own arguments in his subsequent essay. Yet do these arguments stand up?

They are rooted in the account of the soul in *The Elemental Forms.* But apart from issues to do with this account's imaginative use of Spencer and Gillen's ethnography, its attempt to correlate embodiedness and individuality is merely incoherent in terms of Durkheim's own social theory. Embodiedness is a key source of collective life, thanks to the physical and mental highs of effervescence, as well as the material intermediary of the symbol. Society is a key source of individuation, thanks to the division of labour. Nor is it a foursquare defence of the dualism to suggest it should not be taken literally, but is a metaphorical expression of underlying concerns with particular, particularly worrying forms of individualism. So is it possible to dig around in the texts to come up with a more satisfactory interpretation of the dualism and what is at stake in it?

A new annotated critical edition of the essay has been produced by Giovanni Paoletti (2009), and an English translation of his introduction is forthcoming (2012b). His analysis stands out from other commentaries. It is clear, concise, sane and scholarly, in its grasp of the material, negotiation of Durkheim's arguments and handling of his use of the terms 'dualism' / 'duality'. In brief, the analysis is that in the end it is not an essentialist dualism, to do with two 'beings', 'things' or 'substances'. It is a relational duality, concerned with the interlinkage of two aspects of a whole. What is above all at stake, then, can be summarized as a relational duality of 'immanent transcendence' (Paoletti 2009: 28).

Given Durkheim's insistence on a power that can exist only if internal and immanent within individuals but that necessarily goes beyond them to assume a collective, impersonal, transcendent form, it seems to me entirely correct to emphasize this as a relational duality of immanent *transcendence*. That is, it incorporates the aspect of the immanent/particular/individual, but prioritizes the aspect of the transcendent/impersonal/collective. Or this is his aim. Yet does he succeed in it?

A key to everything is the argument in *The Elemental Forms*, repeated in the essay, about a simultaneous process in which the formation of collective forces is bound up with their internalization in the individual consciousness, where it is inevitable that they are themselves individualized (1912a: 356, 382; [1914a] 2005: 43). In the work itself, this is part of an attack on a rival theory of evolution, and in an explicit insistence that the collective is *not* prior to the individual in time. Perhaps it is often nowadays a forgotten argument. It nonetheless has far-reaching implications for understanding Durkheim's commitment to the importance of the collective, and campaign against theories overemphasizing the individual.

He himself was determined to keep on looking for ways to assert the priority of the collective. This could be called the aggressive option, and helped to generate criticism of his worship of 'Society'. But an alternative is to make do with a relational duality of immanence/transcendence, which privileges neither one aspect nor the other and instead just insists on their interlinkage in a same overall process. This is still to insist on the importance of the collective, in a criticism of mere worship of the 'Individual'.

The issue can be brought out through Durkheim's long-running interest in the neo-Kantian problematic of the relation between autonomy and authority in a modern ethic of the person. One of the ways the essay tries to assert the priority of the collective is through assertion of the sheer imperativeness and authority of collective moral forces and ideals. 'When these ideals move our will, we feel led, driven, carried along by unusual energies, which clearly do not come from us but impose themselves on us'. Even in their internalization and individualization within the personality, they retain their transcendent character: 'they command, they inspire in us respect, we do not feel on a level-footing with them' ([1914a] 2005: 42–43).

Yet does this answer Lachelier? His argument is also on neo-Kantian lines. But it is to assert the priority of the individual, thanks to the modern aspiration to autonomy and how it has nowadays emerged as the only legitimate basis of imperativeness and authority. A religious person himself, he is concerned with the transcendence of a spiritual ideal and truth. But he insists it must be the individual's own truth, discovered in an inner quest and struggle for autonomy against all external pressures, not least social pressures and 'religion' as mere social conformism and convention.

Durkheim objected to Lachelier's disdain for ordinary traditional faith and its 'gods of the crossroads' (1913b: 58). But this is an inadequate response from someone committed to an enlightenment that reveals these gods as mystifications, and fails to address what is at stake in a modern ethic of the person, which he himself had rallied round and championed. It is one thing to bring out how it is not simply about the individual, but entails a common collective element. It is another matter to try to prioritize this collective element. It may be true enough that each individual's autonomy is bound up with a collective ideal of the force of reason and with a collective ethic of everyone's status as a person. Yet a basic point of this ideal and ethic is to invest authority in actual individual personalities as centres of autonomous thought and action. Indeed, it is what helps to make it a lost battle to try to counter prioritization of the individual with prioritization of the collective. Instead of an abstract mystificatory privileging of either of these elements, the more mundane but more illuminating task is to understand ways they interlink and interact in modern aspirations – surfacing, among other places, in Kant's kingdom of ends – to a republic, society or commonwealth of persons.

In sum, Durkheim's launch of *The Elemental Forms* raised major issues over how to apply its story of Australia to the contemporary world. In a way, it landed him back in concerns at the heart of his thesis on the division of labour, his essay on a cult of the person, and his lectures on moral education, ethics and autonomy. Even so, a book that had taken him so long had now been completed. Yet he wasn't someone to rest on his laurels. Durkheim was a workaholic, and was no doubt thinking of something to do next. But what?

CHAPTER 8

Towards a New Great Work

Just after publication of *The Elemental Forms* and no doubt in part in recognition of its achievement, Durkheim was appointed in 1913 to the first official chair of sociology in France.[1] In what might be seen as capturing an ambivalence central to the book, he used the ritual of an inaugural lecture to set out his vision of sociology as science. He then went on to develop this in the course that followed, but through a critique of the philosophical claims of pragmatism, which had especially got going in the United States in the 1890s and had attracted attention in France in the 1900s. So two points might be made about a next great work. To apply his vision of sociology, it could not just be in a critique of general philosophical approaches such as pragmatism. He needed an actual field to investigate, and what he eventually decided on was an investigation – or, given all his earlier interest in it, a reinvestigation – of moral life. A way, then, to read texts after *The Elemental Forms* is how they prepare the ground for a new great work on *Ethics*. A way to conclude is how the manuscript of this throws light on his intellectual career as a whole.

For Sociology and Against Pragmatism

It was suggested to Durkheim, during the meeting of philosophers to discuss *The Elemental Forms*, that his approach had similarities with pragmatism. He replied: 'Between me and pragmatism there is the gulf that separates rationalism from mystical empiricism. No confusion is possible' (1913b: 39). This recalls his long-running commitment to a new rationalism, in an attack on empiricists who enlighten nothing and 'spread mystery everywhere' (1897f: 78). It is also consistent with his particular hostility to James's *Varieties of Religious Experience*, expressed in two recently rediscovered texts, a confidential report of 1906 (in Durkheim 2003) as well as a review of the following year ([1907g(2)] 2010). But before turning to his lectures on sociology and pragmatism, something should be said about their background, as well as about the status of the text itself.

The French Reception of Pragmatism

It is understandable enough to identify pragmatism as a general philosophical approach that above all developed in the United States, and to try to say what it is about by going to its different expressions in various original sources, such as the work of James, Dewey and Peirce. But what happened in its export to a sister republic? This raises issues that are clearly brought out by Romain Pudal (2005), in an article based on research for his thesis (2007), which includes a systematic investigation of the French literature on pragmatism between the 1890s and 1920s.

The new 'ism' had an undeniable success, in the sense that it was the subject of an extensive and indeed vast coverage. True, the comment ranged all the way from the enthusiastic to the implacably hostile. But a basic point is that there was little attempt, in any of this, to engage with the actual original sources. Instead, the Americans were overwhelmingly used as ammunition-fodder in internal political, philosophical and ideological battles going on in the Third Republic itself. In effect, 'pragmatism' became a symbol. And it was overwhelmingly a symbol of an anti-intellectualist movement with a whole mixed bag of supporters – such as Gustave Le Bon, Georges Sorel and Henri Bergson, to name a few – but united in opposition to a republican establishment, and in war cries for action against theory, psychology against logic, instinct and faith against reason.

It is this context that helps to explain Durkheim's own attitude to 'pragmatism'. It was impossible to ignore what it had come to represent in his own environment. His course was as much as anything directed against Bergson & Co., rather than James & Co., in an effort to defend the rational values of science as well as the political values of the Republic (Pudal 2005: 94–95). At the same time his lectures stand out from the rest of the literature, as a serious attempt to go to the sources – especially James but also Dewey, whom he admired – and to engage with and examine their actual arguments (96–97). It remains the case that he came out against what he saw as their general position, in a campaign for sociology and against pragmatism.

The Status of the Text

A version of the course was eventually published in 1955 as *Pragmatism and Sociology*, and the status of the text is explained in a preface by the editor, Armand Cuvillier.[2] Durkheim's manuscript had been lost, but it had been possible to obtain two sets of student lecture notes. As editor, then, he wrote these up into a readable text, while in the process fashioning them into a single text. He feels confident that at least some of the passages 'echo' Durkheim's very words. But, he emphasizes, his text is only a '*reconstitution*' of the original course (Cuvillier 1955: 8–9).

Although Durkheim's manuscript remains lost, a third set of student lecture notes has been discovered by Stéphane Baciocchi. It is hoped to edit and publish these in collaboration with Jean-Louis Fabiani. It will then be possible to assess their significance for existing interpretations of the course. Indeed, the new notes include a lecture that is missing from the old edition, and that because of its importance is being made immediately available in *Durkheimian Studies* (see Baciocchi 2012). It is the inaugural lecture of 1913, setting out Durkheim's vision of sociology and leading on to his course on pragmatism. Meanwhile, in approaching the overall course as reconstructed by Cuvillier, a strategy is to dig beyond the surface of the text and detailed arguments that might or might not have been made by Durkheim, in search of basic underlying themes and problematics.

Pure and Practical Understanding

The first half of the text analyses pragmatist works themselves (1955: lectures 1–12). The second half criticizes them in a development of a sociological approach (lectures 13–20). This gets going with a whole wave of arguments (lectures 13–17). In digging around in these, they are concerned with a problematic of pure and practical understanding – which links with a Kantian problematic of pure and practical reason, turning up later on.

The text emphasizes truth as an affair of '*pure speculation and theoretical thought*', while pragmatists reduce things to a practical interest in which '*the true is the useful*' (1955: 137, 151). At the same time it is in a campaign on two fronts, against classic rationalism and against empiricism. The text sides with the pragmatists against classic rationalism, only to criticize their mystical empiricist attack on any rationalism whatever. In effect, then, a task of sociology is to defend an ideal of truth as an affair of pure rather than merely practical understanding. But it is in giving up on a fixed, static, classic philosophical world. Instead, and even or especially in seeing sociohistorical variations between ways of thinking, it is to see theoretical thought as an active creative sociohistorical force and part of 'life'. This term is repeated again and again, no doubt to block its monopolization by Bergson & Co. But 'life' also helps with a basic insistence on the interrelation of thought and action, and with a rejection of any dogma that either 'in the beginning, there is thought' or 'in the beginning, there is action'. In an echo of the philosophical history of Kant (as well as of Hegel and Marx), Cuvillier's reconstructed text instead maintains that, for sociology, 'truth, reason, morality are results of a becoming that includes the entire unfolding of human history' (143).

This is all quite recognizably in line with Durkheim's long-running views. The same can be said about all the arguments against a reduction of truth to the useful. For example, belief in the true can't just be changed with a wand of the will to fit in with whatever seems convenient. 'Truth' can be inconvenient, indeed painful, and acts on consciousnesses with an impersonal, necessitating, obligatory authority (153–58). Or again, it is to emphasize how myth constructs a worldview and cosmology, in a drive towards pure rather than merely practical understanding and in a sheer interest in speculative, theoretical, conceptual thought (159–62). But the text simplifies the picture in *The Elemental Forms*, where myth is simultaneously a cosmology, a history *and* an ethic. In other words, myth is simultaneously an affair of pure *and* practical understanding.

Of course, this in no way means that Durkheim reduces the ethical to the advantageous. But it raises two issues that underlie what is going on in the lectures, and that require digging around to bring out. One is the whole interrelation of pure and practical understanding. The other is the nature of practical understanding itself, and how it entails concerns that do not reduce to usefulness. Thus the lectures emphasize the role of concepts, but they do not distinguish and bring out the importance of ideals. These can include religious, moral, political or indeed economic ideals, but in any case some basic points might be made. The ideal does not reduce to the useful. Ideals are bound up with concepts, theories and worldviews, just as they are bound up with practical commitment and action. The ideal, then, suggests an intertwining of pure and practical reason in webs of belief. What happens, though, in Cuvillier's reconstructed text itself?

Science, Myth, Art and Enlightenment

A whole further wave of arguments begins in lecture 17, with a critique of pragmatism as an approach that is not only utilitarian but individualistic. Pragmatists say 'it is *we* who make the real', except that '*we*, here, is the individual', and they fail to appreciate the importance of a collective dimension. No doubt, in the end, 'it is thought that creates the real'. But it necessarily involves the power of collective energies, and a dynamic in which 'the key role of collective representations is to "make" the higher reality that is society itself' (173–74).

However, the next lecture immediately qualifies this sweeping claim. It is to deny a freedom to create with a wand of the will – even a collective will – any reality whatever. Such an insistence on limits is a continuing Durkheimian theme. It can be traced back all the way to his Latin thesis, with its campaign against a megalomaniac belief in a power to do anything, and with its characterization of social institutions and mentalities as 'things' that resist change at will, even a collective will. But in the journey to *The Elemental Forms*, it is increasingly embedded in a problematic of collective representations that are somehow simultaneously *expressive, creative* and *transfigurative.* Thus the lectures repeat the by now familiar yet still slippery argument that religious beliefs aren't mere illusion (177). Even in all its repetition it remains slippery, since these beliefs *express* an underlying reality yet *create* this reality.

So why, in expressing what they bring into being, can they not create any social reality whatever? A characteristic Durkheimian theme is about limits in the form of a social world's 'conditions of existence'. Yet given that these are not merely crude external factors, but are 'conditions of existence' internally constituted within a social world's own logic and dynamic, what might they be? Again in line with his long-running views, it can be seen in the end as an affair of situatedness within a particular social time and place, but also within a creative evolution and 'becoming that includes the entire unfolding of human history'.

Yet is it still in a vision of a move towards transparence and enlightenment? Or is it in a sociology entailing that a condition of any social world's existence is its more or less inevitable transfiguration and mystification? This issue is central to *The Elemental Forms* and reappears in the lectures in a contrast between two types of truth, the scientific and the mythological. It comes in a discussion of the nature and role of sociology as science, but complete with a standard argument that its task is complex and it has a long uphill road to go. Meanwhile, 'society cannot wait for its problems to be solved scientifically', which leads on to the conclusion:

> There is, and there will always be, a place in social life for a form of truth that will perhaps have a highly secular expression, but that will nonetheless have a mythological and religious foundation. For a long time to come there will be two tendencies in every society: a tendency towards objective scientific truth and a tendency towards subjectively perceived truth, to mythological truth. It is, as well, one of the great obstacles that hold up the progress of sociology. (184)

Far from resolving any ambivalence in *The Elemental Forms*, this is open to quite different interpretations. On the one hand, it registers a belief in a continuing, more or less inevitable power of mythology. On the other, it also registers a refusal to give up and a commitment to a campaign, against the obstacles, for the rationalism of a scientifically informed enlightenment. This is why it is important to look in Durkheim's work for a sociology of sociology, involving a story of its own conditions of existence, development and role in public life.

A distinction made throughout his career is to do with the relation between science and 'art', in the sense of a practical application of theoretical ideas to action. In the sociological landscape of *The Division of La-*

bour, it is especially concerned with the development of a scientific study of moral life and how it can help not only with understanding a modern crisis but with guiding the practical work of reform. This is a work of society itself, so that a key point about the campaign for new intermediate groups is the failure of existing institutions, in a need to develop forums of effective, informed, collective argument. Put another way, it is about the development of an effective democratic public culture.

On the surface, there might seem little or nothing on this in the lectures. But its relevance is that it breaks up the text's simplistic picture of science versus mythology. Instead, it brings in an essential intermediary in the form of an enlightened 'art' and public culture of argument that isn't science, yet that is ready to listen to science – a public culture that gives science an authority it lacks in an environment dominated by mythology.

Indeed, in terms of *The Division of Labour*'s worldview, the picture in Cuvillier's reconstructed text can seem hopelessly incoherent. It appears to imagine a world of consensus, in seeing all sorts of modern mythological truths that 'are accepted without question' and that 'express a unanimous conception' (175, 184). At the same time it appears to imagine a world in which only science runs on a division of labour, different perspectives and respect for one another's views in a culture of public argument (185–87). That is, it appears to be about a miraculous virgin birth of science, as if on its own, rather than as part of a whole wider development, away from unquestioned 'unanimous conceptions' and towards a culture of argument across all of modern social life.

This is why it is important to notice the discussion that in effect links with the Kantian problematic of pure and practical reason, complete with the remark, 'we remain in the Kantian tradition' (202). It is concerned with the role of science in society, complete with science's critique of ordinary lay beliefs. And it is to ask how this critique has any authority, in the sense that it is not only made in a feeling of obligation to speak out, but is listened to with respect. The answer, more or less, is that in the end theoretical understanding depends on practical understanding. It is part of collective life itself. Its authority has its source in 'the authority that opinion gives science' (202), an argument already made in *The Elemental Forms* itself (1912a: 298, 626).

The development of science is bound up with development of a wider public culture in which reason, argument and critique are accorded respect, and indeed are not merely tolerated but take on the character of an obligation. Or in Durkheim's own words, in his essay on a modern cult of the person, its first 'dogma' is the autonomy of reason while its first 'rite' is free enquiry and examination. This was during the crisis of the Dreyfus Affair. Now – up against the use of pragmatism as a new rallying-point of anti-rationalist, anti-republican forces – the lectures can be seen as a continuation of the defence of enlightenment, a defence not just of science but of an ideal of truth as part of a whole wider *ethic*, in a public culture of enquiry, debate and informed collective argument.

The War

The lectures ended only a few months before the outbreak of war, in August 1914. A question, as far as Durkheim is concerned, is how his writings on this traumatic upheaval try to understand it through his sociology. These writings include a long-lost article, 'The Politics of the Future' (1917c), rediscovered and commented on by Jennifer Mergy (2009). She explains in scrupulous detail its background, as well as its sources in his sociology. However, a general point is that it draws overwhelmingly on the sociology associated with *The Division of Labour*. Indeed, there is no mention of the sacred and little trace of *The Elemental Forms*. Moreover, the war-writings have been re-examined as a whole by Irène Eulriet. A general overall picture established by her analysis is again how works such as *The Division of Labour* are a far more important reference than *The Elemental Forms*. Ideas such as solidarity have a key role in his approach, which just 'is not rooted in notions of "sacrifice", "ritual", "sacred" and "profane"' (Eulriet 2010: 71).

Of course, although Durkheim's war-writings have considerable interest, they are not major publications. It is also true that during this time there are still occasional remarks about the sacred. Even so, it seems clear from the evidence that at this stage of his whole intellectual development there is a significant change of direction, away from *The Elemental Forms* and its preoccupation with the sacred. In his plan of a new great work, at the height of his academic success, there is a return to *The Division of Labour*'s core secular rationalist concerns.

Ethics, Sociology and the Study of Moral Life

A manuscript was published in 1920, with a note by Mauss explaining that Durkheim had worked on it more or less throughout 1917 until his death, and that it had been discovered in a file containing a mass of other, related material. This material is important in helping to give an idea of the nature and scope of the project. It would have brought together the many lectures given by Durkheim to do with ethics, but writing up and refashioning them in the more authoritative form of a book. The manuscript itself explains how it is to introduce a project consisting of two volumes, and outlines both the aim and the plan of the first volume, while also indicating the aim of the second. In brief, the aim of the first volume includes a systematic survey and critique of approaches to ethics, but in the process to bring out the issues and methods at stake in developing a science and sociology of moral life. The aim of the second volume is to get on with actual investigations, but in the process to link the science and 'art' of morals in an overall ethics.

Sociology and the Study of Moral Life

Durkheim's project once again involves him in a campaign on two fronts, against an empiricism that refuses to dig around in things for an underlying reality and rationale, but also against a rationalism that believes in access to basic principles without having to dig around in 'facts' at all. His introduction attacks this to defend the very need for research, and the hard slog of 'laborious, methodical, scientific investigation' (1920: 321). Yet to get on with a science that first of all seeks to identify and describe 'moral facts', there is a need to pick out what is 'moral' from what is not. But how?

Durkheim's introduction to a new great work on ethics runs into the same problem as the original introduction to his first great work on the division of labour, and sees the same solution. It is to look for outward visible 'signs' of the moral (321, 324, 325, 331). But he could hardly be clearer that this is merely an initial stage. His manuscript repeats the same message twice over. These preliminary indicators are replaced with others, as investigation develops and gets on with the increasingly complex task of analysis, classification and explanation, in an effort to understand 'the innermost characteristics' of an underlying moral reality (321, n.2, 325).

Where, then, is all this heading as a conception of sociological enquiry and knowledge? Perhaps it might have been to emphasize that from the start empirical 'signs' are bound up with stories of their meaning, that as investigation develops these are replaced with increasingly more sophisticated webs of observation–interpretation, and that in the end it is about a creative interaction – indeed, a creative fusion – of empirical detective work and theoretical reason. Whether or not Durkheim himself would have put things this way, the essential point is that his social science is non-foundationalist. Certainly, it is in a search for an underlying reality that can be brought out and made intelligible. But there is no access to this, except through enquiry that continuously interweaves the empirical and theoretical in developing webs of argument.

In the case of his webs of argument in search of the moral, it involves looking for signs of this in what has 'authority', commands 'respect', is 'obligatory' and imposes itself as an 'imperative' (315, 316, 322). But in linking obligatoriness with rules, it also brings in ideals. Indeed, 'every morality has its ideal', 'embedded in the institutions, traditions and precepts that usually govern conduct' (316). Against empiricism, an essential task is to dig around in these facts for an underlying ideal. Against rationalism, it is impossible to access this through hasty generalizations: 'it is a whole world that has to be explored' (329).

What world? Although each morality varies according to its time and place, it is in the various 'currents' that divide opinion and 'crisscross societies'. Although every morality has its ideal, 'there are always others in process of formation'. The ideal isn't fixed, but 'lives, evolves, continues to change'. There is stagnation 'when traditional morality goes unquestioned', and only periods of conflict are 'morally inventive' (316). Thus although Durkheim himself keeps switching between talk of 'moral facts' and 'moral life', he can be seen as above all concerned with exploration of the world of moral life. As in the lectures on pragmatism, but also and in line with his long-running views, this is a world embedded in the 'facts' of a particular time and place yet simultaneously situated within a 'becoming' that includes the entire unfolding of human history.

It is also how it involves him in a search for elemental forms of moral life – basic and continuing throughout history, even or especially in their variation, change and development throughout history. An essential job of enquiry is to dig around for an idea of 'the moral' embedded in all cultures, and his project's first volume is to begin by asking about the 'signs' that distinguish it from 'other social facts' (331). This is also to ask about the elements of 'individual and collective consciousness' in the moral, in going on to the issue of its 'place in collective life as a whole' (331). However, it is clear that his aim is to link the collective with the impersonal and obligatory as basic elemental forms of the moral. In turn, this is not just an affair of rules, but is very much about ideals. So along with a negative element of obligatoriness, is there not also a more positive element of attachment? It can be detected in the material in his manuscript's file. This includes lectures on the 'unity of two elements: the ideal and duty', and on 'attachment to society', but along with lectures on Kant and the issue of autonomy (314). All these themes are reported in student notes taken in 1908/1909 by Cuvillier (see Durkheim 1975, vol.2: 302–6). The same themes can be found in the lectures on moral education, to do with two elemental forms of all moral life, discipline and attachment, but also with the development of a third essential element in modern aspirations to autonomy.

Ethics

A major objective of Durkheim's investigation of moral life is to link science and 'art' in an overall ethics. Or, in his own words, he is concerned with 'how, from these scientific, theoretical studies, it is possible to deduce practical conclusions' (1920: 331). Thus he writes:

> There is no science worthy of the name that is not ultimately a way to art: otherwise, it would be a mere game, an intellectual amusement, erudition pure and simple. (317)

However, there is a difference as against applied sciences that draw on knowledge as a means to a chosen end. In contrast, ethics lays down ends themselves (319). He then goes on to discuss how only a study of moral life can be the basis of ethics and its construction of the moral ideal, but to emphasize it is not an affair of hasty generalizations and instead 'it is a whole world that has to be explored' (327–29). It is nonetheless in an argument that sees investigation of this world as a way to practical conclusions about the moral ideal of our own, modern times. How, and what is the ideal he might have had in mind?

His introduction's main and indeed only key to how – promising further detail later on – is that it is in an effort to dig around for and bring out 'morality in itself'. This is grounded within and immanent in actual life. But it rises above and transcends 'the deformations it undergoes in ordinary everyday practice', where it is reduced to the level of the 'average' and 'mediocre', and where it is always subject to 'mixed motives', 'reservation' and 'compromise'. Instead, it is morality in its 'purity' and 'impersonality', or, in a word, 'the ideal morality' (330).

This conception of a science of moral life, digging around in search of an underlying logic and reality in the form of an ideal, is not a mere passing thought. In general, it fits in with his whole conception of social science as a simultaneously empirical and rationalist undertaking. More specifically, it fits in with what is known about the material in his manuscript's file. Thus there is documentation of an identical message in two different sets of student lecture notes from around 1909. One is again the set of notes taken by Cuvillier (see Durkheim 1975, vol.2: 297–98). The other was taken by Georges Davy (ibid.: 14–16).[3] As Davy's notes report Durkheim, 'the morality studied by sociology is ideal', a morality that 'men violate all the time', yet that is a collective work of their 'entire group', and an ideal that constitutes 'a set of real forces'. Accordingly, in going from a sociology of moral life to ethics, '*We do not pass from fact to ideal.* We are already in the presence of pure ideals. We go from the ideal to the ideal'.

An objection is that it is still about an impossible passage from 'is' to 'ought'. It is about getting from what is in fact an ideal to what ought to be the ideal. But the objection repeats what Durkheim describes, in his main thesis on the division of labour, as a dogma of mystics through the ages, putting human reason to sleep.

His companion thesis, on social science and enlightenment, helps to launch his lifelong campaign against a megalomania that sees no limit to the power to will, create and attach ourselves to any social world whatever. On the contrary, and as, for example, in a later discussion, 'it is impossible to will a morality other than that implicit in the nature of society' (1906b: 54). The let-out clause is that it is within the situated-ness of living developing aspirations, in a 'becoming' that includes the entire unfolding of human history. There is plenty of room, in these conditions of time and place, for ethics as an 'art' and culture of public argument to negotiate the details of what a science of moral life identifies as the modern world's core ideal.

Indeed, it is in leaving all this room for 'art' that his project for a science could seem an immense labour to little effect. Yet it was once again bound to involve him in a sociological defence of the ideal of a commonwealth of persons. On the one hand, then, there is the business of coming up with evidence of this in his continuing commitment to a web of ideals interlinking solidarity, justice, autonomy and enlightenment. On the other, there is the business of saying why it matters, in the conflicts over the legacy of the Revolution, the battles for a Third Republic, the crisis of the Dreyfus Affair, the trauma of the Great War. But it is also in all the unfolding history, after his death in 1917, of power struggles to defend and achieve something like the ideal of a democratic republic and moral commonwealth.

Conclusion

Durkheim's project of a new great work is a key to any story of his overall intellectual development. The reason is how it undertakes to do a number of interrelated things. One is to construct a whole new programmatic statement of his idea of the nature and role of sociology as science. Another is to bring out what this means in practice, in investigations of a field of central importance, the world of moral life. At the same time it is to link these scientific, theoretical studies with ethics and endorsement of an ideal.

So it is possible to wonder how, if it had been completed, it would have impacted on the career of 'Durkheim after Durkheim' and the history, after his death, of all the many ways in which he has been both used and abused as a 'founding father of sociology'. Investigations of this history, in different countries, at different periods and on different issues, would easily fill many volumes by a host of researchers. To give a few examples, glimpses of his career in Australia can be found in Len Hiatt's *Arguments about Aborigines* (1996), a fascinating guide to his career in Poland, from his lifetime to the present day, is provided in an article by Antoni Sułek (2009) that focuses on *Suicide*, and the story of his reception in Brazil is one of the themes of a collection edited by, among others, Alexandre Massella and Raquel Weiss (2009). Or skipping over how he has fared, for instance, in China, England, Italy, Germany, Mexico, Russia, Turkey and the United States, there is a vast literature on 'Durkheim after Durkheim' in France. A recent general overall sketch is offered by Jacques Coenen-Huther (2010: 127–53), while various particular aspects, issues and episodes are examined, for example, by Isabelle Gouarné (2011), Jean-Christophe Marcel (2001a, 2001b), Derek Robbins (2011), Phillipe Steiner (2005) and in a special edition of the *Année sociologique* edited by Massimo Borlandi (2012). Indeed, merely to compile a reasonably comprehensive bibliography of research and research sources relevant to investigations of Durkheim's post-mortal global career could in itself easily fill a volume.

Rather than even attempting such investigations, I leave them to others who, in a division of labour, are far better qualified for the task. Instead, and partly to claim a bit more freedom to speak in my own voice, I explore some of the questions nowadays raised by Durkheim's work in the following essays on modern times. But in drawing to a close what has been an effort to focus on an understanding of his work itself, it seemed right to end with what is in effect his own last testament.

PART 2
ESSAYS ON MODERN TIMES

Power Struggles

It is careless talk to say that Durkheim was uninterested in power. A discourse of power is already evident in *The Division of Labour*, but is above all mobilized in *The Elemental Forms*. Indeed, a way to begin a Durkheimian exploration of modern times is through power struggles to do with energies of the sacred and forces of the profane.[1] In turn, this involves a distinction between periods of historically momentous change and periods of the more normal and routine. Thus it is possible to see the English, American and French Revolutions as foundational modern events, helping to give birth to an age of democracy through a transfer of sovereignty from king to people. But the French Revolution has a particular significance, to do with a transfer of sacrality.

A Modern 'Transfer of Sacrality'

The idea of a 'transfer of sacrality' is a key theme of a work that launched the career of Mona Ozouf, one of France's leading contemporary historians. This is her study of *The Revolutionary Festival* (1976), somewhat misleadingly translated into English as *Festivals and the French Revolution* (1988). It is not just an individualistic account of particular ceremonial occasions. Her concern is with the conception of the festival as a whole, and the unity and diversity of ceremonies in an overall ritual-symbolic system. Her argument is that the creation of 'the revolutionary festival' was essential to destroy the power of the old regime. This required a transfer, not merely of sovereignty, but sacrality.

The argument generates any number of questions. But it is possible to highlight two main issues. Who is the transfer of sacrality to, and can it just be a bright, festive, non-violent affair?

Power in the old regime involved a mystique of the sacred attaching both to the impersonal, socioreligious, collectively defined office of 'king' and to the actual flesh and blood individual who, by the grace of 'god', was destined to inherit the role. Given this pre-existing ambivalence – as well as a corresponding ambivalence in Durkheimian theory itself – who or what is a modern transfer of sacrality a transfer to? How can it only be from society as represented by a sacred 'king' to society as represented by a sacred 'people', 'nation', '*patrie*' or whatever? Does it not also entail a sacralization of the individuals who, in the history of universal Declarations of Rights, share the same status of a person?

A disturbing question, however, is if a sacralization of everyone as a person depends on a bloodbath. This is bound up with the issue of the nature of the 'transfer of sacrality' itself. The issue is partly to do with the long-running dispute over whether or not there really was such a thing as a revolutionary 'religion'. But it is especially to do with the dynamics of revolutionary 'effervescence'. Thus it is worth recalling the note in *Suicide* on the Revolution:

> In these times of internal struggles and collective enthusiasm, the individual personality had lost some of its value. The interests of country or of party took precedence over everything. The large number of executions arose, no doubt, from the same cause. Killing others came as easily as killing oneself. (1897a: 247, n.1)

In *The Elemental Forms*, it is again the intensity of the collective passions stirred up in times of effervescence that helps to explain acts of extremism and 'the many scenes, sublime or savage, of the French Revolution':

> Under the influence of the general exaltation, the most mediocre or the most inoffensive bourgeois can be seen transformed, whether into hero or butcher. (1912a: 301)

Yet although Durkheim acknowledges destructive forces of the sacred, his overwhelming emphasis is on social rebirth and renewal through 'creative' effervescence. This comes out in a revealing example.

A work by the young, up-and-coming left-wing historian Albert Mathiez, *The Origins of the Revolutionary Cults* (1904), used Durkheim's essay on the definition of religious phenomena to maintain that the cults constituted a religion. He was then promptly accused of failing to realize they were merely 'religious phenomena without being religions', in a review by Mauss (1905: 297). But it is mistaken to assume that Mauss was always the voice of Durkheim. On the contrary, *The Elemental Forms* approvingly quotes Mathiez to insist that the revolutionary cults constituted a genuine religion, complete with 'its own dogma, symbols, altars and festivals' (1912a: 306). What is revealing, then, is how Durkheim just leaves out one of his source's main arguments. The Revolution involved a religion thanks to its intolerance, fanaticism and 'destructive rage against the symbols of other cults' (Mathiez 1904: 12).

In sum, it is all very well to emphasize creative effervescence. But how can a 'transfer of sacrality' sweep away a whole vast symbolism entrenching the power and mystique of the old regime, unless it unleashes more demonic energies?

Iconoclasm

Mathiez gives a long list of examples of the iconoclastic destruction of old regime symbols – paintings, statues, monuments, churches, relics, tombs and even the corpses of the royal dead. He then cuts his list short by remarking that the examples are so numerous they could fill a large volume (Mathiez 1904: 38). In any case, it is only part of the story.

Thus there were proposals to pull down the entire palace of Versailles and erase it from memory. But these remained proposals, which were never adopted. What is often forgotten is that the revolutionaries themselves invented the term 'vandalism'. This was in a campaign to defend something else they helped to invent, the idea of a 'cultural heritage'. A key problem in the launch of a new era of enlightenment was how to destroy objects as old regime symbols, while conserving them as cultural artefacts. At least part of the solution was seen as the development of the institution of 'the museum' – whether as a use for former churches and palaces, or as a place to display objects now reframed as works of art or as cultural artefacts with intrinsic historical interest as well as educational value.

In turn, however, this generated continuing controversy over the actual nature of 'the museum' – for instance, as itself a form of cultural vandalism, removing and ransacking objects from their original setting, or fragmenting into bits and pieces what had been created as a whole. It could still be argued that Durkheim was right to emphasize ideals. The underlying problem in all the issues bound up with iconoclasm is what a new era of enlightenment is about.

It is pious just to accuse the revolutionaries of intolerance. Emancipation from the old regime required intolerance, and attack on the very idea of a homogeneous Catholic France. Yet was it in a misguided attempt to replace one fiction of a monolithic social-sacred order with another? It isn't much of a revolution to come up with a new version of the old myth of one 'king' and one 'faith'. A radical transfer of sacrality is to some sort of simultaneously communitarian and liberal-pluralist ideal of a commonwealth of persons. But the trouble is not simply to figure out, in philosophical conversations, what it might look like. It is if great social movements towards this liberal ideal arise from power struggles that devalue the individual personality.

Iconocide

Louis XVI, the anointed king of France, was transformed by the events of 1789 into Louis XVI, the constitutional king of the French. He did not last long in this office. In 1792, a newly elected Convention declared a republic, and decided to put the king on trial as well as to try him itself. He was found guilty of treason, sentenced to death, and executed, in a public ceremony, on 21 January 1793. Yet was his real 'crime' not so much anything he had done, but who he was and what he symbolized? The physical destruction of the individual who embodied the old order could be seen as an extreme type of iconoclasm. It calls for a name of its own, and could be termed 'iconocide'.

The establishment of a republic entailed an effort to break with the mystique of kingship, in outraged talk of 'superstition', 'idolatry' and the 'magic talisman of royalty'. Even so, what has the trial and execution of a symbol got to do with enlightenment?

The best short guide to the period as a whole is William Doyle's *The French Revolution* (2001), while the best detailed study of the episode in question remains David Jordan's *The King's Trial* (1979). To simplify, however, the conflicts within as well as outside the new Convention over what to do about the king can be seen as involving four basic options:

1. Lenient politics: against both the trial and the execution;
2. Lenient justice: for the trial but against the execution;
3. Harsh justice: for both the trial and the execution;
4. Harsh politics: against the trial but for the execution.

What, roughly, was the Convention's make-up, and how did it split on these lines?

It had around 750 members. About 200 might be identified as 'Girondins', and about 100 might be identified as 'Jacobins'. Neither of these groupings constituted an organized modern party. Both of them depended on persuasion to win support, issue by issue, from the ranks of the assorted 450 or so delegates nicknamed 'the Marsh'.

A small minority of the Convention's members consistently spoke out and voted for a form of lenient politics. This is also the position defended by Ferenc Fehér (1987), who represents the view that the whole episode of the king's trial and execution marked a catastrophic setback for modern liberal democratic ideals, and instead signposted the route to totalitarianism and terror.

The vast majority of delegates were divided between lenient and harsh justice. Some of those voting for the trial but against the execution expressed a principled objection to all capital punishment. It was a way to perpetuate the old order's barbarism, rather than to inaugurate a new era of enlightenment. The Girondins manoeuvred to delay any decision about a trial, but in the end joined in with the majority that voted to proceed with it, while most of those who then voted for the death sentence did so with reluctance and with various reservations. This is also the position defended by Michael Walzer (1974), who supports the trial but with reservations about the execution, and who represents the view that the whole episode was an essential part of killing off kingship in the long bumpy ride to democracy.

Last but not least, the Jacobins campaigned for harsh politics, denouncing the trial and demanding the king's immediate execution. But in going over the different options, the way to start is with the trial itself.

The Trial

The main explicit public argument for the trial was that it would be a show trial, in the sense of helping to symbolize and enact the ideals of a new era of justice. It would demystify kingship by teaching equality before the law, and that no one, not even a king, was above it. A hitch was that Louis, in his office as constitutional head of the state, had been expressly granted immunity from legal prosecution. A lot of time was spent on how to get round this. Yet Louis himself made no attempt to hide behind his immunity. So in a way it was a non-issue.

More worrying, perhaps, were the tendencies to brush aside due process. These are gone over in an obviously pro-royalist account by the Girault de Coursacs (1982). But they are also documented, in detail, by Jordan. The Convention, in charging Louis with treason and trying him itself, acted as judge, jury and prosecution rolled into one. It excluded witnesses on the accused's behalf. It excluded the accused himself from its hearings, except for two appearances. It interrogated Louis, at his first appearance, on a long list of allegations and supporting material, but refused to let him or his lawyers read these beforehand. Indeed, it did not let him have the help of lawyers at all, until prior to his second and final appearance. Even then, only a few days were allowed for the preparation of his defence, and relevant material was still withheld. There was no provision for the accused to appeal against either the verdict or the sentence, and he was executed the day after the final vote to condemn him to death.

But the most fundamental concern to do with due process is that ideals of justice require a presumption of innocence until proved guilty. Accordingly, a root and branch objection is that any such presumption had become politically impossible. The trial would be a show trial, in the sense that it would be a mockery.

It was a version of this objection that was pressed by the Jacobins, as in a memorable speech – reprinted, symbolically enough, during the reign of the last French king – by Robespierre (1840: 5–18). There could only be one verdict, the verdict already given by the people. 'Louis was deposed for his crimes', and 'Louis cannot therefore be judged; he has already been judged'. To put the king on trial is to put the revolution on trial with him. If Louis can really still be the subject of a trial, he can be presumed innocent and he can be acquitted. But this is politically unthinkable. If the king is acquitted, 'where is the revolution?'

The point that the trial was bound to be a sham can be made in a different way. The standard of due process and evidence required in a court of law is one thing. The kind of inference and evidence relied on in the arena of political action is another. It had helped to justify the overthrow of the monarchy on the belief that Louis could not be trusted, that he had never really accepted the new constitution, and that he was working to restore the old regime. This rapidly became a self-confirming belief, in the sense that it no longer mattered what the king did or did not do. Any action was automatically suspect, and seen as yet further proof of his guilt. For example, he was accused of deliberately setting out to weaken the army, in a plot to bring about France's defeat and so his own return to power. But if, as the Girault de Coursacs maintain, he did his best to strengthen the army, he could as readily have been accused of doing so to use it against the people, again in a plot to return to power. In fact, at one time he had been accused of precisely that.

An especially symbolic case concerns the affair of the hidden cabinet, which was discovered, stuffed full with private and confidential documents, in the royal apartments. In a study of the episode by Andrew Freeman (1989), it emerges that little detailed use was made of the documents to convict the king. Instead, they were exploited as general propaganda. They were presented as an obviously incriminating mass of evidence and telling sign of the true, secret character of Louis – a man who, behind the public façade, was as duplicitous as any king.

What this rhetoric helps to reveal is the character of the trial itself. Louis was trapped by his old identity, unable to say or do anything that could dispel belief about his real underlying motives, given who he had been and what he personified. But the same forces ensnared the entire legal process in a contradiction – between an enlightened philosophical idealism to do with the trial *as* a symbol, and a murkier social logic to do with the trial *of* a symbol.

The trial *as* a symbol was intended to exemplify a new era of justice. Yet it went far beyond an attempt to bring to book the crimes of a constitutional official. It entailed the trial *of* a symbol, in its settling of accounts with 'Louis the Last' and relic of a long line of dead sacred kings. Thus part of the story is that some of the accusations were about his role during the old regime itself. But it misses the point to make too much of this, and how it violated basic principles of justice in turning the clock back to criminalize what had not been crimes at the time. On the one hand, the main accusations were about his role as new constitutional head of state. On the other, these were inextricably bound up with who he had been and what he continued to symbolize. In the end, it was believed that Louis the constitutional official must be guilty of treason, thanks to his inescapable historical collective identity as Louis the mystical sacred king.

So why did the Convention decide to go ahead with a legal process that the Jacobins attacked as a sham and the Girondins wanted to avoid? The calls and overwhelming vote for a trial came from the mass assorted ranks of 'the Marsh'. This is a reason for seeing a form of legal process as more or less inevitable. It is also a reason for looking for an explanation, not in mere political manoeuvrings, but in wider collective mentalities. Accordingly, it might be suggested that the pressures for a trial combined three different although interrelated currents of belief in justice.

The most fundamental could be seen as a demand for a public narrative that recorded, commemorated and vindicated the events leading to a republic. Putting the revolution on trial with the king is precisely the point of this process. It is because the drama has already been enacted that it needs to be re-enacted.

At the same time it could be seen as linking with a demand to put Louis through a public ritual that confronted him with his past, involved him in a confession and expiation, and made clear to him and everyone his change of status.

But it remains contradictory thanks to a perhaps inevitable call for a trial as the paradigmatic form of legal process. Instead, it was essentially a form of sacred drama, in the way it combined theatre, narrative, symbolism and a rite of passage to enact the nation's transition to a republic and the king's transition to man and citizen.

The Execution

An implication of the idea of a modern cult of the person is that Louis's execution was a double iconocide. He was tried, convicted and guillotined as a symbol of an old 'magical' institution. But this also meant killing a symbol of humanity and an embodiment of the sacred status he now shared with everyone. If the new era of enlightenment needed to demystify a king, how could it be by the solemn collective decapitation of a man?

Fehér, while accepting the king's guilt but in opposing both the trial and the execution, envisages a solution in which Louis 'retires, derided and humiliated, to the humble private life of a fully employed citizen' (1987: 104). Yet why see it as a step down? A member of the Convention, also looking for an alternative way to make an example of the king, emphasized 'the more impressive spectacle' of Louis 'returning with his family to the class of citizens, the only one nature sanctions' (speech of 1792, J-M. Rouzet 1898–99: 423). In a more famous intervention, Tom Paine – author of *The Rights of Man*, hero of the American Revolution and a deputy to the Convention – pleaded with it to exile Louis and his family to France's sister republic across the Atlantic, again to take up the life of a citizen. Even so, were those against the execution an insignificant minority? Was the killing of the king an inevitable part of killing off kingship itself?

On the issue of the verdict, the Convention came up with a practically unanimous expression of Louis's guilt – 99 per cent – with a few 'diverse declarations' and with no one voting for an acquittal. On the issue of the execution, in contrast, there was uncertainty and confusion. The following discussion is based on the different voting figures in the long, punctilious analysis by Jordan.

A start can be made by counting 288 votes for some form of imprisonment or exile, 361 votes for the execution, and 72 variously ambiguous votes for the death sentence, subjecting it to variously envisaged terms of postponement. Thanks to these votes, but also because there was then a further ballot on the possibility of a reprieve, there are three main ways of calculating how the Convention split between 'regicides' supporting the execution and 'antiregicides' opposing it (see table 2.1.1).

As the different calculations indicate, the expression of regicide sentiment was in the range of 50 to 55 per cent. The expression of antiregicide sentiment was in the range of 50 to 45 per cent. This hardly suggests the inevitability of the execution thanks to a vast overwhelming tide of feeling. If the voting patterns on the execution suggest the inevitability of anything, it is the inevitability of a conflict between equally powerful forces and currents of sentiment.

Jordan, with reason, emphasizes the key role of the final vote on a reprieve, and its 'unambiguous' majority to go ahead with the execution. But he then goes on to talk of an 'inexorable logic' (1979: 199), in which the Convention finally made the only decision that was possible – killing Louis, in the interests of the Revolution. Again, however, a humble empirical question is what kind of 'inexorable logic' swept away only 55 per cent of those voting, while leaving as many as 45 per cent

Table 2.1.1 The Convention's Votes on the King's Execution

	First Pattern[1]	Second Pattern[2]	Third Pattern[3]
For	361 = 50%	387 = 54%	380 = 55%
Against	360 = 50%	334 = 46%	310 = 45%
Majority	1	53	70

1. Counts all ambiguous votes as against the execution
2. Counts 26 ambiguous votes as for the execution, and 46 as against
3. The votes for execution rather than reprieve

SOURCE: based on the analysis in David Jordan, *The King's Trial* (1979: 239–48)

unstirred and unmoved. At the same time, of course, there is also the judgmental question of whether or not the 'logic' was correct, and if it is really in the democratic interest to execute symbols, to set aside basic rights and principles of due process, or to do whatever else is considered expedient and necessary.

It is important, in asking about all this, to return to the general nature of power struggles. To what extent are they conflicts between different energies of the sacred? To what extent are they an affair of forces of the profane? In the case of attempts to launch a new era, it is especially important to ask about power struggles involving the mystique of grandiose ideals but also the politics of compromise, humbug, wheeler-dealing, dirty hands and this-worldly realism.

Mystique and Politics

Durkheimian social science entails a search for some sort of underlying logic. But it is a logic with the built-in possibility of going in different directions and generating a variety of scenarios. A way to understand this is through the abstract nature of modern ideals, complete with their conflicting interpretations. Thus if the Revolution helped to launch a whole new discourse, it wasn't a discourse that came with an inexorable logic leading in a single direction – whether, as in one view, to a reign of democracy, or, in another, totalitarianism and terror. It came with the inexorable logic of a multitude of disputes within the revolutionary movement itself, in power struggles over the very conceptualizations of 'the nation', 'the people', 'liberty', 'equality', 'justice', 'the individual', 'the person', and how to put them together in a vision of a commonwealth.

This involves an explicitly idealistic concern with power struggles over grandiose hopes and aspirations. But it can link in a number of ways with interest in class struggles. An example is Durkheim's own account of a modern crisis. There is also the long history of variously left-wing accounts of the Revolution itself – as in the work of Mathiez, Jaurès, Lefebvre, Soboul and so on – and a brief yet illuminating guide to this history is provided by François Crouzet (1999).

Another link, however, is with conflicts centred round the issue of 'constitutional' and 'revolutionary' government. A key expression is in speeches given in 1793 and 1794 by Mathiez's hero, Robespierre (1840: 511–25, 539–67). His appeal to 'constitutional government' might be seen as invoking an essentially liberal ideal of a commonwealth. Yet while 'the object of constitutional government is to maintain the republic, that of revolutionary government is to inaugurate it'. Revolutionary government therefore requires extraordinary action, effort and energy, in a war not only against the republic's external enemies but against its 'enemies within'. In order to prepare the ground for a constitutional government of civic liberties and individual rights, it is necessary to subordinate them to the overriding collective interest of establishing the republic itself. 'To the good citizen, the revolutionary government owes the full protection of the nation, to the enemies of the people it owes only death.' If it is a 'despotism of liberty', it is in the cause of liberty. Although in normal times a people's republic runs on virtue, in revolutionary times it must run on 'virtue and terror'.

In a way, then, the whole argument comes wrapped in mystique. Its mobilization of republican ideals is a mobilization of the sacred, even or especially as an expression of demonic energies, in a vision of virtue through terror, and an imagery of purification through death and the scaffold.

It is nonetheless a mystique inextricably bound up with politics, and it is possible to try to identify some basic forms. One of these is the politics of dirty hands, in which high-minded ends justify ruthless means. At the same time it entails a politics of calculation, juggling ends and means to strike a balance between them. The enemies within included 'moderates', endangering the Revolution with agitations that things had gone too far. But they also included 'extremists', endangering the Revolution with agitations that things had not gone far enough. In turn, a crucial issue in such calculations is to do with a politics of the slippery slope. Is a supposedly transitional revolutionary arrangement an introduction to a more permanent 'dictatorship', postponing 'constitutional government' to a forever receding future, or dropping the idea completely? In any case, the business of separating out the sheep from the goats and 'good citizens' from 'enemies within' – hiding behind a 'mask' of patriotism – was part of a whole wider politics. This is the politics, not just of dirty hands, but dirty tricks. More or less everyone was caught up in it, accusing each other of plots, lies, slander, hypocrisy, double-dealing, sell-outs, opportunism, corruption. As summarized in a study by Geoffrey Cubitt (1999: 77), 'the language of conspiracy was a common currency', 'an idiom of mutual and general recrimination'.

So where does all this leave the picture of the Revolution as a foundational modern event? Any story of a new era of enlightenment and its transfer of sacrality is complicated, not just by the unleashing of demonic, murderous energies, but by the role of politics. Indeed, this is a source of the disagreements involving Mauss, Mathiez and Durkheim.[2] In effect, Mauss represented the views of an older, established republican historian, Alphonse Aulard, when he insisted that the revolutionary cults were so politicized they merely imitated religious phenomena and were not genuinely religious. It was this orthodoxy that was challenged by Mathiez, with the support of Durkheim. But it was someone else who, in an essay published shortly before *The Elemental Forms*, reshaped debate through a whole general view of the relation between 'mystique' and 'politics'.

Charles Péguy identified himself as a republican, a socialist and a Catholic. Yet in his disillusionment with politics, he was especially scathing about the politics of republicanism, socialism and the Church. He is difficult to categorize, except, perhaps, as a quintessential rebel and member of the awkward squad. His essay is about a modern world that lives off ideals it always betrays. 'Everything begins in mystique and ends in politics' (Péguy [1910] 1957: 31). If there is an inexorable logic of modern times, it is how every form of ideal – religious or secular, right-wing or left-wing – gives birth to a politics that, like a parasite, eats away at and destroys it. In its dependence on the mystique of Christianity, while taken up with worldly institutional interests and calculations, the Church is no exception to the rule but its 'most eminent' example (135). Yet if only because politics depends on what, in eating away at, it lives off, mystique never dies out. The germ of idealism survives, and Péguy ends with a vision of how, one day in an hour of crisis, an energy that now appears dormant will rise up again and '*they will see what we are still capable of doing for the Republic*' (254).

A Return of the Sacred?

One of many possible criticisms of Péguy's essay is that it is merely romantic to assume a foundational time of pure idealism. In the Revolution, mystique and politics were from the very beginning wedded together in a sort of unholy alliance. On the other hand, his essay brings out how it is nowadays merely simplistic to imagine a pure, genuine, non-politicized religion. This is also why it can be both romantic and simplistic to go on about a return of the sacred. Like Péguy's essay, *The Elemental Forms* worries that idealism has fallen on hard times in a modern moral mediocrity. And like the essay, it ends with a vision of how, one day, idealism will rise up again in a new moment of creative effervescence. Yet, a hundred years on, this can have the appearance of an illusion.

In a way it doesn't matter if the forces of the profane have more to do with the sordid commercialism that worried Durkheim, or the sordid politics that worried Péguy, or the sordid utilitarianism that worried them both. In a way it also doesn't matter to produce bits and pieces of evidence about a continuation of the sacred. What counts is the overall state of play, and if there are nowadays only fleeting incursions of the sacred in a world dominated by the profane. What counts, specifically, is if the vision of a commonwealth is merely utopian. On the one hand, it might not seem very Durkheimian to give up hope in this key ideal. On the other, it can also seem fundamental to his approach to acknowledge social reality. So is it time to accept that the forces he spent his whole career opposing have at last won out?

Hope

Durkheim's work is full of hope, but comes with only a few scattered remarks on the topic. It needs to be explored with the help of more systematic accounts, and a place to begin is with the account of hope developed by the French Catholic philosopher, Gabriel Marcel. This is especially in a work written during the occupation of France in the Second World War, and in an essay during the threat of a third. In one, he identifies the core of hope as 'I hope in thee for us' (Marcel 1944: 81). In the other, 'hope is perhaps nothing but an active struggle against despair' (Marcel 1951: 71).[1]

Elemental Forms of Hope

A familiar approach to hope identifies it with hope that something or other will come about. But Marcel is highly suspicious of hope merely in the form of hope-that. Instead, he is concerned with hope as a quality of character or virtue, anchored in a network of relations. Hope, as a virtue, is an active struggle to hold on, against the going to pieces of despair. At the same time it is embedded in the solidarity of a network of relations. It is a holding on through the solidarity of hope-for – where one's own hope is bound up with hope 'for us', and the self escapes isolation through forming, in attachments with others, what he calls 'the city' of the individual personality. But the foundation of this 'city' is the communion of hope-in – hope in a 'thee' at once inside and beyond each individual, an inner immanent force and a transformative, transcendent power.

Marcel leaves open the identity of this 'thee', in his search for a broad, inclusive, non-sectarian account. Yet it is clear that for him, personally, hope in 'thee' is hope in God. At the same time it is how, in the end, his 'city' and stronghold of hope incorporates two basic general forms of hope-that. One is a rock-bottom hope, that all is not lost in the struggles of this world. The other is a glorious hope, of salvation in the kingdom to come.

Even so, he remains especially concerned with the issue of this world's secular hopes-that, since he is especially worried about forms reducing them to whatever the individual desires. These work against and weaken hope, breaking down its stronghold to let in the going to pieces of despair. A fundamental reason is to do with his distinction between worlds of 'being' and 'having'. The hope he defends is anchored in a communitarian world of being and belonging. The hopes he criticizes are about an individualistic world of having and possessing. These are the hopes that are a fast track to despair, through their vulnerability to life's ups and downs. They are a constitutive part of the isolated atomistic self, and how it can easily go to pieces, since built round the individual's own particular wants and material interests and desires.

Accordingly, a fundamental theme shared with Durkheim is to do with the 'city' of the individual yet communitarian personality – the 'I' of hope 'for us' – but under siege from modern forces of alienation and anomie. At the same time it raises the question of the kinds of webs of links and relations that might nowadays act as an effective stronghold against these forces. Durkheim's campaign for new intermediate groups is precisely not about the present-day existence of a robust, resilient stronghold of hope. It is about a way ahead to this in the future, a way ahead obstructed by the very forces of alienation and anomie it is hoped to overcome. It can nonetheless be seen as a commitment to reform that shares, with Marcel, the language of effort and active struggle, and a sense of a dour, obdurate belief in the need to keep going.

A difference involves the whole issue of effervescence. For Marcel, writing during the German occupation, 'it is difficult to interpret as hope the idolatry shown by vast collectivities, bewitched by their leaders' (1944: 75). Moreover, he passes over all the explosive upsurges of hope in messianic and millenarian movements throughout the history of religion. In contrast, these fill the pages of the monumental study of hope by the Marxist philosopher Ernst Bloch (1959). They are also central to the work on the sociology of hope by Henri Desroche (1973). But Desroche, although drawing on *The Elemental Forms*, gives up on its search for change through a new time of effervescence. So it is important to recall the chequered career of effervescence in Durkheim's own thought, complete with criticism of a pathological manic agitation, and of upsurges of a naive enthusiasm soon followed by bitter disenchantment. A neo-Durkheimian sociology of hope, while including investigation of times of effervescence, can go to Durkheim himself to question the faith placed in them in *The Elemental Forms*.

In any case, there is a more fundamental difference. Marcel's bedrock of hope is hope in God. The Durkheimian candidate is to do with hope in society. At the theoretical core of *The Elemental Forms*, hope in society can be seen as hope in the energies of special times of the sacred that create, constitute and renew the world of social life itself. At the theoretical core of *The Division of Labour*, hope in society can be seen as hope in an unfolding dynamic that creates, constitutes and shapes the modern world, and in the process generates efforts and aspirations towards a commonwealth. Either way, however, there are formidable problems for a neo-Durkheimian sociology of hope, and the work of Desroche helps to bring these out.

It represents a general weariness, nowadays, with false dawns, not least with calls for change through a new time of revolutionary ferment and effervescence. Yet on the one hand, giving up on effervescence can risk giving up on the whole interconnected theory of society and the sacred in *The Elemental Forms* itself. On the other, it is also a collapse of the foundations of *The Division of Labour* that Desroche's work might be seen as helping to signal. It represents a general weariness, as well, with stories of progress and a march towards utopia.

In effect, these stories of a new Jerusalem to come secularized a religious glorious hope of salvation in the kingdom to come. But what is involved in converting a glorious hope into something more mundane? The very logic of the conversion entails a scaling down, from the full-blown to the semi-sacred. Indeed, it might not stop there. Perhaps a bright idealistic secularized hope can live off religious energies for a while. Then in one way or another, to do with forces of secularization itself, it fizzles out.

Idealistic Hope

The American philosopher Richard Rorty makes an impassioned plea, in *Achieving Our Country*, for holding on to idealistic, even utopian hope.

> You have to be loyal to a dream country rather than to the one to which you wake up every morning. Unless such loyalty exists, the ideal has no chance of becoming actual. (Rorty 1998: 101)

Yet this is why there is a need to distinguish idealistic hope from a utopian free play of the imagination. Idealistic hope isn't about utopia, in the sense of a secular version of the kingdom in all its final stationary perfection. As in Durkheim's work, it is about aspirations and commitments to act to achieve something like a commonwealth, but in which things are never perfect and there is always a field wide open to our efforts.

So this is one way in which a commonwealth scales down the kingdom. Another way, of course, is that the individual has no prospect of salvation in an eternal life to come. But what actual difference does this make to present hope, embedded in the here and now?

An essential element of idealistic hope 'for us' is concern for future generations, long after one's own death. A key factor, here, is again the 'city' of the individual personality, with a sense of belonging to a community that stretches across time and links the dead, the living and the not yet born. It is nonetheless a 'city' and stronghold of a present hope, anchored in the here and now. So the question again arises of a stronghold nowadays under siege, from forces that in one way or another tend to shape the individual's identity around a radically separate self – an 'I' hoping for 'me' – whether, in a religious case, an 'I' alone with God, or, with secularization, merely alone.

It is worth repeating that what is involved in the question is a rise of modern individualism, not in a same single inevitably atomistic form, but in struggles between different forms. This is basic to understanding Durkheim's work and why it entails a dynamic that can go in different directions. It is also why his work has roots in a French liberal tradition, concerned with an ambivalence in which individualism can spell authoritarianism rather than a free society and commonwealth. In turn, the tradition has roots in a reinterpretation of Montesquieu to grapple with the events of the Revolution and their implications. It includes works such as Benjamin Constant's *Ancient and Modern Liberty* (1819), but not least Alexis de Tocqueville's *Democracy in America* (vol. 1: 1835, vol. 2: 1840).

America

In terms of doing social theory through concrete investigations rather than grandiose up-in-the-air abstractions, there is a basic similarity between Durkheim's *Elemental Forms* and Tocqueville's *Democracy*. One is a case study of Australia, as a laboratory of religion. The other is a case study of America, as a laboratory of a new era. In general, it involved concern with the link between democratic institutions and underlying social attitudes, both as 'habits of the heart' and 'habits of the mind' (Tocqueville [1835] 1951: 300). In particular, it latched on to and helped to spread the term 'individualism', which had started up in France in the 1820s.

> Individualism is a calm, considered sentiment that disposes each citizen to isolate himself from the mass of his fellows and to draw apart along with his family and friends, in such a way that, after having thus created a little society for his own use, he gladly leaves the larger society to itself. (Tocqueville [1840] 1951: 105)

So, as the argument continues, a reason why there is an inherent modern tendency to individualism plus authoritarianism is that concentrating on private affairs and leaving the larger society to itself is in effect to leave it under the power of government. Thus like Constant before him, Tocqueville warned against what he clearly regarded as the social monstrosity of a mass of atomized individuals under an authoritarian and indeed despotic state. But where Constant essentially relied on general political theory to speculate how individuals could also be citizens, Tocqueville's laboratory unearthed a solution in which Americans, for all their individualism, 'are always joining together with one another'.

> Wherever, at the head of a new undertaking, you see the government in France and in England a great lord, you are sure to find, in the United States, an association. (113)

The answer to a modern contradiction, formulated in French liberal theory, had already been worked out in practice in America. Individuals are drawn into citizenship thanks to a vast web of intermediate groups and associations.

Or at any rate, Tocqueville has become a classic reference in debate on these issues. An update can be found in two works in particular, Robert Bellah and team's *Habits of the Heart* (1985, new edition 1996), and Robert Putnam's *Bowling Alone* (2000). However, *Habits of the Heart* is especially concerned with attitudes, *Bowling Alone* with relations.

> The dominant theme is simple: For the first two-thirds of the century a powerful tide bore Americans into ever deeper engagement with the life of their communities, but a few decades ago – silently, without warning – that tide reversed and we were overtaken by a treacherous rip current. Without at first noticing, we have been pulled apart from one another and our communities over the last third of the century. (Putnam 2000: 27)

But in an equivalent of the new preface to *The Division of Labour*, the new preface to *Habits of the Heart* brings together concerns with attitudes and relations, in a trenchant account of a nation in crisis and increasingly divided, above all by class. Yet like Durkheim's new preface, it runs up against the same problem. It is how reform can get going through a renewal of intermediate groups – in the process renewing wider aspirations and ideals of a commonwealth – when this is so powerfully blocked by the forces that generate disconnectedness. Or, more generally, the problem is what can keep social idealism alive, during a time when its strongholds are crumbling and all might seem lost.

Grand Narrative

Hope is a matter of 'weapons and luck', according to Rorty (1989: 91). In a way this is a secularized version of 'Praise the Lord and pass the ammunition', a naval chaplain's exhortation at Pearl Harbour in 1942. Belief in effort and agency is expressed, in straight-talking terms, in both these cases. The difference is that the notion of 'luck' is secular. It is part of the whole issue of what happens to hope, when loosened from an anchorage in religious worldviews and narratives.

In the modern West, this has essentially involved a secularization of Christianity and its grand narrative's key elements and problematics. But in whatever form, nothing happens in it by chance. In whatever form, it is a narrative of destiny, ending with the coming of the kingdom and the final glorious triumph of good over evil.

In mainstream traditions, it is a narrative in which some things are revealed, while others remain mysterious, hidden and unseen. Again in mainstream traditions, it is about God as a continuing active power within human lives, rather than as a mere external force or creator of a universe that is then left to run on the clockwork of inexorable laws. At the same time, in these traditions, it is about a God of grace as well as of justice. It is also in a concern with free will, rather than the determinism of a wholly preordained fate. So in a way it is about hope in ourselves as agents. But it is as an integral part of hope in God, in coping with life at its bleakest, as well as in working towards ideals in this world, rather than merely waiting around for the coming of the kingdom in the next.

True enough, according to a criticism that became often repeated by secularists, Christianity entails a blocked hope, giving up on any real transformation of this world and substituting an illusory, imagined triumph of the kingdom in another realm. Yet Christianity is not in fact a monopoly of ruling classes or conservatives. Again and again, it has been mobilized by radical social movements. Indeed, it can be seen as a strength that imagination of the kingdom incorporates resolve to hold on through the worst of times, together with aspirations and commitments to social change. But it is in a set of rock-bottom and idealistic hopes held together by the glue of the transcendent, and faith in God.

Secularization dissolves this glue, yet with different consequences, thanks to all the different possible ways of unpacking Christianity's grand narrative and its hopes and problematics. However, a start can be made by distinguishing deterministic from non-deterministic options, and by taking Durkheimian grand narrative as a key form of the non-deterministic approach.

In the first place, it is a narrative of enlightenment, in an effort to dig around in the obscurity of things and uncover the unseen. But what especially characterizes it is an effort to bring to light and understand, as in the French liberal tradition, a modern dynamic that can go in different directions and generate a variety of social worlds, yet that in the process generates deep-rooted aspirations only realizable in the world of a commonwealth. In turn, this is why it is about a logic that comes with an altogether crucial role not just for agency but enlightened agency and intervention, to 'direct the course'. It can be debated to what extent it is also about a logic with a necessary place for the contingent, and chance or luck. But in Durkheim's work itself, the discourse that combines with the idea of a modern dynamic and the social forces involved in it is overwhelmingly a discourse of struggle, effort and agency, rather than mere sheer chance or luck. Indeed it can be suggested, in terms of his commitment to an enlightened rationalism, that the so-called 'contingent' is essentially mystical empiricist talk for what so far remains hidden but can be dug around in and eventually understood. In any case, there is a fundamental implication of any and every form of secularized non-deterministic narrative. It scales down hope, from the inevitable to the possible. It gives up on stories of destiny and a conclusive final outcome. But this is precisely why it involves refusal to accept that all is lost.

In contrast, any and every form of secularized determinism is a route to despair, when it eventually emerges that the march to destiny is to what seems conclusive, final defeat. Or at least this is what might be suggested by reading Rorty and his critique, in *Achieving Our Country*, of the American 'cultural' left. In a long tradition they look at the nation with the help of the French, but with the help of writers such as Michel Foucault, and it is 'to mock the very idea that democratic institutions might once again be made to serve social justice'. They withdraw into a private world of systematically negative deconstruction, in which they are 'spectators rather than agents'. It is nonetheless to spread, in the public domain, a 'principled, theorized, philosophical hopelessness' (Rorty 1998: 36–37).

Or could it be upgraded to rock-bottom hope? It hardly matters, if what is instead needed is a vision of a dream country. All the same, a question is if an alternative to going to pieces in despair is to keep going with a rock-bottom hope, but having abandoned any faith in ideals.

Rock-bottom Hope

In looking for representations of modern secular rock-bottom hope, a leading candidate must be the work of Albert Camus and writings such as

The Myth of Sisyphus (1942) and *The Rebel* (1951). An iconic image, in *The Myth of Sisyphus*, is of a forever repeated, apparently futile struggle to push a rock to the top of a mountain, only for it to fall back down again. But as a new English edition explains, 'this book declares that even within the limits of nihilism it is possible to find a way to go beyond nihilism' (Camus 1955: 7). An essay of the same time comes with another iconic image: 'In the middle of winter, I learnt at last there was in me an invincible summer' (Camus 1954: 158).

Foucault's work also has its iconic images. One of the most famous, in *Discipline and Punish* (1975), is about the modern birth of the prison but also of the whole of society as a sort of prison – a 'carceral city' – controlling individuals through a vast web of relations of power and domination. This still comes with a rock-bottom hope in forms of resistance. But it gives up on any more idealistic hope. It involves its own recycled version of the myth of Sisyphus, in a resignation to the endless rise and fall of one historically specific system of domination after another.

However, is there a change in his later work, and interest in an ethic of 'care of the self'? In a text not long before his death, he writes:

> Maybe the target nowadays is not to discover what we are, but to refuse what we are. We have to imagine and to build up what we could be to get rid of this kind of 'double bind', which is the simultaneous individualization and totalization of modern power structures … We have to promote new forms of subjectivity through the refusal of this kind of individuality which has been imposed on us for several centuries. (Foucault 1982: 216)

This remains anchored in concern with forms of resistance. But it now comes with a fusion of rock-bottom and idealistic hope, in which any emancipatory vision of what 'we could be' must be worked out in the actual activities of critique, refusal and resistance. So in a way it is about hope in an unseen ideal, and in energies able to construct it. In turn, it is perhaps not too shocking and transgressive to suggest it is about hope in energies of the sacred, as against forces of the mundane. It draws on a whole long-running tradition in its attack on forces that produce individualism plus an authoritarian state. At the same time it mobilizes energies bound up with a whole long-running mystique of freedom.

This links with an analysis in Paul Cohen's *Freedom's Moment* (1997). It is about the 'consecrated heretic', a role pioneered in France by Rousseau, then quickly taken up by Robespierre. In the case of the twentieth century, his analysis covers such diverse figures as Péguy, Sartre and Foucault. But he looks beyond differences, to bring out common themes in a 'heretical tradition'. From Rousseau on, it involves a sweeping critique of established society and its brand of individualism. This is partly thanks to the inner slavery of domination by materialism, and egoistic interests and desires. But it is bound up with the incarceration of the 'social' individual, forever living in the eyes of others. A basic common horror is of dependency, in any form, and its route to subservience. A basic common ideal is personal freedom, as an affair of independence, integrity and care of the self.

So there is again a fusion of rock-bottom and idealistic hope, in struggles to achieve this freedom that are central to the heretical hero's actual or legendary life story, as well as to the heretical tradition's own version of grand narrative. It is just that its idealism might not stretch very far unless it includes society, and unless hope in struggles for one's own freedom includes hope in struggles for everybody's freedom as part of a commonwealth.

A route to alienation is a mystique of freedom that rules out any form of solidarity. Cohen's 'heretics' have tendencies in this direction, thanks to their worries about dependency. But it is especially in worries about any form of established organization, network of apparatuses and institutionalized authority. An enduring hope is in upsurges of energies against these. It is another matter to expect the power of such energies to last, without being ground down, corrupted and betrayed by the forces of a mundane politics. The heretical tradition's grand narrative is not about progress but repetition, and 'the rise and fall of freedom's moments' (Cohen 1997: 156).

Put another way, it is about freedom's effervescent moments. It is about what 'we could become', yet only in brief episodic special times. In the end it comes down to rock-bottom hope, in a renewal of resistance, rather than a reformation of society. It might be that Foucault's later work represents a wish to break with this, and so not merely with his earlier writings, but with an entire heretical tradition embedded in French culture. In any case, it is instructive to return to the hope on offer from Camus.

The Rebel asks why the whole modern movement of revolution turned sour, and produced a state running on mystification, oppression and terror. At least part of the answer is to do with the death of God, but rebirth in secular form. This involves the utopianism of a kingdom of ends to come, while serving to justify any means, however murderous, in the here and now. Crucially, it also involves the conversion of reason and history into objects of faith, making everything fit into the dialectics of a vast theoretical system, empowered with God-like knowledge of a 'totality'. Giving up on all this is not to give up on rebellion, but to develop it as a 'philosophy of limits' (Camus 1951: 357).

As argued in his introduction, rebellion creates solidarity – a 'solidarity born in chains', reacting against humiliation and looking for respect, in the stirrings of an impassioned affirmation of 'what, in man, must always be defended' (29–32). These stirrings draw the individual out of egoism and solitude, to become conscious of a common subjection, and in rising up against this to assert a common identity. 'I rebel, therefore we are' (36).

The essay then works towards an all-important concluding discussion. In emphasizing the need for limits, this focuses on two main issues. One is to do with freedom and justice. The other is about the use of violence.

Rebellion comes with aspirations to both freedom and justice as part of solidarity. But a lesson of revolutionary experience is how these come into conflict. Absolute freedom rules out justice. Absolute justice rules out freedom. The only solution is to struggle to negotiate a relative freedom and a relative justice – not simply relative as against a particular absolute abstract ideal, but relative to and limited by each other as part of a set of values bound up with solidarity.

The issue of violence again requires struggle to negotiate a way through values in tension with one another. Absolute opposition to violence makes the world of power safe from any movement of resistance. Absolute endorsement of violence licenses murder. It redivides the world into persons and non-persons, in a destruction of individuals whose common human status it is the point of rebellion to assert and 'consecrate' (347). It amounts to what I have suggested calling iconocide. For Camus, in any case, it isn't something to normalize with a clear conscience, but a 'desperate exception' (348).

A brief passage then connects all this with another far-reaching, if familiar issue. It is how rebellion, in generating the solidarity of a collective 'we are', generates a new individualism – in effect, a new secular ethic consecrating everyone's status as a person. Rebellion is a force for social renewal, through its struggle to create and recreate a collective 'we are'. But it is through an individualism – clearly entailing an ethic of the person – in which 'on my own account, in a sense, I stand up for the common dignity that I cannot allow to be debased in myself or in others' (367).

In sum, the essay links rock-bottom hope in resistance with a vision of rebellion as a struggle to assert and negotiate a set of values that are bound up with one another, but in a relationship of mutual limitation and tension. These are identifiable as values bound up with one another in the French Revolution and its continuing modern legacy. At core, they are to do with freedom, justice, solidarity and each individual's collective status, rights and obligations as a person. True, it is in a horror of utopianism. Even so, can the hope represented by Camus be seen as involving some sort of relatively idealistic hope in a commonwealth of persons?

A clear, detailed examination of his social and political writings can be found in John Foley's *Albert Camus* (2008). They are also illuminated, through a comparative approach, in Jeffrey Isaac's *Arendt, Camus, and Modern Rebellion* (1992). This investigates the characteristic features of a 'rebellious politics', including its critique of a conventional democratic system operating through institutions such as the state, parties and parliaments. But it is one thing if the critique merely looks for an alternative system. It is another if its actual underlying message is the inadequacy of every system and how any attempt 'to choose a single vision of democratic politics is futile' (Isaac 1992: 258).

A rebellious hope in a commonwealth isn't to fix the system, once and for all. It is to do with ideals that mean there is always a field wide open to our efforts. With each successive effort, 'injustice and suffering will remain' and 'will not cease to be an outrage' (Camus 1951: 374). A rebellious, awkward squad's politics is the inconvenient thorn in the flesh that is integral to what a commonwealth is about, in a continuing need to rethink, renegotiate and reassert a set of core values centred round concern with human solidarity. 'It is this prioritization of solidarity, and the demands of relative freedom and relative justice that stem from it, that are at the heart of Camus's contemporary relevance' (Foley 2008: 172).

An Endnote

Durkheim's campaign for new intermediate groups, to help get going a developing process of reform, could be seen as concerned with the institutional framework and overall system of a democratic politics. Yet as in his repeated use of the example of Socrates, his work can also be seen as entailing an interest in a rebellious politics, forever arising from within society to express aspirations that challenge any existing, established system. But the choice of Socrates as a symbol of the rebel is perhaps a revealing symbol of Durkheim's own commitment to the intellectual life and world of science and philosophy. It is possible to nominate many other examples from many different kinds of milieux, including, not least, the arts. Indeed, Camus himself is nowadays best known for his novels, rather than his other work. So a way to end an essay on hope is to open up links with the creative, transformative power of art.

In *The Elemental Forms*, after all, art has a key role in creative, socially transformative effervescence, the rite that is picked out as special is the enactment of myth as drama, and there is a poetry inherent in the whole business of the sacred. This involves a practical aesthetics of hope, and how art is a powerful medium of asking about and exploring issues to do with 'god', society, the human condition. But there is also a pure aesthetics of hope. It is the art itself that is a sort of sanctuary of the soul, and a way, even in the middle of winter, to feel a sense of an invincible summer.

Art

The aim, here, is to explore what might be called a 'total aesthetics'.[1] It builds on the account of art in Durkheim's *Elemental Forms*, but also in Mauss's *Manual of Ethnography*. These sources are essentially concerned with traditional forms of art. However, they help to bring out an issue to do with a far-reaching development nowadays. This is the impact of repro art – the art made possible by modern mass reproductive techniques.

Total Aesthetics

One of the reasons for talking of a total aesthetics is to get away from narrow, restrictive assumptions. Instead, it is to ask about art as an activity that can take form in, among other things, music, dance, drama, mime, acrobatics, flower arranging, codpieces, face paintings, face masks, hairstyles, earrings, tattoos, carvings, ground drawings, murals, drinking vessels, banquets, raves, gospel sessions, and, not least, the creation of a whole atmospherics.

It is also to get away from modern culture-bound assumptions that frame art as 'Art'. Instead, for example, an event might be primarily framed as a religious event rather than an art event, or an object might be primarily framed as a religious object rather than an art object.

At the same time it is concerned with the importance of mobilizations of a whole combination of art forms, as in Durkheim's paradigmatic case of drama, and what is more generally seen by Mauss as the 'mixing of the arts' ([1947] 2007: 69). But it is centrally concerned with art as a collective event. Because this involves the creative collective electricity of a live collective enactment – in secular as well as religious events – it will be discussed as 'sacred art'.

Sacred Art
Sacred art includes the performative arts, such as song, music, dance and drama. But it doesn't exclude objects, such as paintings or sculptures. On the contrary, it means asking if and how these have a role in art as an event.

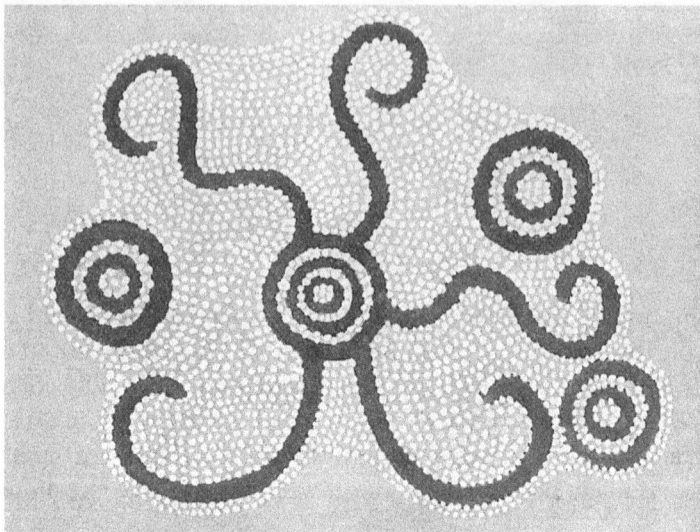

Figure 2.3.1. Ground Drawing of the Warramunga People
(created for one of the ceremonies associated with the Wollunqua)
SOURCE: Spencer and Gillen (1904: 737)

The ground drawings, specially created for the ceremony to do with the snake Wollunqua and then immediately destroyed, constitute a clear example. Along with the account of their social role, an idea of their aesthetic power is given not just by the description but by the photographs and reproductions of them in Spencer and Gillen (1904: 243–46, 737–43; see figure 2.3.1). The same applies to the churingas, with their many different designs, extensively illustrated in Spencer and Gillen (1899:129–50; 1904: 268–77, 725–36; see figure 2.3.2). But churingas are enduring objects, hidden between ceremonies in places poetically described by Durkheim as like 'a temple, at the threshold of which all the bustle of profane life starts to die away' (1912a: 188). Altar paintings, on permanent open view between ceremonies in a church, are different.

However, churingas and altar paintings can share the same fate if removed or indeed looted from their original environment for display, as decontextualized objects, in the museum of Art. This involves a move away from any core notion of what, thanks to a role in collective occasions, counts as sacred art. It is necessary to come up with another term for objects that are essentially framed as having their own independent status, and what might be suggested is 'iconic art'.

On the surface, *The Elemental Forms* is unconcerned with such questions. In contrast, the *Manual of Ethnography*'s account is explicitly organ-

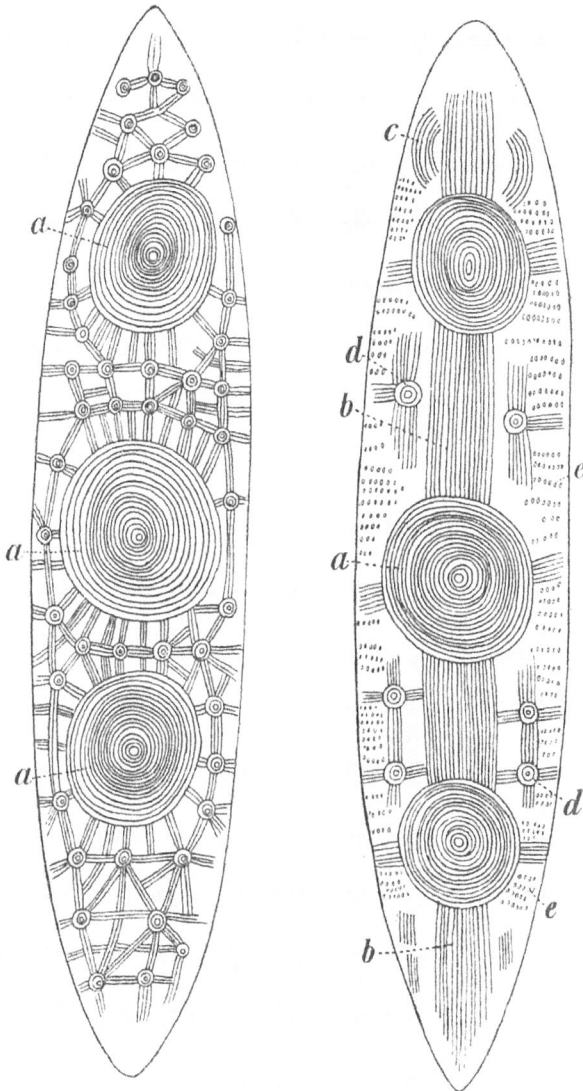

Figure 2.3.2. A Churinga of the Arunta People
(wood, with designs on both sides associated with the frog totem)
SOURCE: Spencer and Gillen (1899: 146)

ized round a distinction between 'plastic arts' to do with objects such as paintings and 'musical arts' to do with enactments such as song, dance or drama. This distinction is not very satisfactory and needs a rethink.

The account begins with what is presented as a key site of the plastic arts (Mauss [1947] 2007: 77–79). This is bodily art, divided into the 'cos-

202 | Essays on Modern Times

metics' of direct bodily ornamentation and the 'finery' of indirect ornamentation. It might be wondered if 'cosmetics' is an entirely adequate
term for a range of practices that includes head crushing. In any case, it
seems bizarre to centre these practices round objects. The 'cosmetics' of
face painting, hair styling, tattooing and so on are above all to do with
art as a performance, in general helping to enact an individual's identity, but especially mobilized in participation in collective events. The
same applies to the 'finery' of face masks, rings, jewels, clothes. These
aren't mere objects, but, after all, are 'intended for wearing' (74). Indeed, the discussion concludes with the ritual importance of the mask.
It can represent a spirit or ancestor and, when put on and worn, effects
a total transformation in which 'the individual is other than himself'
(78–79). A similar point had already been made in *The Elemental Forms*,
in describing scenes of effervescence in which 'sorts of masks' are worn
that not only help to effect the individual's uplift and total transformation, but above all communicate and 'materially represent this internal
transformation' (1912a: 312).

In sum, bodily art is certainly a key site of art, but art as an event. Cases
of cosmetics and finery such as face paintings and face masks are like cases
of objects such as ground drawings, churingas or altar paintings. Thanks
to a core, integral role in collective occasions, they are part of sacred art.

Mauss continues his account with a section on 'the ornamentation
of everyday objects', and follows this with another on special objects that
constitute what he calls 'ideal' art ([1947] 2007: 79–83). What is involved
is a distinction between the everyday and the iconic. It is about the design
and ornamentation of everyday utilitarian objects such as furniture, in
contrast with special non-utilitarian objects such as paintings that have
their own independent status and accordingly constitute iconic art. But it
needs rethinking in terms of two sets of distinctions, between the everyday
and the special as well as between the sacred and the iconic.

Thus, as already suggested, his analysis fails to cope with the objects,
cosmetics and finery that are all part of sacred art thanks to their role
in special events. But it is also inadequate in coping with everyday art. A
necessary way to approach this is again not merely through objects but
practices. It is not just that the ornamentation of everyday utilitarian
objects such as furniture might help to construct a living room as an
everyday sacred space and central site of domestic activities. It is also to
do with how he remarks that 'the labour involved in a musical drama
is infinite' (89), but how a simpler, everyday counterpart of drama can
be found in his discussion of oral storytelling (91–92). This is missing
from *The Elemental Forms*. Yet even if it is only an echo of elaborate sacred
drama, everyday oral storytelling is an altogether key case of sacred art.

An Intrinsic Link between the Social and the Aesthetic

It is all very well for philosophers to go on about art through a focus on objects such as paintings. But it is more or less a guarantee of missing something basic – an intrinsic link between the social and the aesthetic, built into the live collective enactments of sacred art. Oral storytelling is one of many examples, while drama is another. Or there is how 'in an Australian corroboree, men, women and children dance and sing: everyone is simultaneously actor and spectator' (Mauss [1947] 2007: 89). A sort of brute theoretical fact, in everyone's singing and dancing, is a union of the social and the aesthetic.

The simultaneous involvement as actors and spectators of all members of a gathering is a paradigmatic case of this union. As at a gospel session, everybody joins in the singing, swaying, clapping and creation of a collective 'high'. Another modern but more secular example might be the rave. It is anyhow essential to go through a range of cases, helping to bring out a range of issues. They include a need to rethink effervescence, the tension in live art between organization and spontaneity, and the existence of any such thing as a 'work' apart from actual performances. But a way to start is with the group it is conventional to call 'the audience' or 'the spectators'.

These terms are inadequate to describe gatherings at events such as a pop concert. Calling them 'the audience' is as if they merely listen to the music. Calling them 'the spectators' is as if they merely watch the whirling, gyrating, pierced, ringed, tattooed, erotically clad bodies and flashing lights, smoke and atmospherics of a pop act. They themselves are part of the act, with their own finery, cosmetics, singing, swaying and jumping around. Like Mauss's Australian corroboree, it is still a type of event in which everyone's energetic participation is an essential ingredient of its aesthetic power and success.

At the same time it helps to bring out the issue of organization and spontaneity, at stake in Durkheim's remark, 'an organized tumult is still a tumult' (1912a: 309). A key aspect of this is to do with styles of participation. In all sorts of settings – a jazz session, a country and western festival, cabaret, stand-up comedy, the circus – genteel restraint is very much *not* the norm. Instead, excited involvement is the rule. It is a way in which organized spontaneity is still spontaneity. It is not, however, just in a need for at least some preparation and planning. It is to do with events that draw on a basic cultural model of how to go about things. But, as in a jazz session, it is a cultural model organized round expectations of collective creative interaction, improvisation and spontaneity.

In contrast, 'high' art has become a site of norms of restraint. Indeed, it might even amount to organized anti-effervescence. As at a theatre, members of what can be appropriately cast as 'the audience' are expected to focus in silence on the play. True enough, an audience is considered an essential part of the show and this is not just thanks to ordained brief moments of applause. During the ordained long stretches of silence, there are many ways in which audience and actors can interact, develop a rapport that is valued as helping to lift up a performance, and inject it with spontaneous creative sparkle. It is nonetheless in a style of participation requiring a concentrated focus on events on the stage. It also involves issues it is possible to bring out through examples that centre round three compositions by Stravinsky, *The Rite of Spring*, *Apollo* and *Oedipus Rex*.

Famously, *The Rite* sparked off a riot at its first performance in 1913, but is now conventionally hailed as having been a revolutionary piece and has an established place in the modern repertoire.[2] So even if it no longer generates riots, can it still generate effervescence?

Certainly, *The Rite*'s wildness and frenzy can be contrasted with *Apollo*'s calm and restraint. But it is also possible to contrast both of them with the complex range of emotions, ideas and references going on in *Oedipus Rex*. The three examples, taken together, suggest a need to get away from any assumption that just identifies effervescence with a dionysian 'tumult' going on throughout the whole of an assembly.

In the case of the audience, *The Rite*'s music, dance and atmospherics might arouse a sort of enjoyment of frenzy, but hardly, confined in their seats, the orgasm of a total dionysian high. *Apollo*'s music, dance and atmospherics might seem more consistent with the audience's actual situation. Yet it is also about stirring up in them an enjoyment and relish. But it is a relish in restraint, and the serenity of an apollonian high. *Oedipus Rex* is different again, with its music, song, spoken narrative and modern take on an ancient disturbing drama. In general, however, it can be seen as an example of all the forms of art concerned with stirring up, fomenting and counter-pointing a mix of thoughts and emotions.

In the case of performers on the stage, perhaps they are sometimes so involved that they collectively take off into a total bodily-mental high, even if this is never fully shared and experienced by the audience. There is still a need to rethink effervescence in terms of different types of high, varying with different types of aesthetic, cultural models, styles of participation and relationships between audience and performers in an assembly as a whole.

These variations across the live arts are important enough in themselves. But they are also interlinked with variations around the issue of the very existence of a 'work', apart from actual performances.

Mauss warns, in discussing traditional oral storytelling: 'Do not seek the original text, *for there is none*; the narrator improvises, and his contribution may be far-reaching' ([1947] 2007: 92). Put another way, there is just a model of a story. The model may exist in a collective memory shared by both narrator and audience, but is actualized only in performances that draw on it. These flesh out the story, in a version that comes complete with its own touches, flourishes, inventions and overall rendering and interpretation. The same applies throughout the live arts, but in differences that range from the absence of any script to an entire elaborate ensemble of texts. In cases such as enactments of *The Rite of Spring*, the texts consist of musical scores, choreographic notations, costume and set designs, director's guidelines and so on. Yet however detailed and elaborate, they are still in effect like models, brought to life only in and through performances. These draw on, flesh out and actualize them, in versions that come complete with their own particular flourishes and inventions, as well as their own particular overall account and interpretation. The ensemble of texts does not so much constitute a definitive 'work' as a basis of infinitely variable enactments. In any case, from the construction of textual ensembles to their enactment in actual performances it is indeed in what Mauss calls an 'infinite' labour. Moreover, although it is in a chemistry that depends on the creativity of individuals, it is above all in the interaction and in the chemistry and creativity of an immense collective collaborative labour. In other words, it is again in an intrinsic link between the social and the aesthetic.

This can be found in one form or another throughout the live arts. Yet is there a dimension of the social that is not just to do with art as an event, but is part of a set of elements common to all the arts?

Practical and Pure Aesthetics

The Elemental Forms can be seen as generating the claim that art always involves a combination of practical and pure aesthetics. The practical aesthetic element is to do with a sacred, social symbolism. The pure aesthetic element is to do with enjoyment in the art itself. This pure aesthetic *jouissance* can in turn be seen as involving three ingredients, the sensuous, the imaginative and the poetic.

Durkheim warns against looking for purpose and significance in a rite's every action: 'some have no purpose', and there are scenes of 'jumping, whirling, dancing, shouting, singing, without it always being possible to give a meaning to this agitation' (1912a: 545). To develop his example, it is about a sheer creative relish in the sensuous – sounds, rhythms, movements, bodily techniques, contacts, smells, shapes, textures, colours...

But he also sees enjoyment in a free, imaginative play of ideas. This constructs worlds of fantasy, in particular in tales of monsters and the macabre (543), but in general sweeps beyond any serious social symbol-

206 Essays on Modern Times

ism in 'free creations of the mind' (545). Indeed, it is why there is a need to fill out his account with a third pure aesthetic ingredient, bound up in his concern with the serious business of drama, and that thanks to his view of the sacred as poetry could be called the poetic.

Sacred drama enacts sacred myth, yet which is not just an exercise in fantasy but part of life in earnest. Myth is how a society represents 'man and the world', and is both 'an ethic and a cosmology at the same time as a history' (536). This might by why myth, even as a basic bare-bones model of a story, has a force and fascination of its own. But if a powerful social symbolism always attracts efforts at its expression through art, it is the power of art that helps to create, constitute, renew and reinforce the power of myth. Art fleshes out a skeletal bare-bones story into versions that come complete, not just with touches of the sensuous or flourishes of the imaginative, but a whole poetic energy. It is about enjoyment in the very force, skill and technique of a representation, say, of Our Lord's Agony and Crucifixion – even if an essential job is to channel attention away from the art, and concentrate concern on the mythic significance and symbolism of the Crucifixion itself.

All the same, it is one thing to insist that it is important always to look for a combination of pure and practical aesthetics. It is another matter if a fusion of art and symbolism can always be found. A reason has to do with developments in modern art and how they involve what might seem a paradox. A long-running move has been away from art's embeddedness in a religious, social-sacred setting, in a tendency to frame things just as Art. It can be seen as already at work in the Revolution. But it especially took off in the nineteenth century, according to Mauss ([1947] 2007: 82). In any case, it is perhaps surprising that he fails to notice or discuss how the emergence of a modern category, Art, has come with a multitude of disputes over what counts as art. Indeed, since at least the end of the nineteenth century, there has been a non-stop effervescence of different 'isms' – impressionism, realism, surrealism, dadaism, modernism, primitivism, minimalism and whatever. A way, then, to try to begin to make sense of what is going on is through two nowadays iconic images. One is René Magritte's gently ironic representation of a pipe with the caption, 'this is not a pipe'. The other is Marcel Duchamp's crueller image of *The Mona Lisa* with a beard and moustache.

Magritte's joke about representational art can be seen as symptomatic of a movement towards radically anti-representational art and abstraction and formalism. This may well have had origins in art that still retained representational elements, while becoming increasingly interested in sounds, rhythms, textures, shapes and colours just in themselves. But it was the arrival of pure abstraction and formalism, concentrating on pure aesthetic explorations of the sensuous, that has especially contributed to the difficulty of always finding a social symbolism. Of course, many continued to play the old traditional game of searching for a sign and arguing over its meaning, unable or unwilling to understand the message of art that comes with the caption, 'this is not a symbol'.

Duchamp's *Mona Lisa* with a beard and moustache instead comes with the caption, 'this is anti-Art'. Another example is the transfer of a urinal from the ambivalent sacred–profane underworld of the lavatory, for display upstairs in the purer realm of the Salon of Art, complete with an authenticating Signature of the Artist. Duchamp began his series of 'ready-mades' with a bicycle wheel mounted on a kitchen stool, then continued with a bottle rack and a urinal, first exhibited in 1917. As he is supposed to have said much later: 'I threw the bottle rack and the urinal in their faces as a challenge and now they admire them for their aesthetic beauty'. This was quoted by the surrealist, Hans Richter (1965: 207–8), as if from a letter written to him by Duchamp, complete with an authenticating precise date. But it may have been a spoof, in which they agreed on a bogus, earnestly academic representation of a chat between them (Tomkins 1996: 414–15). In any case, the urinal has long since been installed as a pioneering classic of modern art. Despite any original revolutionary intentions to storm the barricades and overthrow Art, the effect has been to reshape and renew a modern social category, in the very process of being absorbed into it.

Indeed, this is nowadays where to look for an underlying social symbolism. There has been one wave after another of avant garde attacks on an old regime, but in which each soon loses its power to shock and joins an ever-expanding museum of Art. It is in a non-stop effervescence, if in two different yet interacting currents. Like the one celebrated in *The Elemental Forms*, there is the creative excitement during the brief moments of each successive avant garde wave itself. Like the one worried about elsewhere, there is the manic agitation gripping a whole world of art, establishment and all, ceaselessly moving on from the old to seek – not just the glitz, thrill, scandal, shock – but the very newness of the new. The social symbolism of each ism's caption, 'this is the new', is to be found, not just through old games of hunt the meaning, but in its play with the modern social-sacred category of Art itself. Yet, it might be protested, what has *The Mona Lisa* with a beard and moustache got to do with beauty? Merely to ask the question is gloriously to miss the point.

A Universal Criterion of Aesthetics?

Mauss can seem quite conservative, in that he not only assumes a universal criterion of aesthetics but identifies it as beauty ([1947] 2007:

68). Durkheim is more radical, in that he discusses art without even mentioning beauty and is instead concerned with creative energies, to do with a necessary 'surplus' (1912a: 545).

It can be quite attractive to approach art as fundamentally an affair of creative energies, but that can come in many different forms, including, nowadays, the cult of excitement in the new. More traditionally, they include the fascination of beauty, the force of the austere, the wildness of the dionysian, the explosiveness of farce, the cruelty of satire, the spine-chilling horror of tales of the monstrous and the macabre, the power of a complex mythic drama... But how might such an approach run into trouble with counter-examples, or, more constructively, how might it help with understanding them?

A way to begin is with a distinction between foreground and background art. The job of foreground art is to absorb attention, through its power and energy. The job of background art is not to absorb attention, thanks to a lack of power and energy. Or rather, it is how this contributes to the impact of a totality. Tinkly baroque table-music is an essential background part of the total aesthetics of the glittering chandeliers, sumptuous food, perfumed bodies, painted faces and powdered wigs of an old-regime court banquet. At the same time it raises an issue of style, but particularly the style of a general atmospherics and whole ensemble. Mauss notes how some cultures 'decorate everything; others decorate next to nothing' ([1947] 2007: 79). It is possible to go on from this to contrast two styles of ensemble, the 'cornucopian' and the 'minimalist'. Cornucopianism fills every part of an environment with items each of which can be foreground art and a focus of interest in themselves, and it is this clamour and competition for attention that generates the overall, even engulfing effect. Minimalism clears an environment of anything with an interest of its own, so that everything imposes a concentration on the ensemble itself. Both styles obliterate, in their own fashion, a distinction and interaction between foreground items and background art. In practice, and in between these two ideal-typical extremes, a perennial aesthetic issue is the balance of power between foreground and background within a totality.

This includes issues arising from modern switches of the environment of traditional art. In at least some cases, it can wipe out the impact of foreground art, as with the removal of a painting of *The Madonna* from a church's altarpiece, to become merely one *Madonna* among many in a long endless line in a museum. There is almost no need to give them each a beard and moustache, since the basic work of subversion has been accomplished already. Or again in at least some cases, another way to sap aesthetic energy is by changing the environment of background art. A basic pattern of court table-music during the old regime was to herald the royal entrance with a dramatic fanfare of drums and trumpets, soon settling down to repetitive tinkliness for the rest of the meal. It is one thing, then, if a modern concert includes the fanfare in its programme. It is another if, in the interests of 'authenticity', it consists almost entirely of background baroque. This is a recipe for the atmospherics, neither of a banquet nor a concert, but a museum lecture.

Essentially similar points could be made in returning to modern art itself. It is possible to become absorbed in the energy of a painting that consists only of an expanse of white, even or especially if it is an expanse of intense sheer white, without any tonal or textural variation whatever. It is another matter if it is merely one of many such paintings, lined along an art exhibition's walls. Or a sort of degree-zero concert might offer a programme of pieces that all play nothing. Yet even in actual cases, where only a single piece plays nothing, how can it absorb attention and have aesthetic power?

Robert Rauschenberg's paintings of expanses of white helped to inspire John Cage's *4′ 33″*, divided into sections of varying length but playing nothing for four minutes thirty-three seconds. First performed in 1952 at the appropriately entitled Maverick Concert Hall, it is now a modern classic, with earnest discussions of the power of a 'silence' that is quite unlike the acoustic nothingness imagined in an ideal-type of silence, but instead consists of the audience's own sounds and movements. Put another way, then, its power depends on the organized transgression of a genteel norm. The audience is expected to concentrate attention on the performance on stage, yet it is on musicians who play nothing, and attention is thrown back on to the audience themselves. The effect isn't simply to encourage them to create and improvise, through their own 'silence', their own music. The dramatic switch of focus emphasizes the involvement and participation in all live art of a gathering – a participation that is essential for the energy of the art itself.

In sum, much can be said for an approach to traditional as well as modern art in terms of creative energies. But it doesn't add up to a single overall universal criterion of art, pinning down its nature, fixing its boundaries with other things and unlocking all its secrets and mysteries. Indeed, it might be wondered if the way to get on with investigations of aesthetics is to chase after the rainbow of an essence of 'art'. In any case, there is a need to consider a feature of the modern world that goes unnoticed both in *The Elemental Forms* and the *Manual of Ethnography*, but that affects the whole relation between art and society.

Repro Art

Mass reproductive technology makes possible new genres of art, which could accordingly be called 'neo-repro' art. A paradigmatic eighteenth and nineteenth century case is the rise of the novel, while a paradigmatic twentieth century case is the rise of the film. It also makes possible the mass reproduction of copies of musical performances, paintings and so on, which could accordingly be called 're-repro' art. But both through the creation of new genres and the reproduction of traditional forms, it is a force for far-reaching change in the role of art in society. A basic point is that repro art makes art available and accessible as never before.

A Downside

Reading the millionth imprint of a novel is to read the novel itself, while watching the millionth screening of a film is to watch the film itself. A downside, however, is that it is through a mechanistic technology that eliminates the creative energies of spontaneity, interaction and involvement that are essential elements of art as a live collective event. A worry, then, is if repro art is a gravedigger of sacred art.

The novel has become a modern hallowed site of Literature. Yet in contrast with traditional collective oral storytelling, it generates an individualized, atomized, mass readership, without any close, direct and meaningful relationship either with one another or with the author. Indeed, it is a key site of a modern Dictatorship of the Author. True, there is the reader's personal response, along with collective debate, and changing collective currents of fashionability and evaluation. There is nonetheless a brute fact about the text, as laid down in the printed page and reproduced in the first as well as the millionth copy. It simply does not allow for all the interactive participatory energies that go into a collectively told story, and that spontaneously vary and re-vary things from one telling to another.

The cinema is a less dramatic example in that it developed as a collective occasion and gathering, far from tending to dissolve this. It was a key twentieth-century form of collective ritual in individual lives and generated its own collective electricity. Yet whatever the interactive hubbub and excitement going on in the cinema itself, the film cuts off audience and performers from each other. Although allowing the assembly to express their feelings, it simply does not permit any real immediate power of input into events on the screen. And thanks to TV, DVD, etc., it is vulnerable to the same mass technological processes of individualistic consumption as literature. As a way to watch films, the cinema's heyday is over. Or in running through some of the main twentieth-century forms of theatre – a town's local rep, the summer seaside variety show, the travelling circus, the music-hall – this, too, can sound like one of history's casualty lists. The cinema and the theatre survive. The case for gloom is if they have become as marginalized as each other, in an advanced age of atomized, departicipatory repro art.

On The Other Hand...

Repro art is still art. Indeed, genres such as the novel and the film come with a vast protean energy and aesthetic power of their own. But this gets only so far in addressing worries about a modern scenario in which privatized, individualistic art might be becoming hegemonic. A general strategy in addressing these concerns is to look for patterns, not of an emerging dominance, but of mutual stimulation and interaction. One way to do this is to explore the interrelation between literature, film and theatre as a modern classic trio of the arts. Another way is to ask about the mass reproduction of art such as music or painting.

Again a basic point, here, is how mass reproduction makes accessible as never before an immense range of music and painting. Another basic point, in turn, is how this can stimulate interest in going to hear live musical performances, or in going to see the original paintings themselves – in visits to the museum as a shrine of art, or to the special blockbuster exhibition as a carnival of art. However, there is a fundamental problem with iconic art. It is the ambivalent status of a treasury of artefacts as objects belonging to a common cultural heritage but also as objects of private ownership. This generates disputes over how museums come to possess which particular bits of whose cultural heritage, and over restitution to rightful claimants. At the same time it is why so much iconic art disappears into a private world away from public view, or even into bank vaults away from anyone's view. These problems are to some extent created by repro art and the interest and value it invests in iconic art. In sum, the interaction of repro and iconic art is bound up with the idea of a treasury of artefacts for show in museums and exhibitions as part of a public culture. Yet it is also bound up with major issues and obstacles in the achievement of this public culture.

Although a treasury of artefacts can include objects such a piece of music's original score, it is without raising the same problems for a public culture of music's actual performances. These events can be held anywhere whatever the location of an original score, if, indeed, any exists. It is anyhow a model, to be fleshed out and actualized in performances, whether in a studio, a recording of a live performance, or a live performance itself, but also in interaction between these forms of enactment. This interaction can work in various ways, influencing the repertoire as well as the style of what is played live and what is recorded, feeding into knowledge of particular musical pieces, artists and composers, but not least in stimulating interest in live music itself and going to hear, absorb and participate in it in the atmospherics of a collective event.

A particular type of event that stands out is the festival. It constitutes a hard-core case of art centred round a gathering. It is difficult or indeed pointless to attempt to substitute it with a reproduction, and yet it has a flourishing place in modern culture.

The Festival

A way to explore things is through George McKay's *Glastonbury: A Very English Fair*, and Jean-Louis Fabiani's account of the festival of theatre at Avignon and the festival of film at Cannes.

As McKay explains straightaway, his focus on Glastonbury is also to bring out a wider movement that he discusses as 'festival culture'. This has many diverse sources, and comes in many different forms. But its festivals are about 'idealism, being young, getting old disgracefully, trying to find other ways, getting out of it, hearing some great and some truly awful music, about anarchy and control' (McKay 2000: preface). An important part of his book sketches out a 'time-line of festival culture' (87–114). He begins this in the 1950s, with the launch of the Edinburgh People's Festival, organized by various left-wing and nationalist groups to balance the elitist, often non-Scottish Edinburgh Festival, founded, just after the war, in 1946. He continues the story through the 1970s, with the launch of events such as the Stonehenge Free Festival as well as Glastonbury itself, and brings it up to the 1990s with events such as the urban 'Reclaim the Streets' street parties in London. A discussion of these brings out the approach and concerns of the organizers in their own words:

> 'A carnival celebrates temporary liberation from the established order; it marks the suspension of all hierarchy, rank, privileges, norms and prohibitions. Crowds of people on the street seized by a sudden awareness of their own ideas and creations. It follows then that carnivals and revolutions are not spectacles seen by other people, but the very opposite in that they involve the active participation of the crowd itself' (quoted in McKay 2000: 79).

But the theme of generating active participation in some sort of organized spontaneity – Durkheim's 'an organized tumult is still a tumult', echoed in McKay's 'anarchy and control' – runs through his whole account of the ideals, issues and tensions that help to constitute what is essentially an anti-establishment festival culture, involving a form of rebellious politics to reclaim culture and art from an elitist 'high art'.

Active participation is also a theme – if in a very different, not so very 'English' context – of Fabiani's account of the festivals at Avignon and Cannes, and in a concern with what he discusses as a 'public culture'. Both these festivals, as he explains, had various earlier sources. But they were founded and actively sponsored by the state just after the end of the Second World War, in a mood of hope and in a general effort to reconstruct French identity through a renascence of French art. However, a quite specific ideal was to convert the festival's gatherings from 'spectators' to 'participants', so that a quite specific feature of its organization is not just to lay on artistic events but to make these part of a forum of active public argument, reflection and debate (Fabiani 2005: 60–62). On the one hand, then, it is undoubtedly possible to identify elements of Durkheimian 'ritual'. But it is in sophisticated forms, shot through with an ironic, reflexive 'distancing', and involving characters who are highly argumentative in a sort of Durkheimian multitude of disputes, so that it is necessary to escape the spell of a Durkheimian picture of effervescence as a sort of delirium in scenes of the wildest excitement. The 'rave' is definitely not the model to apply in trying to understand what is going on in the modern festival (63). I would very much agree, while making the point that it is also not the model to apply to McKay's overall account of anti-establishment festival culture, whether in getting going with the Edinburgh People's Festival, or in developing through many different yet interacting forms such as Glastonbury, Stonehenge and 'Reclaim the Streets' street parties. On the contrary, it seems to me, a basic model is the existential rite of sacred drama, but injected with a large dose of Fabiani's elements of a modern, ironic, reflexive distancing, in the effort to think, argue and ask about key contemporary issues through participation in the festival as a live, collective art event.

Fabiani is particularly concerned with how, in modern tendencies towards a mass individualized consumption of art, the festival is a way to renew and reaffirm the value of a public culture in a republican society (64). However, a basic point about Glastonbury as 'a very English fair' is not so much that it is 'English' but that it is republican. Its origins owe nothing to official state sponsorship, and it is in a continuing battle against capture by commercial forces as well as against absorption and integration into an establishment's 'public culture'. It inevitably comes with tensions that undermine any simplistic notion of solidarity, and indeed that are part of the whole modern problematic of solidarity itself. But it is in the very effort to avoid capture, absorption and integration that it is a way to renew and reaffirm the value and ideal of a republican public culture.

In sum, and recalling Mona Ozouf's concern with *the* festival rather than merely with different particular individual festivals, it is worth digging around in all the many modern examples in search of an idea – or ideal – of the festival itself, as a hard-core case of modern sacred art, that is, of art as a live, participatory, collective event. However, this is not just to make an academic theoretical point about it as a modern hard-core case of total aesthetics. It is also to do with how art has become an essential modern sanctuary of the soul, in trying to cope with and survive the forces of capitalism, or at least what Durkheim once described as a sordid commercialism.

Surviving Capitalism

The issue of solidarity is fundamental to Durkheim's effort to develop a social science. It drives the concerns, at the outset of his career, with the division of labour. It underlies the quest, later on, for the sacred. It makes a return, at the end of his life, in the plan for a work on ethics. So perhaps it is the way to conclude with some thoughts about his overall project and modern times.

Class-divided Society

Modern societies lurch along in a crippled solidarity because they are class-divided societies, whether class conflict is 'latent or acute' (*The Division of Labour*'s new preface) or 'latent or overt' (*The Communist Manifesto*). Or at least this is a picture that emerges in trying to understand Durkheim's social science and his worries over a world in crisis. They especially involve worries to do with aspirational constraints, exploitative contracts, alienation and a 'sordid commercialism'.

Aspirational Constraints and Modern Ideals

Durkheim's account locates a basic source of modern class conflict in a blockage, in various ways, of modern aspirations and ideals. A key aspiration is to equality, in the form of a universalizing ideal of everyone's same status as a citizen and a person. But the ethic of the person doesn't exist in isolation. It is part of a web of aspirations to do with ideals of a society of freedom, equality, justice, solidarity and dynamic energies in which everyone can live up to their potential. A key form of blockage of this whole set of aspirations is the exploitative contract. Why?

An all-important Durkheimian theme is that exchange is a necessary but only a superficial aspect of relations within a division of labour. Accordingly, the damage done by exploitative contracts is in no way simply to do with injustice in exchange. The malaise goes much deeper, in a poisoning of the whole social milieu of work itself. An explicit Durkheimian concern is with vast inequalities of unmerited wealth, which he especially identified with inherited wealth and a class-divided society of 'rich and poor at birth'. But an implication of his account is the damage done by any vast inequalities that, in shaping the terms of exchange between members of different classes, shape what is in effect a relation of masters and servants rather than of morally equal, mutually respected persons. This is such a fundamental blockage of modern aspirations and demands that it is a guarantee of class conflict, whether 'latent or acute'.

Yet given the power of these aspirations as social and moral forces, how is it that they can be frustrated in actual social relations?

Anomie, Alienation and a 'Sordid Commercialism'

Durkheim's main worry over anomie is to do with economic anomie, and his main explanation of economic anomie is to do with alienation. This is about a radical separateness, but at the same time links with a 'sordid commercialism'. Alienation as a radical separateness involves a sort of modern contradiction. In a way there is increasing macrosocietal interconnectedness, thanks to mass markets, mass production and globalization. Yet it is together with forces of microsocial disconnectedness, in which 'labour' and 'capital' are not just abstract economic categories but become the basis of social gulfs that isolate individuals from one another. They are not just ranked in different classes. They are physically separated and segregated in what are almost different planets.

So how might a development of new occupational guilds involve any significant change? There is once again a need to distinguish between Durkheim's functionalist, republican and moral discourses of solidarity. There is something seriously inadequate with his functionalist vision of a transformation of work into a scene of dynamic collaborative interaction between 'vibrating cells' and 'organs of an organism'. It is difficult to see how his new guilds will achieve anything without a fundamental switch away from old regime relations of masters and servants, towards a republicanization of work as a cooperation between equals and persons. In turn, this is thanks to a fundamental shift in the moral basis of solidarity, as an affair of mutual respect and attachment. Whether or not there was once upon a time an old regime of harmony, respect and attachment between individuals related as masters and servants, the Revolution killed it off as an ideal of the modern era.

On the one hand, then, Durkheimian hope in a renewal of the guild is in effect about development through work, as a moral milieu of everyday attachments, contacts, links and relations, of an everyday basis of an actual, deep-rooted respect for persons. On the other, this helps to bring out worries over a world of mere lip-service to rights. An isolation that is not just social but physical is an essential modern way in which one class treats others as if subpersons, through relationships without relations and a macrosocietal connectedness of microsocial disconnectedness. In contrast with old regime masters and servants living cheek by jowl, they are exploited from a distance, located as far out of sight and out of mind as possible.

At the same time it is in a world infected by a 'sordid commercialism' and belief in self-interest as the basis of the operation of society. An insistent theme, from the beginning to the end of Durkheim's career, is a critique of this 'economism', and it applies all the way through, to the 'economistic' homeland of economic life itself. In the last article he published, he makes clear his long-held view that 'economic activity is something eminently social', and welcomes the transformation of industries run for private profit into 'genuine public services' ([1917c] 2009: 4–5).

This is undoubtedly to welcome a transformation to something different from what has often been understood as 'capitalism'. At any rate, talk of 'capitalism' had by Durkheim's time become a standard feature of the vocabulary not only of orthodox economics but socialism. A problem, then, is that it is not a standard feature of his own vocabulary. Throughout his career he avoided use of the term in his own voice, and as part of his own explanation and account of a crisis in economic life that he located at the heart of the modern world. Why?

A clue is in a debate between Durkheim and the socialist, Hubert Lagardelle, criticized as a 'prisoner of the Marxist materialist formula'. Unconcerned with webs of social and moral life, he reduces the worker to the abstract status of a 'producer' and accordingly resurrects the ghost of abstract 'economic man' (1905e: 286–90). In reply, Lagardelle denies that he ignores the social, moral and other ingredients of life as a whole, but insists that the worker's economic condition and status is primary, and everything else depends on this. Obviously, the debate was heading nowhere. Yet at least it suggests a reason for Durkheim's reluctance to use the term 'capitalism' as part of his own approach. It is too closely associated with a sordid economism – on the left, as well as the right – that makes the world of material interest the foundation of the realm of society.

True enough, the crisis in economic life is a crisis he himself locates at the heart of modern society. But economic activity is pre-eminently social, and the crisis going on in it is pre-eminently a social, moral crisis. As he explains in his lectures on socialism, the key to the issue 'is not the state of our economy, but much more the state of our morality' (1928: 297). Or again, although he begins with a definition of socialism in terms of a demand to organize economic activity, he goes on to emphasize how this requires an organization that is social as well as moral. And he ends with a critique of the Saint-Simonians for attempting the 'impossible', in trying to get from economics to ethics. Instead, it is necessary to rebuild morality itself, through moral milieux with the power to regulate economic life and to meet needs by controlling selfishness (351).

It is true enough, too, that although Durkheim's account of modern everyday scenes of injustice is about modern everyday scenes of class conflict, he was against raising the banner of class war as the way to the future. Instead, his campaign for what is in effect a form of guild socialism is about leaving behind class war and moving towards a cooperative commonwealth. At the same time it is about leaving behind a sordid economism and moving towards a moral commonwealth. In both these aspects, it is about rebuilding solidarity – yet not, miraculously, out of nothing, but out of materials of social and moral life already to hand. What, then, are his basic materials?

Rebuilding Solidarity

Durkheim sets out to rescue the division of labour from its pathological forms, in the view that it is still the main modern route to solidarity in everyday life. This is above all in a concern with its continuing centrality, not just as an economic but a social activity, and as a source of the solidarity of attachment in webs of everyday contacts, links and relations. It is why he looks to the division of labour as a moral force, and to work as a moral milieu. It is also bound up with his insistence that functional diversity entails moral diversity, helping to generate different outlooks, attitudes and characters. In republican terms, there are two main implications, or two aspects of the same basic implication. Work is or ought to be a key modern site of the individual's development as a socially attached yet distinct and autonomous personality. Not least, work is or ought to be a key modern site of cooperative effort and interaction between morally equal persons, ready to recognize, draw on and pool one another's talents, and to negotiate ways round inevitable problems, disagreements and disputes. Is it realistic, then, to aspire towards the republicanism of Durkheim's spontaneous division of labour? Yet what is realistic about settling for a constrained division of labour, with its systematic blockage of modern ideals?

Put another way, Durkheim also sets out to rescue ideals that he sees as powerful moral forces and energies generated by the modern world itself, but, through their very frustration, feeding into a situation of crisis, malaise and class war. It is no solution to try and pick and choose between these ideals, whether, say, in a sacrifice of freedom for equality, or of equality for freedom. It is necessary, as in Camus's 'philosophy of limits', to search for forms of their mutual influence and interaction in a rootedness in solidarity. For Durkheim as for Camus – in their quite different voices, experiences and times – a crucial concern is with how the freedom of the individual is bound up with a solidarity of collective life, and with establishing the connection. This is easier said than done. But as in an essay by Susan Stedman Jones (2009), a way of appreciating the nature and significance of Durkheim's search for a collective life that is pluralist rather than authoritarian is to trace its roots in social, political and philosophical struggles in nineteenth-century France. Another way is to return to his campaign for new intermediate groups and how it involves a set of interrelated concerns with republican ideals, moral milieux and an effective social organization.

Rebuilding solidarity depends on translating the energy of these powerful yet vast abstract ideals into a practical moral code. This in turn means rebuilding, especially in economic life and through the division of labour as a social force, attachment in the webs of relations of particular, definite moral milieux. But it also means the development of a social organization that is pluralist, rather than either too diffuse and anarchic or too concentrated and monolithic. Durkheim sometimes discussed these as separate risks. However, what worried him most was their modern combination in the 'sociological monstrosity' of a mass of atomized individuals under an authoritarian, centralized state. Accordingly, what are his worry's fundamental, underlying sources?

On the one hand, he saw no future for a withering away of the state. He maintained that everything pointed to its continuing and indeed growing role. On the other, this is a reason for his alarm at a withering away of civil society. His campaign for a renewal of the guild is about many things. But it is not least about a renewal of citizenship, through a pluralist commonwealth that counterbalances the state with an effective, powerful organization of intermediate groups.

In sum, Durkheim's account of the modern world comes with a whole set of concerns and materials to think about and draw on. Even so, it might be wondered how far it can help with understanding a 'crisis of transition' that is still with us, and that is clearly bound up with the economy, however bound in with society.

Economy and Society

A way of taking on board Durkheim's reservations about the term 'capitalism' is to emphasize that it focuses on an economic system, rather than society. As an economic system, capitalism arose, developed and continues to make its career in worlds of society. A way of taking this further is through the work of a pioneer of economic anthropology, Karl Polanyi (1944), and his account of how, among tribal peoples, the economy is 'embedded' in society. But it is to add that capitalism, in its own fashion, is also embedded in society. The question is in what fashion.

The Keynesian Interlude

Capitalism has a long track record of surviving one crisis after another. Indeed, *The Division of Labour* was written during a major economic downturn in Europe, and especially in France, between 1873 and 1895. The lectures on socialism were given just at the beginning of recovery from this period, but were published just before the stock-market crash of 1929, followed by the Great Depression of the 1930s. However, after two world wars, the depression and the threat of the Red Menace, capitalism was reformed in significant and even dramatic ways in the period from the late 1940s to the 1970s. These included policies of full employment, the nationalization of key industries in a 'mixed economy', the development of the welfare system, the reduction of inequalities of income and wealth, and, linked with all this, the stabilization of financial markets not only by their regulation but in a macromanagement of demand through state and international institutional intervention. So the period can be characterized in a number of ways. But since it became associated with the ideas of John Maynard Keynes, and began to come to an end with various events in the late 1970s, it could be known as the Keynesian interlude.

In the case of market stabilization, a basic pattern can be brought out from research discussed and cited by Alex Callinicos (2010: 35). The level of financial crises was halved between 1945 and 1971, compared with the pre-1914 era of Durkheim's time. But, again compared with this era, it doubled between 1973 and 1997. Or, compared with the Keynesian interlude, the level of crises in the succeeding period increased so much that it quadrupled. Whatever might be claimed for the succeeding, so-called 'neoliberal' period, it has a long and well-documented record of failure as a way to avoid the havoc of financial crises and economic slumps. Some of the most serious incidents are described by Gérard Duménil and Dominique Lévy ([2000] 2004: 86–97), in a work of empirically based analysis that made clear there was an even bigger crash to come, and that duly came in 2008.

In the case of inequality, a basic pattern can be brought out from research discussed and cited by David Harvey (2005: 17). This concentrates on the rich, to track their share of income in the US, the UK and France between 1913 and 1998. In 1913, on the eve of the Great War, a mere 0.01 per cent of the population took around 8.5 per cent of total income in the US, 11.5 per cent in the UK, and 8 per cent in France. By

1979, which effectively marks the end of the Keynesian interlude, their share had fallen to 2 per cent in the US, 1 per cent in the UK and 2 per cent in France. By 1998, after twenty years of Anglo-Saxon 'neoliberalism', it had bounced back to 6 per cent in the US and 3.5 per cent in the UK, but remained at 2 per cent in France. Clearly, compared with the similarity between these three homelands of capitalism during the Keynesian interlude, different trends in inequality have now been going on in them. Clearly, too, a fuller picture depends on a range of measures of inequality that track long-term historical changes in a range of countries with some or other form of a capitalist system. But where the trend is on the up, towards vast inequalities approaching a level unknown since Durkheim's time, why worry about it?

An answer can be found in a seminal study by Richard Wilkinson and Kate Pickett (2009). This draws on a mass of data and research, and undertakes a systematic comparison of what are in effect the world's capitalist economies that are the richest (by average income) as well as the most populous (3 million plus). So while it leaves plenty of scope for further, more comprehensive investigations, it is already quite an ambitious exercise. A key factor that emerges, again and again, is the degree of inequality. As they summarize their findings: 'most of the important health and social problems of the rich world are more common in more unequal societies'. The problems affect all groups of a population, but are 'from three times to ten times as common in more unequal societies' (173). It is an inequality that comes with low levels of trust, generosity, well-being and educational attainment, and with high levels of violence, crime, drug addiction and mental illness. So it is not surprising that they discuss these societies as 'dysfunctional societies' (173–93). However, a number of comments might be made.

In setting out to explain how inequality can have such a far-reaching, simultaneously physical, psychological and social impact, they draw on research on the hidden injuries of class and emphasize the damage done by hierarchical caste-like relations of superior and inferior. But there is a need to situate this in the context of a modern world that comes with ideals of everyone's equality as a person, and indeed that generates furious opposition to the very use of a language of 'class', yet while also generating lip-service to rights and glib talk of already living in a 'classless' society. In other words, a factor in the modern world's injuries of inequality is that they rub in the gap between ideals of respect for everyone as a person and actual everyday experiences.

At the same time it is in the context of modern ideals of justice and what counts as morally legitimate wealth. A factor in modern injuries of inequality is unfairness, not least thanks to unearned wealth. Thus the study examines how high levels of inequality come with low levels of social mobility through the influence of rich and poor at birth. But it also looks beyond this, in a discussion of the vast inequalities created in corporate boardrooms. For example, it cites how in 2007 top US companies paid their chief executives over 500 times more than the average for their employees. An even more revealing statistic is how this differential had increased by around ten times since 1980 – at the end of the Keynesian interlude and beginning of the 'neoliberal' period. It is difficult to believe that the differential increased because executives became ten times better at their jobs, or workers became ten times worse. Instead, and what the study might have done more to emphasize, it is part of a wider picture of a redistribution of wealth, away from the many, to the very, very few – not just to 10 per cent, or even 1 per cent, but a tiny fractional 0.01 per cent. Moreover, the most recent evidence indicates that these inequalities are continuing to become greater and greater, and that in the wake of the crisis of 2008 the very, very rich are now richer than they were before.[1] Again, then, how can it be because they have become so much better at earning a well-deserved living, or everybody else has become so much worse?

It is no doubt interesting to discuss the claims of 'neoliberalism' as a theory. However, its essential ideas are neither very new nor very liberal. They regurgitate a crude free-market doctrine that the eminent Scottish economist John McCulloch described, in 1848, as the policy of a parrot.[2] They were also refuted, in detail, in edition after edition of one of the great works of the time, John Stuart Mill's *Principles of Political Economy* (1848 to 1871). In practice, the so-called 'neoliberal' period is to do with a massive reconcentration of wealth and power, in a return to an inequality of the old regime but in the conditions of a world of modern ideals and aspirations. This is a basic contradiction, and an underlying force at work that guarantees a 'dysfunctional society'. It is also why it remains, inescapably, a variation of how capitalism is embedded in a social and moral world. Wilkinson and Pickett help to bring out how it comes with different profiles of inequality and associated problems in different local social and moral environments. What the crash of 2008 helped to drive home, at least to a wider public if not to a mammonite sect of bankers, speculators, corporate executives and fellow-travelling politicians, is how it involves a general overall crisis in which what is at stake – to echo Durkheim – is not just the 'state of the economy' but the 'state of morality'.

The Crash of 2008

Some initial reflections on the crisis, exploring it in a Durkheimian perspective, are offered in a set of essays by Steven Lukes (2009), Mike Gane

(2009) and Edward Tiryakian (2009b). A key theme is to do with Durkheim's critique of anomie and alienation, or, put the other way round, his belief in moral regulation, anchored in the solidarity of attachment in microsocial relations. Thus Lukes ends with a discussion of concerns that the financial rampage lacked control by official, statutory bodies, but emphasizes that 'moral regulation was absent and, indeed, never even contemplated'. In turn, however, development of moral regulation is bound up with development of solidarities rooted in social life, and this is part of how, in his view, the crisis raises 'many questions about the future of capitalism as we have known it'. But the question with which he concludes is if and how it might help to generate wide-ranging public debate about 'the morality of capitalism' itself (Lukes 2009: 18).

The nature of the stakes can be appreciated from Gane's essay on the 'paradox of neoliberalism', to do with how it embeds the economy in society. In bringing out the paradox, he especially draws on Durkheim's view of socialism as a demand to link the economy with an overall social organization that includes the state. This is how, in its own fashion, 'neoliberalism' is a socialist project. To link the economy with society, it 'inserts the market principles of competition and enterprise at every conceivable site, extending not contracting the sphere of intervention of the state' (Gane 2009: 21). One of the main ways is its use of the state to develop and extend techniques of the population's self-surveillance, controlling individuals by shaping them into market contestants who manage themselves as 'human capital'. But perhaps the most important way is its use of the state to impose a form of market competition on groups and institutions in every sector of social life, in education, health, welfare, charities, the police service, the arts... This is done by a system of targets, scores, assessment exercises, league tables and so on. It is in a sort of market-style game, in which 'the advantage to government is that the result is legitimised by the very participation of the players' (25). In sum, the 'neoliberal' project emerges from the essay as a misbegotten socialism, in its effort to make the market principle itself the way to integrate economy, society and state.

But this is why, in a more familiar Durkheimian view, it emerges as yet another version of a sordid economism, in yet another route to atomized individuals and an authoritarian state. So to the extent that it has succeeded in embedding its economistic attitudes deep within civil society and the state, Lukes might seem overhopeful in looking to a wide-ranging public debate about 'the morality of capitalism', and more realistic in wondering where, nowadays, there are the bases for a rebuilding of morality through a rebuilding of solidarities. This is the question that underlies Tiryakian's reflections on what he emphasizes is a '*systemic* crisis', in no way limited to economic institutions. 'Other pillars of societies have been affected by moral deregulation, like the educational, kinship and political institutions – key intermediary structures between the individual and the State' (Tiryakian 2009b: 29).

In recalling Durkheim's concern with the moral and civic role of education, he worries, not unlike Gane, about a tendency in which education 'is seen as a commodity whose goal rests with obtaining certificates, and diplomas that are stepping stones to better material conditions' (32). Outside the school, moreover, far-reaching changes are going on in domestic life. Durkheim was a firm believer in marriage, and had seen its long-term intimate relations as a paradigmatic case of solidarity. But this might nowadays seem a lost cause. Tiryakian goes over statistics on marriage, cohabitation, same-sex unions, single parent households and divorce that indicate similar general trends both in Europe and the US. They point to 'new patterns in the making', generating challenges of how to interpret them but also of how to come up with constructive proposals for reform, in ways that are relevant to and 'motivate new generations' (35–36).

Let us suppose, however, that reform takes place on Durkheimian lines. It is in aspirations to a commonwealth of persons, that can be variously characterized as a pluralist, cooperative and moral commonwealth. It involves a liberal pluralist politics in which the state is counterbalanced by a powerful web of intermediate groups throughout civil society, but in which the state itself has been won back for the republic and recovered democratic legitimacy as an essential coordinating agent of social life. It also involves initiatives, through this framework of everyone's citizenship and same moral status as a person, to create a dynamic world of everyone's freedom to fulfil their potential, to overcome the injustice of vast suffocating inequalities due to unearned, unmerited, private wealth, to develop forms of decentralized collective ownership and control, and to make industry first and foremost an affair, not of individual profit, but public service and cooperative enterprise and effort.

So if this leaves the disaster of the 'neoliberal' period behind, at the same time it goes beyond limitations of the Keynesian interlude – such as the managerialist centralism of welfare and of nationalized industries – that helped to make it vulnerable to attack. Yet is its fate also to become, not a turning point in the history of a modern world in crisis, but merely another interlude?

Durkheim 'hoped to "moralize" capitalism', according to Lukes (2009: 16). This is true enough, in terms of his hopes in a way to get going a process of reform. It is misleading, in terms of his hopes in a process that continues to develop and indeed never stops, in fresh challenges in which there is always a field wide open to effort. Thus while setting out his own views on the need for far-reaching change – such as the development of forms of decentralized collective ownership and control of wealth – he consistently refused to work these up into a blueprint of the good society, and instead consistently maintained that the evolution of reform is a matter for society itself in a 'politics of the future'. On the one hand, then, it is difficult to pin down Durkheim's own views to a belief *either* in a civilized, radically reformed capitalism *or* in going beyond it altogether as the only way of overcoming the forces of a sordid commercialism. On the other, it is possible to argue that his views home in on this as a basic issue to be sorted out in the effort, struggle and experience of working towards a commonwealth.

Accordingly, it is instructive to turn to modern Marxist accounts of the crisis, on offer, for example, from Callinicos (2010), Duménil and Lévy ([2000] 2004) and Harvey (2005, 2010). These home in on the economy but with attention to its various social, simultaneously local and global contexts, analyse it in detail but with various disagreements about what is going on, yet nonetheless come up with a similar core message. A lesson of the Keynesian experience is that any regulation and reform of capitalism can be no more than an interlude. It will be swept away by the very dynamics of capitalism, as and when necessary, and as has happened in the 'neoliberal' period.

But it is also instructive to turn the clock back to the 1930s, and to a little known episode in the career of Durkheim after Durkheim. He was commonly denounced by Marxists of the time as a bourgeois stooge, and in response to these attacks a more nuanced and sympathetic picture was given in a paper by René Maublanc, a former student of Durkheim's who had converted to Marxism. He gave the paper in 1934, although it has only recently been published (Maublanc 2011), together with a discussion of his text and its background in an essay by Isabelle Gouarné (2011). The text is of interest in many ways, but is of interest, here, for two main reasons.

In commenting on *The Elemental Forms*, he is concerned with taking on board its account of the importance of the sacred in the origins of social life, and argues it is time to give up on faithful reproductions of the line on 'primitive' economy and society that Marx and Engels based on what is now a long out of date, discredited ethnology. In commenting on *The Division of Labour*, he puts his finger on a central mystery of its account of a modern crisis, yet without bringing out and acknowledging how it can also involve a problematic of solidarity in Marxist interpretations. The mystery is Durkheim's official line on a crisis due to exceptional, abnormal circumstances, rather than anything inherent in the very nature of the division of labour and its modern development in everyday scenes of alienation, exploitation and class conflict. At one level, the problematic for Marxist interpretations is how these scenes can indeed be described as pathological. At a perhaps more fundamental level, it is to do with Maublanc's insistence on the key modern importance of the division of labour, not only for Durkheim but for Marx, as a set of relations between individuals. So it might be put this way. Capitalism depends on a division of labour and accordingly lives off a world of relations, attachments and society that in the process it turns into a frontline of modern class war. Yet these are ineliminably cooperative relations, in the very activity of work itself, and form an essential basis of rebuilding solidarity in modern everyday life. Or it might be put another way. Capitalism simultaneously lives off and eats away at solidarity, but which is why it cannot survive if it destroys what it depends on and might outgrow it.

The Worm in the Bud

A passage in *The Elemental Forms* throws particular light on Durkheim's view of the profane and its relation with the sacred.

> In ordinary days, individual and utilitarian preoccupations are uppermost in minds. Everyone sees to their personal task on their own account; it is above all, for most people, about meeting the demands of material life, and the principal motive of economic activity has always been self-interest. (1912a: 497)

Even in Durkheimian Australia, self-interest is never far away but is kept in check by the flowering and effervescence of solidarity in special times of the sacred.

This also illuminates something very basic about *The Division of Labour*. It digs around for sources of solidarity in ordinary everyday life itself, and indeed in the ordinary everyday homeland of self-interest, the sphere of economic activity. However, it is in coming up against a form of self-interest that isn't just a given of human nature or of a universal abstract 'economic man'. It is self-interest as socially and culturally constructed in the modern world and its economic life.

There are at least two main interlinking ways in which the entrepreneur's self-interest is shaped and defined in a capitalist economy. One is central to Durkheim's concerns. It is to do with the pursuit of gain through generalized market-exchange, while treating the division of labour as if a mere instrument of this and mechanism to be exploited, in a systematic blindness to its character as a social and moral milieu in webs of ineliminably cooperative relations between persons. The other was never adequately tackled by Durkheim, but is central to Marxist concerns. It is to do with a never-ending drive for profit, through a never-ending search for investment and reinvestment in any form of social wealth that can be appropriated as private capital. These are historically specific ways of constructing self-interest in an overall package, in turn feeding into a system that can develop with important particular variations and different particular far-reaching consequences. But at bottom it is how capitalism, like a worm in the bud, lives off what it eats away at.

A way to conclude, though, is with a core Durkheimian concern about its impact on the world of society as a world of ideals. A classic capitalist doctrine is that private profit is the route to the public good. It has been taken apart again and again since the early nineteenth century. Yet it has been merely repeated again and again in the 'neoliberal' period, in a disregard of historical experience and in an unprecedented epidemic of crises. It is still being repeated after the latest disaster, on course to another.

So a question is if it is simply another case of how, through the ages, as well as through capitalism's own successive phases of development, a ruling class survives thanks to the wrapping up of its self-interest in an ideology. Thus although the 'neoliberal' period came with widely quoted remarks to the effect that greed is good, these merely recycled an eighteenth century quip about private vice and public benefit. The less scandalous, more usual form of official rhetoric drew on standard modern ideals of freedom, rights, fairness, equal opportunity, progress, the democratic way of life. Even after the latest disaster, and in policies that continue to fill the trousers of a few while paying for their failures by imposing austerity on the many, it is in talk of fairness, everyone's equal sacrifice, pulling together and pulling through, rebuilding the Big Society, etc. In helping to feed cynicism about politicians, the damage this does is not just to do with a theft of the republic, but a theft of the very language of a republic and a moral commonwealth.

A mystery that remains is the apparent contradiction between feeding distrust, through abuse of this language, and a successful ideology. At the same time a Durkheimian perspective suggests a need to distinguish the problematic of ideology and a loss of illusions from the issue of transfiguration and transparence.

Ideology involves the wrapping up of a particular cultural construction of self-interest in a particular world of society and its ideals, but in such a way that self-interest is the main underlying driving force. Transfiguration, for Durkheim, is essentially about the mystification of a world of society and its ideals, but in such a way that the sacred is a pre-eminent, impersonal, collective power, going over and beyond self-interest and effective enough to limit and regulate forces of the profane. Indeed, throughout his career he believed not only that self-interest can never be a foundation of ethics but that it can always be brought under control by the moral world of society, whether transfigured in forms of the sacred or demystified and transparent. Yet how is this still possible?

In 1885, in a speech that at the time became famous and as part of a campaign against 'the excessive inequality in the distribution of riches', the English politician Joseph Chamberlain asked: 'What ransom will property pay for the security which it enjoys?'[3] This question was undoubtedly one of the underlying factors in the long struggles for justice that resulted, after two world wars, a devastating depression and under the threat of communism, in the Keynesian interlude. But what can seem a turning point in the situation nowadays is a change in the whole balance of forces. It is as if 'property' calculates it is in a position to pay little or no ransom for its security, to hollow out the state, to free-ride on civil society and to risk placing this under immense strain in increasing vast inequalities of wealth and a massive concentration of private economic and financial power. Public opinion might express any amount of moral outrage. But it is diffused, disorganized and doesn't count. It has been denied the effective voice that was central to Durkheim's campaign for reform.

The Division of Labour, written so long ago, is full of hope. Yet the fundamental reason for this has not gone away. Ideals of a commonwealth and struggles to defend and work towards these are part of the modern world, even if forces that variously corrupt, frustrate or block them are part of it too. In any case, and whatever might happen in a politics of the future, attachment to an ideal gives meaning to life in the here and now. It is a way of holding on to the soul, to keep going and not give in. There is every reason, perhaps more than ever, for obstinate rock-bottom hope.

Notes

Introduction

1. This is based on the two indispensable biographies of Durkheim, by
   Steven Lukes (1973) and Marcel Fournier (2007). It also draws on
   a conference that the latter organized at Epinal in 2008, presenting
   new research on Durkheim's social origins and background, including the career of his local Jewish community from the late eighteenth to the early twentieth centuries. Publication of this research,
   edited by Fournier, is still awaited. Meanwhile, on the much debated
   question of Durkheim's Jewish identity, see, e.g., W.S.F. Pickering
   (1994) but also Matthieu Béra (2011). This is the most important
   recent investigation of the issue, with discoveries of crucial, hitherto
   unknown biographical information.

Chapter 1

1. The relation between Kantian and Durkheimian ethics is examined
   in an earlier book (Watts Miller 1996). This has detailed references
   for the discussion that follows, not just on Kant's work itself but on
   Kant's career in France and as interpreted in Durkheim's own milieu.
2. This is based on two pieces of evidence. Durkheim uses a passage
   from Rousseau that only became widely known in an influential new
   edition of 1896. He also mentions 'my course on Rousseau' in a letter of around 1897 (Durkheim 1998: 63; cf. Fournier 2007: 149).
3. On the Dreyfus Affair, and Durkheim's role in it, see Fournier (2007:
   365–90). The crisis split French society, and was sparked off by the
   case of a Jewish army captain found guilty of treason.
4. This has become accepted as the date of these lectures, and was first
   put forward by Philippe Besnard (1993).
5. See Watts Miller (1996), chapter 8.

Chapter 2

1. William Doyle (2001) is the best short up to date guide to the Revolution. Alfred Cobban (1965) remains an accessible, authoritative guide to the arrival and establishment of the Third Republic, as well as to the crisis of the Dreyfus Affair.
2. On the battle of rites and symbols, and its role in the construction of French collective memory and identity, a key source is the collection edited by Pierre Nora (1984–92).
3. See, especially, *Trésor de la langue française*, edited by B. Quemada (1992).

Chapter 3

1. This generally unnoticed switch from 'Jews' to 'Hebrews', between a thesis completed in 1892 and a new edition completed in 1901, is all the more intriguing in light of another recent discovery. The author registered himself as 'David Durkheim' in the census of 1891, but as 'Emile Durkheim' in the census of 1901 (see Béra 2011).

Chapter 4

1. The title of this chapter is owed to Philippe Steiner, chair in sociology at the Sorbonne. At a seminar in Paris in 2009, when I was floating some of the ideas of my research, he clarified things with the suggestion that what I was concerned with was 'an intellectual crisis'.
2. Like the switch from 'Jews' to 'Hebrews', these are so far generally unnoticed changes between *The Division of Labour*'s editions of 1893 and 1902, but form a crucial piece of actual empirical evidence in asking about the 'revelation' of 1895, on which so much theoretical ink has been spilt.
3. On Frazer's influence on the creation, production and reception of *The Native Tribes of Central Australia*, see the biography of Spencer by D.J. Mulvaney and J.H. Calaby (1985: 178–80, 185–86). On Spencer and Gillen's impact on the theories of Frazer in particular, but also on the whole course of the debate on totemism, see Frederico Rosa (2003).

Chapter 5

1. On Radcliffe-Brown and the history of British social anthropology, see the indispensable, authoritative work by George Stocking (1995).

2. 'The lectures might be said to constitute the initial draft of *The Elementary Forms*' (Pickering 1984: 79).
3. See his letters of July 1908 (1975: vol.2, 467) and November 1908 (1998: 390).
4. For details of the controversy over the ethnographies of Spencer and Gillen and of Strehlow, which became a *cause célèbre* in Australian anthropology, see Mulvaney and Calaby (1985: 378–96).
5. For an informed, recent analysis of the work's treatment of conceptual thought and the categories, see Susan Stedman Jones (2012). For an overall account of the relation between sociology and philosophy in Durkheim's writings, see Giovanni Paoletti (2012a).

Chapter 6

1. See Mulvaney and Calaby (1985: 220–21).
2. For an illuminating discussion of internationalism in *The Elemental Forms*, see David Inglis (2011). On the meaning and importance of the idea of a 'human *patrie*' in Durkheim's work in general, see Watts Miller (1996: 151–54, 244–46).
3. There is an essential maxim to guide investigating Durkheim's work: 'Read What Durkheim Read' (Borlandi 2000).

Chapter 7

1. There appears to have been little response from Jewish writers. But there was a review by Salomon Reinach (1912), discussed in recently discovered letters to him from Durkheim (2010: 30).

Chapter 8

1. To be more exact, the chair in education to which he was appointed in 1906 was converted to a chair in education and sociology. See Fournier (2005: 820–21).
2. Cuvillier was one of a number of Durkheim's former students who became sympathetic with Marxism, and who in a nowadays largely forgotten episode sought in the 1920s and 1930s a rapprochement between Durkheimianism and Marxism. See Isabelle Gouarné (2011).
3. There is yet again a need to acknowledge a debt to Steven Lukes. It was during research for his thesis that he was given access to various, now invaluable documents. These include the student lecture notes shown to him by Cuvillier and Davy, and reproduced in appendices to volume 2 of his thesis (Lukes 1968).

Essay 1

1. Modern power struggles between forces of the sacred and forces of the profane are also explored, for example, by Michel Maffesoli (1988).
2. On the relation between Durkheim, Mauss and Mathiez, see also Edward Tiryakian (2009a).

Essay 2

1. For the best short guide to Marcel's philosophy of hope, see Joan Nowotny (1979).

Essay 3

1. This is an extensively revised version of an earlier article (Watts Miller 2004). One of the main changes is to bring in the lectures on aesthetics by Mauss (1947), while another is to take on board the comments of Jean-Louis Fabiani (2005). It is also in the context of the collection of essays on Durkheim and art edited by Alexander Riley et al. (forthcoming).
2. For a detailed account of the first performance and public reception of *The Rite*, see Richard Buckle (1980: 346–62).

Essay 4

1. For example, according to a report by Merill Lynch and Capgemini on the world's 'high net worth individuals', their total wealth rose from around $33 trillion in 2008 to around $43 trillion in 2010 (*The Guardian*, 23 June 2011, 31). According to a report by the UK High Pay Commission, the share of the top 0.1 per cent rose to 5 per cent of all earnings in 2010. This involved an income increase of just over 64 per cent since 1996, compared with an average income increase of just over 7 per cent. A continuation of these trends would see the top 0.1 per cent taking 14 per cent of national income by 2030, the same as in 1900 (*The Independent on Sunday*, 15 May 2011, 4–5). According to a report by the Resolution Foundation, in line with this but looking at things another way, the trend in the UK and the US is towards a sharp decline in middle and lower incomes both in real terms and as a share of national GDP (*The Observer*, 22 May 2011, 30–31).
2. 'The principle of *laissez-faire* may be safely trusted to in some things but in many more it is wholly inapplicable; and to appeal to it on all

occasions savours more of the policy of a parrot than of a statesman or a philosopher', discussed and quoted by Arthur Taylor (1972: 22).

3. Discussed and quoted by Derek Fraser (1973: 130).

References

Note: references to works published by Durkheim during his lifetime are based on the dating-enumeration system developed by Steven Lukes (1973) and W.S.F. Pickering (1984).

Anon. 1899a. Review of B. Spencer and F. Gillen, *The Native Tribes of Central Australia*, *Notes and Queries* 9: 338–39.
——— 1899b. Review of B. Spencer and F. Gillen, *The Native Tribes of Central Australia*, *Journal of the Anthropological Institute* n.s. 1: 330–32.
Baciocchi, S. 2012. 'Durkheim's Inaugural Lecture and the Course on Pragmatism and Sociology', *Durkheimian Studies/Etudes durkheimiennes*, 18 (forthcoming).
Baruzi, J. et al. 1926. *Philosophes et savants français du XXe siècle: extraits et notices*, vol.3. Paris: Alcan.
Bellah, R. et al. 1996. *Habits of the Heart: Individualism and Commitment in American Life*, 2nd ed. Berkeley, California: University of California Press.
Béra, M. 2011. 'David, Emile: les ambivalences de l'identité juive de Durkheim', *Durkheimian Studies/Etudes durkheimiennes* 17: 121–50.
Besnard, P. 1993. 'De la datation des cours pédagogiques de Durkheim á la recherche du thème dominant de l'œuvre', in F. Cardi and J. Plantier (eds), *Durkheim, sociologue de l'éducation*. Paris: Harmattan, pp. 120–30.
Bloch, E. [1959] 1986. *The Principle of Hope*, 3 vols, trans. N. Plaice, S. Plaice and P. Knight. Oxford: Blackwell.
Borlandi, M. 2000. 'Lire ce que Durkheim a lu: enquête sur les sources statistiques et médicales du *Suicide*', in M. Borlandi and M. Cherkouai (eds), Le Suicide *un siècle après Durkheim*. Paris: Presses Universitaires de France, pp. 9–46.
Borlandi, M. (ed.). 2012. Les Formes élémentaires de la vie religieuse *un siècle après*, special edition of *L'Année sociologique* 62 (1).
Boutroux, E. 1895. *De l'Idée de loi naturelle dans la science et la philosophie: cours professée à la Sorbonne en 1892–1893*. Paris: Lecène, Oudin.
Brunschvicg, L. 1939. *La Raison et la religion*. Paris: Alcan.

Buckle, R. 1980. *Nijinsky*. Harmondsworth: Penguin.

Callinicos, A. 2010. *Bonfire of Illusions: The Twin Crises of the Liberal World*. Cambridge: Polity Press.

Camus, A. 1942. *Le Mythe de Sisyphe*. Paris: Gallimard.

—— 1951. *L'Homme révolté*. Paris: Gallimard.

—— 1954. *L'Eté*. Paris: Gallimard.

—— 1955. Preface to *The Myth of Sisyphus*, trans. J. O'Brien. London: Hamish Hamilton, p. 7.

Cobban, A. 1965. *A History of Modern France, vol.3, 1871–1962*. Harmondsworth: Penguin.

Coenen-Huther, J. 2010. *Comprendre Durkheim*. Paris: Armand Colin.

Cohen, P. 1997. *Freedom's Moment: An Essay on the French Idea of Liberty from Rousseau to Foucault*. Chicago: University of Chicago Press.

Constant, B. [1819] 1980. 'De la Liberté des anciens comparée à celle des modernes', in Constant, *De la Liberté chez les modernes: écrits politiques*, ed. M. Gauchet. Paris: Le Livre de Poche, pp. 491–515.

Crooke, W. 1899. Review of A.H. Keane, *Man, Past and Present, Journal of the Anthropological Institute* n.s. 2: 185.

Crouzet, F. 1999. 'French Historians and Robespierre', in C. Haydon and W. Doyle (eds), *Robespierre*. Cambridge: Cambridge University Press, pp. 255–83.

Cubitt, G. 1999. 'Robespierre and Conspiracy Theories', in C. Haydon and W. Doyle (eds), *Robespierre*. Cambridge: Cambridge University Press, pp. 75–91.

Cunow, H. 1894. *Die Verwandtschafts-Organisationen der Australneger*. Stuttgart: Dietz.

Cuvillier, A. 1955. Preface to Durkheim, *Pragmatisme et sociologie*. Paris: Vrin, pp. 7–26.

—— 1975. Notes of 1908/1909 on lectures by Durkheim on morality, in Durkheim 1975, vol.2: 292–312.

Davy, G. 1975. Notes of 1908/1909 on lectures by Durkheim on morality, in Durkheim 1975, vol.2: 12–22.

Desroche, H. [1973] 1979. *The Sociology of Hope*, trans. C. Sperry. London: Routledge and Kegan Paul.

Doyle, W. 2001. *The French Revolution: A Very Short Introduction*. Oxford: Oxford University Press.

Duménil, G. and D. Lévy. [2000] 2004. *Capital Resurgent: Roots of the Neoliberal Revolution*, trans. D. Jeffers. Cambridge: Harvard University Press.

Durkheim, E. 1885a. Review of A. Schaeffle, *Bau und Leben des sozialen Körpers*, in Durkheim 1975, vol.1: 355–77.

—— 1885b. Review of A. Fouillée, *La Propriété sociale et la démocratie*, in Durkheim 1970: 171–83.

—— 1886a. 'Les Etudes de science sociale', in Durkheim 1970: 184–214.

—— 1888a. 'Cours de science sociale: leçon d'ouverture', in Durkheim 1970: 77–110.

—— 1888b. 'Le Programme économique de M. Schaeffle', in Durkheim 1975, vol.1: 377–83.

—— 1888c. 'Introduction à la sociologie de la famille', in Durkheim 1975, vol.3: 9–34.

—— 1890a. 'Les Principes de 1789 et la sociologie', in Durkheim 1970: 215–25.

—— 1892a. *Quid Secundatus Politicae Scientiae Instituendae Contulerit*, in Durkheim 1997: 7–74.

—— 1893a. *De la Division du travail social* (thesis). Paris: Alcan.

—— 1893b. *De la Division du travail social: étude sur l'organisation des sociétés supérieures* (commercial edition). Paris: Alcan.

—— 1893c. 'Note sur la définition du socialisme', in Durkheim 1970: 226–35.

—— 1895a. *Les Règles de la méthode sociologique*. Paris: Alcan.

—— 1895b. 'L'Enseignement philosophique et l'agrégation de philosophie', in Durkheim 1975, vol.3: 403–34.

—— 1895e. 'L'Etat actuel des études sociologiques en France', in Durkheim 1975, vol.1: 73–108.

—— 1897a. *Le Suicide: étude de sociologie*. Paris: Alcan.

—— 1897e. Review of A. Labriola, *Essais sur la conception matérialiste de l'histoire*, in Durkheim 1970: 245–54.

—— 1897f. 'Sur l'œuvre de Taine', in Durkheim 1997: 75–81.

—— 1898a(i). Preface to *L'Année sociologique* 1: i–vii.

—— 1898a(ii). 'La Prohibition de l'inceste et ses origines', *L'Année sociologique* 1: 1–70.

—— 1898a(iv)(1). Review of J. Kohler, *Zur Urgeschichte der Ehe*, *L'Année sociologique* 1: 306–19.

—— 1898a(iv)(2). Review of E. Grosse, *Die Formen der Familie und die Formen der Wirtschaft*, *L'Année sociologique* 1: 319–32.

—— 1898b. 'Représentations individuelles et représentations collectives', in Durkheim 1924: 1–48.

—— 1898c. 'L'Individualisme et les intellectuels', in Durkheim 1970: 261–78.

—— 1899a(i). Preface to *L'Année sociologique* 2: i–vi.

—— 1899a(ii). 'De la Définition des phénomènes religieux', *L'Année sociologique* 2: 1–28.

—— 1899a(iv)(3). Review of A. Hagelstange, *Süddeutsches Bauernleben im Mittelalter*, *L'Année sociologique*, 2: 306–9.

—— 1899a(iv)(10). Review of H. Cunow, *Die ökonomischen Grundlagen der Mutterherrschaft, L'Année sociologique* 2: 316–18.

—— 1899a(iv)(11). Review of M. Kovalevski, *L'organizzazione del clan nel Daghestan, L'Année sociologique* 2: 318–20.

—— 1899a(iv)(13). Review of S. Ciszewski, *Künstliche Verwandschaft bei den Südslaven, L'Année sociologique* 2: 321–23.

—— 1900a(8). Review of B. Spencer and F. Gillen, *The Native Tribes of Central Australia, L'Année sociologique* 3: 330–36.

—— 1900a(9). Review of F. Boas, *The Social Organization and the Secret Societies of the Kwakiutl Indians, L'Année sociologique* 3: 336-40.

—— 1901a(i). 'Deux lois de l'évolution pénale', *L'Année sociologique* 4: 65–95.

—— 1902a(i). 'Sur le totémisme', *L'Année sociologique* 5: 82–121.

—— 1902b. *De la Division du travail social*, 2nd ed. Paris: Alcan.

—— 1905a(i). 'Sur l'organisation matrimoniale des sociétés australiennes', *L'Année sociologique* 8: 118–47.

—— 1905a(ii)(2). Review of M. Pellison, *La Sécularisation de la morale au XVIIIe siècle, L'Année sociologique* 8: 381–82.

—— 1905e. Contribution to discussion on internationalism and class struggle, in Durkheim 1970: 282–92.

—— 1906a(19). Review of A. Howitt, *The Native Tribes of South-East Australia, L'Année sociologique* 9: 355–68.

—— 1906b. 'Détermination du fait moral', in Durkheim 1924: 49–116.

—— 1907b. Letter of 8 November to editor of *Revue néo-scolastique*, in Durkheim 1975, vol. 1: 402–5.

—— 1907f. 'La religion: origines', in Durkheim 1975, vol.2: 65–122.

—— 1907g(2). Review of W. James, *L'Expérience religieuse*, in 2010 *Durkheimian Studies/Etudes durkheimiennes* 16: 15–16.

—— 1909c. 'Examen critique des systémes classiques sur les origines de la pensée religieuse', *Revue philosophique* 67: 1–28, 142–62.

—— 1909d. 'Sociologie religieuse et théorie de la connaisance', *Revue de métaphysique et de morale* 17: 733–58.

—— 1911b. 'Jugements de valeur et jugements de réalité', in Durkheim 1924: 117–42.

—— 1911e. *De la Division du travail social*, 3rd ed. Paris: Alcan.

—— 1912a. *Les Formes élémentaires de la vie religieuse: le système totémique en Australie*. Paris: Alcan.

—— 1913b. 'Le Problème religieux et la dualité de la nature humaine', in Durkheim 1975, vol.21: 23–59.

—— 1914a. 'Le Dualisme de la nature humaine et ses conditions sociales', in Durkheim 1970: 314–32 (tr. in Durkheim 2005).

—— 1917c. 'La Politique de Demain', in 1999 *Durkheimian Studies/*

Etudes durkheimiennes 5: 8–12 (tr. in Durkheim 2009).

———— 1918. 'Le Contrat social de Rousseau' (lectures of around 1897), *Revue de métaphysique et de morale* 25: 1–23, 129–61.

———— 1919. 'La Conception sociale de la religion' (talk of 1914), in Durkheim 1970: 305–13.

———— 1920. 'Introduction à la morale' (manuscript of 1917), in Durkheim 1975, vol. 2: 313–31.

———— 1921. 'La Famille conjugale: conclusion du cours sur la famille' (lecture of 1892), in Durkheim 1975, vol.3: 35–49.

———— 1924. *Sociologie et philosophie*, ed. C. Bouglé. Paris: Alcan

———— 1925. *L'Education morale* (lectures probably of 1898–99), ed. P. Fauconnet. Paris: Alcan.

———— 1928. *Le Socialisme* (lectures of 1895–96), ed. M. Mauss. Paris: Alcan.

———— 1938. *L'Evolution pédagogique en France*, 2 vols (lectures of around 1905), ed. M. Halbwachs. Paris: Alcan.

———— 1950. *Leçons de sociologie* (lectures based on a manuscript of 1898–1900), ed. H. Kabuli. Paris: Presses Universitaires de France.

———— 1955. *Pragmatisme et sociologie* (reconstructed from student notes of lectures of 1913–14), ed. A. Cuvillier. Paris: Vrin.

———— 1970. *La Science sociale et l'action*, ed. J-C. Filloux. Paris: Presses Universitaires de France.

———— 1975. *Textes*, 3 vols, ed. V. Karady. Paris: Minuit.

———— 1997. *Montesquieu* (1892a and 1897f, with parallel tr.), trans. W. Watts Miller and E. Griffiths, ed. W. Watts Miller. Oxford: Durkheim Press.

———— 1998. *Lettres à Marcel Mauss*, eds P. Besnard and M. Fournier. Paris: Presses Universitaires de France.

———— 2003. *L'Evaluation en comité: textes et rapports de souscription au Comité des travaux historiques et scientifiques 1903–1907*, eds S. Baciocchi and J. Mergy. Oxford and New York: Durkheim Press/Berghahn Books.

———— 2004. *Durkheim's Philosophy Lectures: Notes from the Lycée de Sens Course, 1883–1884*, trans. and eds N. Gross and R.A. Jones. Cambridge: Cambridge University Press.

———— 2005. 'The Dualism of Human Nature and its Social Conditions', trans. I. Eulriet and W. Watts Miller, *Durkheimian Studies/Etudes durkheimiennes* 11: 35–45.

———— 2009. 'The Politics of the Future', trans. J. Mergy and W. Watts Miller, *Durkheimian Studies/Etudes durkheimiennes* 15: 3–6.

———— 2010. 'Lettres à Salomon Reinach', ed. R. Benthien, *Durkheimian Studies/Etudes durkheimiennes* 16: 19–35.

————— 2012. 'Leçon d'ouverture, 1913', ed. S. Baciocchi, *Durkheimian Studies/Etudes durkheimiennes* 18 (forthcoming).

Durkheim, E. and M. Mauss. 1903. 'De quelques formes primitives de classification', *L'Année sociologique* 6: 1–72.

————— 1913. Review of E. Durkheim, *Les Formes élémentaires de la vie religieuse, L'Année sociologique* 12: 94–98.

Eulriet, I. 2010. 'Durkheim and Approaches to the Study of War', *Durkheimian Studies/Etudes durkheimiennes* 16: 59–76.

Fabiani, J-L. 2005. 'Should the Sociological Analysis of Art Festivals be Neo-Durkheimian?', *Durkheimian Studies/Etudes durkheimiennes* 11: 49–66.

Fauconnet, P. 1920. *La Responsabilité: étude de sociologie*. Paris: Alcan.

Fehér, F. 1987. *The Frozen Revolution: An Essay on Jacobinism*. Cambridge: Cambridge University Press.

Ferneuil, T. 1889. *Les principes de 1789 et la science sociale*. Paris: Hachette.

Fison, L. and A.W. Howitt. 1880. *Kamilaroi and Kurnai*. Melbourne: George Robertson.

Foley, J. 2008. *Albert Camus: From the Absurd to Revolt*. Montreal: McGill-Queens University Press.

Foucault, M. [1975] 1977. *Discipline and Punish: The Birth of the Prison*, trans. A. Sheridan. London: Allen Lane.

————— 1982. 'The Subject and Power', in H. Dreyfus and P. Rabinow, *Michel Foucault: Beyond Structuralism and Hermeneutics*. London: Harvester, pp. 208–226.

Fouillée, A. 1880. *La Science sociale contemporaine*. Paris: Hachette.

Fournier, M. 2007. *Émile Durkheim (1858–1917)*. Paris: Fayard.

Fraser, D. 1973. *The Evolution of the British Welfare State*. London: Macmillan.

Frazer, J. 1887. *Totemism*. Edinburgh: Adam and Charles Black.

————— 1899. 'Observations on Central Australian Totemism', *Journal of the Anthropological Institute* n.s. 1: 281–86.

Freeman, A. 1989. *The Compromising of Louis XVI: the Armoire de Fer and the French Revolution*. Exeter: University of Exeter Press.

Gane, M. 2009. 'The Paradox of Neoliberalism', *Durkheimian Studies/Etudes durkheimiennes* 15: 20–25.

Girault de Coursac, P. and P. 1982. *Enquête sur le procès du roi Louis XVI*. Paris: Table Ronde.

Gouarné, I. 2011. 'Marxisme et durkheimisme dans l'entre-deux-guerres en France', *Durkheimian Studies/Etudes durkheimiennes* 17: 57–79.

Hartland, S. 1899. Review of B. Spencer and J. Gillen, *The Native Tribes of Central Australia, Folk-Lore* 10: 233–39.

Harvey, D. 2005. *A Brief History of Neoliberalism*. Oxford: Oxford University Press.

——— 2010. *The Enigma of Capital and the Crises of Capitalism*. London: Profile Books.

Hiatt, L.R. 1996. *Arguments about Aborigines: Australia and the Evolution of Social Anthropology*. Cambridge: Cambridge University Press.

Howitt, A.W. 1904. *The Native Tribes of South-East Australia*. London: Macmillan.

Hubert, H. 1905. 'Étude sommaire de la représentation du temps dans la magie et la religion', *Annuaire de l'Ecole Pratique des Hautes Etudes, Section des Sciences Religieuses*: 1–39.

Inglis, D. 2011. 'A Durkheimian Account of Globalization: the Construction of Global Moral Culture', *Durkheimian Studies/Etudes durkheimiennes* 17: 103–20.

Isaac, J. 1992. *Arendt, Camus and Modern Rebellion*. New Haven: Yale University Press.

Janet, P. 1887. *Histoire de la science politique dans ses rapports avec la morale*, 2 vols, 3rd ed. Paris: Alcan.

Jevons, F. 1899. 'The Place of Totemism in the Evolution of Religion', *Folk-Lore* 10: 369–83.

Jordan, D. 1979. *The King's Trial*. Berkeley: University of California Press.

Lévi-Strauss, C. [1949] 1969. *The Elementary Structures of Kinship*, trans. J. Bell et al., ed. R. Needham. London: Eyre and Spottiswoode.

——— [1962] 1966. *The Savage Mind*. London: Weidenfeld and Nicolson.

Lukes, S. 1968. *Emile Durkheim: An Intellectual Biography*, 2 vols, D. Phil. thesis. Oxford: University of Oxford.

——— 1973. *Émile Durkheim: His Life and Work*. London: Allen Lane.

——— 2009. 'The Current Crisis: Initial Reflections', *Durkheimian Studies/Etudes durkheimiennes* 15: 15–19.

MacKay, G. 2000. *Glastonbury: A Very English Fair*. London: Victor Gollancz.

Maffesoli, M. [1988] 1996. *The Time of the Tribes: The Decline of Individualism in Mass Society*, trans. D. Smith. London: Sage.

Massella, A, R. Weiss et al. (eds). 2009. *Durkheim: 150 Anos*. Belo Horizonte: Argvumentvm.

Marcel, G. 1944. *Homo Viator: prolégomènes à une métaphysique de l'espérance*. Paris: Aubier.

——— 1951. 'Structure de l'espérance', in G. Marcel, *Dieu vivant*. Paris: Seuil, pp. 71–80.

Marcel, J-C. 2001a. *Le Durkheimisme dans l'entre-deux-guerres*. Paris: Presses Universitaires de France.

——— 2001b. 'Georges Bataille: l'enfant illégitime de la sociologie durkheimienne', *Durkheimian Studies/Etudes durkheimiennes* 7: 37–52.

Marett, R.R. 1900. 'Pre-animistic Religion', in Marett 1909: 1–32.

——— 1904. 'From Spell to Prayer', in Marett 1909: 33–84.

———— 1908. 'The Conception of Mana', in Marett: 1909: 115–41.

———— 1909. *The Threshold of Religion*. London: Methuen.

———— 1914. *Anthropology*. London: Williams and Norgate.

Marett, R.R, and T.K. Penniman (eds). 1932. *Spencer's Scientific Correspondence with Sir J.G. Frazer and Others*. Oxford: Clarendon Press.

Marion, H. 1880. *De la Solidarité morale*. Paris: Germer Baillière.

Mathiez, A. 1904. *Les Origines des cultes révolutionnaires 1789–1792*. Paris: Société Nouvelle.

Maublanc, R. 2011. 'Marx et Durkheim' (paper of 1934), *Durkheimian Studies/Etudes durkheimiennes* 17: 8–54.

Mauss, M. 1900. Review of Spencer and Gillen, *The Native Tribes of Central Australia*, *L'Année sociologique* 3: 243–44.

———— 1904. 'L'origine des pouvoirs magiques dans les sociétés australiennes', in Mauss 1969, vol.2: 319–69.

———— 1905. Review of A. Mathiez, *Les Origines des cultes révolutionnaires*, *L'Année sociologique* 8: 296–98.

———— 1906. 'Essai sur les variations saisonnières des sociétés eskimo', *L'Année sociologique* 9: 39–132.

———— 1909. *La Prière*, in Mauss 1969, vol.1: 357–477 (tr. in Mauss 2003).

———— 1928. Introduction to Durkheim, *Le Socialisme*. Paris: Alcan, pp. v–xi.

———— 1937. Introduction to Durkheim, 'Morale professionnelle', in Mauss 1969, vol.3: 500–5.

———— 1938. 'Une catégorie de l'esprit humain: la notion de personne', *Journal of the Royal Anthropological Institute* 68: 263–81.

———— 1947. *Manuel d'ethnographie*, ed. D. Paulme. Paris: Payot (tr. in Mauss 2007).

———— 1969. *Œuvres*, 3 vols, ed. V. Karady. Paris: Minuit.

———— 2003. *On Prayer*, trans. S. Leslie, ed. W.S.F. Pickering. Oxford and New York: Durkheim Press/Berghahn Books.

———— 2007. *Manual of Ethnography*, trans. D. Lussier, ed. N.J. Allen. Oxford and New York: Durkheim Press/Berghahn Books.

Mergy, J. 2009. '"The Politics of the Future": An Unknown Text by Durkheim'. *Durkheimian Studies / Etudes durkheimiennes* 15: 7–14.

Mill, J.S. [1848–71] 1965. *The Principles of Political Economy with Some of Their Applications to Social Philosophy*, in *Collected Works of John Stuart Mill*, vols.2–3, ed. J.M. Robson. Toronto and London: University of Toronto Press.

Montesquieu, C.S. [1748] 1876–78. *L'Esprit des Lois*, in Montesquieu, *Œuvres complètes*, vols.3–6, ed. E. Laboulaye. Paris: Garnier.

Mulvaney, D.J. and J.H. Calaby. 1985. *'So Much That Is New': Baldwin Spencer 1860–1929, A Biography*. Melbourne: University of Melbourne Press.

Nora, Pierre (ed.). [1984–92] 1996–98. *Realms of Memory: The Construction of the French Past*, 3 vols, trans. A. Goldhammer. New York: Columbia University Press.

Nowotny, J. 1979. 'Despair and the Object of Hope', in R. Fitzgerald (ed.), *The Sources of Hope*. Oxford: Pergamon Press, pp. 44–66.

Ozouf, M. [1976] 1988. *Festivals and the French Revolution*, trans. A. Sheridan. Cambridge: Harvard University Press.

Paoletti, G. 2009. 'Introduzione: Identità personale e legame sociale', in Durkheim, *Il dualismo della natura umana e le sue condizioni sociali*. Pisa: Edizioni ETS, pp. 5–29.

——— 2012a. *Durkheim et la philosophie: représentation, réalité et lien social*. Paris: Classiques Garnier.

——— 2012b. 'Durkheim's "Dualism of Human Nature": Personal Identity and Social Links', trans. A. Zhok, *Durkheimian Studies/Etudes durkheimiennes* 18 (forthcoming).

Péguy, C. [1910] 1957 *Notre jeunesse*. Paris: Gallimard.

Pickering, W.S.F. 1984. *Durkheim's Sociology of Religion: Themes and Theories*. London: Routledge and Kegan Paul.

——— 1994. 'The Enigma of Durkheim's Jewishness', in W.S.F. Pickering and H. Martins (eds), *Debating Durkheim*. London: Routledge, pp. 10–39.

——— 2008. 'The Response of Catholic and Protestant Thinkers to the Work of Emile Durkheim: With Special Reference to *Les Formes élémentaires*', *Durkheimian Studies/Etudes durkheimiennes* 14: 59–93.

Polanyi, K. 1944. *The Great Transformation*. New York: Rinehart and Co.

Pudal, R. 2005. 'Durkheim et la réception du pragmatisme en France', *Durkheimian Studies/Etudes durkheimiennes* 11: 86–102.

——— 2007. *Les Réceptions du pragmatisme en France (1890–2007): histoires et enjeux*, Ph.D. thesis. Paris: EHESS.

Putnam, R. 2000. *Bowling Alone: The Collapse and Revival of American Community*. New York: Simon and Schuster.

Quemada, B. (ed.). 1992. *Trésor de la langue française*, vol.15. Paris: Gallimard.

Radcliffe-Brown, A. 1913. 'Three Tribes of Western Australia', *Journal of the Royal Anthropological Institute* 43: 143–94.

——— 1918. 'Notes on the Social Organization of Australian Tribes', Part 1, *Journal of the Royal Anthropological Institute* 48: 222–53.

——— 1923. 'Notes on the Social Organization of Australian Tribes', Part 2, *Journal of the Royal Anthropological Institute* 53: 424–47.

——— 1930–31 'The Social Organization of Australian Tribes', *Oceania* 1: 34–63, 207–46, 322–41, 426–56.

Reinach, S. 1912. 'Une étude sur les religions primitives', *Revue critique des livres nouveaux* October: 153–54.

Richter, H. 1965. *Dada: Art and Anti-Art.* London: Thames and Hudson.

Riley, A., W.S.F. Pickering and W. Watts Miller (eds). forthcoming. *Durkheim, the Durkheimians and the Arts.* Oxford and New York: Durkheim Press/Berghahn Books.

Robbins, D. 2011. 'From Solidarity to Inclusion: the Political Transformations of Durkheimianism', *Durkheimian Studies/Etudes durkheimiennes* 17: 80–102.

Robespierre, M. 1840. *Œuvres de Maximilien Robespierre*, vol.3. Paris: Laponneraye.

Rorty, R. 1989. *Contingency, Irony and Solidarity.* Cambridge: Cambridge University Press.

——— 1998. *Achieving Our Country.* Cambridge: Harvard University Press.

Rosa, F. 2003. *L'Âge d'or du totémisme: histoire d'un débat anthropologique (1887–1929).* Paris: CNRS Éditions.

Rousseau, J.J. [1762] 1964. *Du Contrat social,* in Rousseau, *Œuvres complètes,* vol.3, eds J.Starobinsky et al. Paris: Gallimard, pp. 279–346.

Rouzet, J-M. 1898–98. Speech of 15 November 1792, in *Archives Parlementaires,* 1st series, vol.53: 423.

Rudler, F.W. 1899. President's Address, *Journal of the Anthropological Institute* n.s. 1: 312–23.

Schulze, L. 1891. 'Aborigines of the Upper and Middle Finke River', *Transactions of the Royal Society of South Australia* 14: 221–43.

Simpson, G. 1933. Preface to Durkheim, *The Division of Labour in Society,* trans. G. Simpson. New York: Macmillan, pp. vii–xi.

Sorel, A. 1887a. *Montesquieu.* Paris: Hachette.

——— 1887b *Montesquieu,* trans. G. Masson. London: Routledge.

Spencer, B. 1899. 'Some Remarks on Totemism as applied to Australian Tribes', *Journal of the Anthropological Institute* n.s. 1: 275–80.

——— 1927. *The Arunta,* 2 vols. London: Macmillan.

Spencer, B. and F.J. Gillen. 1899. *The Native Tribes of Central Australia.* London: Macmillan.

——— 1904. *The Northern Tribes of Central Australia.* London: Macmillan.

Stedman Jones, S. 2009. 'Moral Humanism and the Question of Holism: Historical Reflections', *Durkheimian Studies/Etudes durkheimiennes* 15: 64–84.

——— 2012. 'Forms of Thought and Forms of Society: Durkheim and the Question of the Categories in *Les Formes élémentaires*', *L'Année sociologique* 62 (1) (forthcoming).

Steiner, P. [2005] 2011. *Durkheim and the Birth of Economic Sociology,* trans. K. Tribe. Princeton: Princeton University Press.

Stocking, G. 1995. *After Tylor: British Social Anthropology 1888–1951.* Madison: University of Wisconsin Press.

Strehlow, C. 1907–11. *Die Aranda- und Loritja-Stämme in Zentral-Australien.* Frankfurt: Baer.

Sułek, A. 2009. '*Le Suicide* in Poland: Analysis of the Spread and Reception of a Sociological Classic', *Durkheimian Studies/Etudes durkheimiennes* 15: 41–63.

Taylor, A. 1972. *Laissez-faire and State Intervention in Nineteenth-century Britain.* London: Macmillan.

Tiryakian, E. 2009a. 'Durkheim, Mathiez, and the French Revolution: The Political Context of a Sociological Classic', in E. Tiryakian, *For Durkheim: Essays in Historical and Cultural Anthropology.* Farnham: Ashgate, pp. 89–113.

———— 2009b. 'Durkheim's Reflection on the Crisis: But Which One?', *Durkheimian Studies/Etudes durkheimiennes* 15: 26–38.

Tocqueville, A. [1835–40] 1951. *De la Démocratie en Amérique*, 2 vols, ed. J-P. Mayer. Paris: Gallimard.

Tomkins, C. 1996. *Duchamp: A Biography.* New York: Henry Holt and Co.

Walzer, M. 1974. *Regicide and Revolution.* Cambridge: Cambridge University Press.

Watts Miller, W. 1996. *Durkheim, Morals and Modernity.* London: UCL Press.

———— 2004. 'Total Aesthetics: Art and *The Elemental Forms*', *Durkheimian Studies/Etudes durkheimiennes* 10: 88–118.

———— 2005. '*Dynamogénique* and *Élementaire*', *Durkheimian Studies/Etudes durkheimiennes* 11: 18–32.

Wilkinson, R. and K. Pickett. 2009. *The Spirit Level: Why More Equal Societies Almost Always Do Better.* London: Allen Lane.

Index

Mulvaney, D. J. and J. H. Calaby,
112, 230–31
museum, xii, xviii, 8, 177, 200,
207–8, 211
mystification, 13, 152–54, 159,
165, 195, 227
mystique, 175, 177–78, 183–85,
194–95; and politics, 183–85
myth, x–xiii, 8, 15, 56–57, 82–83,
85, 87, 96, 115, 120–21, 146–
47, 164–66, 177, 194, 197,
206, 208; and mythological
truths, xi, 165–66

nanja, 132
nation, 38, 129, 176, 183–84, 191,
193
naturism, 101, 104–5
negative/positive cult. *See* cult,
ritual
negative/positive solidarity. *See*
solidarity
neoliberalism, 220, 222–23, 225,
227
Nora, Pierre, 230
Nowotny, Joan, 232
nurtunja, 114

obligation, 10, 33–35, 60–61. 166,
196
occupational groups, xiv, xvi, 4–
5, 17, 20–21, 26–29, 32, 40,
61–65, 69–73, 76, 78; and
corporations, 27, 70. *See also*
guilds
old regime, 3, 6, 22, 24, 31, 175–
78, 180–81, 207–8, 216–17,
222
organic solidarity. *See* solidarity
ownership. *See* wealth
Ozouf, Mona, 175, 213

Paine, Tom, 182
Paoletti, Giovanni, 157–58, 231
pathologies, 3–7, 20, 29, 32, 56,
63, 77, 188, 218, 226. *See also*
crisis, malaise
Péguy, Charles, 185–86, 194
Peirce, Charles, 162
person, 1–2, 4–6, 14–15, 41–42,
48, 68, 102, 107, 131, 136–37,
158–59, 176, 181, 183, 196,
215–18, 221, 224, 227
pertalchera, 132
piacular rite. *See* ritual
Pickering, William, viii, 155, 229–
30
Pickett, Kate. *See* Wilkinson
pluralism, 42, 72, 155, 177, 219,
224; and diversity, 39, 44, 55,
68–69, 218; unity and diversity,
139, 175
poetry, 144, 148–50, 152, 154,
197, 205–6
Polanyi, Karl, 220
politics, xiv, 1, 23–26, 31, 38–39,
71–72, 162–64, 178–86, 191,
195, 197, 212, 219, 222, 224,
228; and mystique, 183–84
positivism, xi, 8
power. *See* discourse of energy,
force, power
power struggles, 175–86
pragmatism, 161–67
prayer. *See* ritual
presentism, xii
problematics: action and belief,
111, 114–16, 156–57, 163;
agency and structure, 53–56;
consciousness and structure,
50–52; creative and expressive,
126–27, 129, 164–65; individual
and collective, 56–57, 116–
19, 133–36, 157–59; modern

www.ingramcontent.com/pod-product-compliance
Lightning Source LLC
Chambersburg PA
CBHW060031030426
42334CB00019B/2269